IMAGES
of America

AROUND TIMPSON

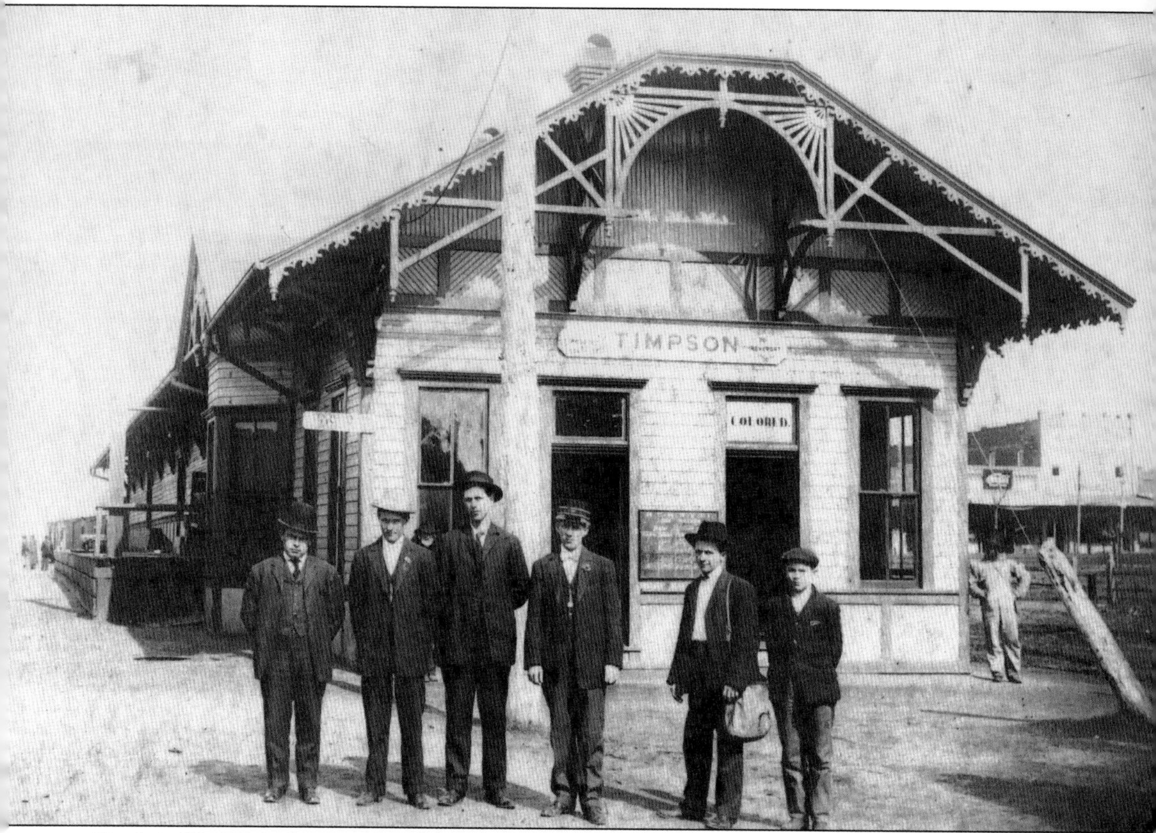

On July 29, 1894, the entire rail line between Houston and Shreveport was converted, in one day, from three-foot (narrow gauge) to 56.5-inch gauge (standard gauge). In October 1899, the Southern Pacific Railroad gained control of the Houston East and West Texas Railroad. A new depot was then constructed near the town square, across from Park Plaza. The railroad agent and local businessmen stand in front of the depot. (Courtesy of Timpson Area Genealogical and Heritage Society.)

On the Cover: Billingsley's Grocery was conveniently located on Bremond Street in downtown Timpson. Billingsley first sold groceries from his home, then built a store in the Shady Grove Community. In 1944, he moved to Timpson and opened the business he operated until his retirement in 1964. Pictured here in 1948 are, from left to right, Lloyd Goolsby, Bailey Ramsey, owner Travis Billingsley, J.R. Carter, and Bob Towns. (Courtesy of Lou Nell Billingsley.)

IMAGES
of America

AROUND TIMPSON

Timpson Area Genealogical
and Heritage Society

ARCADIA
PUBLISHING

ISBN 978-0-7385-8484-3

Published by Arcadia Publishing
Charleston, South Carolina

Printed in the United States of America

Library of Congress Control Number: 2011925215

For all general information, please contact Arcadia Publishing:
Telephone 843-853-2070
Fax 843-853-0044
E-mail sales@arcadiapublishing.com
For customer service and orders:
Toll-Free 1-888-313-2665

Visit us on the Internet at www.arcadiapublishing.com

Dedicated to Beth Shepherd,
who, as archivist for 20 years, diligently preserved the
Timpson Area Genealogical and Heritage Society
records that made this compilation possible

Contents

Acknowledgments		6
Introduction		7
1.	Railroad Boomtown	9
2.	That Old-Time Religion	41
3.	School Days	53
4.	Community Life	67
5.	They Served Their Country	91
6.	Tenaha, Timpson, Bobo, and Blair	103
7.	Small-Town Heyday	109

ACKNOWLEDGMENTS

Bill O'Neal first introduced the Timpson Area Genealogical and Heritage Society (TAGHS) to Arcadia Publishing's *Images of America* series when he presented a program for the society in September 2009 and showed us his book *Carthage*. Without his encouragement, suggestions, and time, this effort might never have been started, or finished.

Fannie Watson graciously loaned us her compiled information about Shelby County schools. Etoula Watson's research on early homes in Timpson provided the information used to write those captions. Timpson First United Methodist Church let us use their building more than once and furnished many exceptional church and community images. Individuals in the community not only shared their precious photographs, but also helped us identify any others that they could.

Tempie Green Pike coordinated the project and did a little of everything. Special thanks go to Jim and Jan Barrett, who, during the final months, volunteered in Tempie's place at the TAGHS library on Fridays so that she could work on the book.

Other TAGHS members who collected photographs, wrote captions, took photographs, researched information, and/or proofed the copy were Tad Bailey, Jan Barrett, Jim Barrett, Sandra Brownlow, Thomas Franks, Tom McClellan, Jim Patterson, Earnest Parker, David Pike, Shannon Ramsey, Beth Shepherd, and Martha Wigley Wheeler.

Much of the research information used in this publication came from the 52 years of Timpson newspapers that TAGHS had the foresight to have digitized. Additional information came from *Timpson, Texas Area History, 1800–2002*, published by TAGHS in 2003. The quarterly *Tap Root* publication, edited by David Pike, provided several leads and well-researched information that was used throughout the book. David Pike also proofed the contents for historical accuracy.

This is not a complete history of the Timpson area. It is only the history as shown by the photographs we were able to secure and had the information to describe. Unfortunately, because of space limitations, we were not able to use all of the images we received. Unless otherwise noted, images are provided by the Timpson Area Genealogical and Heritage Society.

Three acquisitions editors from Arcadia Publishing—Luke Cunningham, Winnie Rodgers, and Simone Monet-Williams—were enthusiastic, encouraging, and responsive throughout the process and made our jobs easier.

INTRODUCTION

When Timpson was founded in 1885, there were only three towns in Shelby County, Texas: Shelbyville, the old county seat, in the southern portion; Buena Vista, in the western portion; and, in 1866, a new county seat named Center because it was located in the center of the county. Still, Shelby County was without a railroad.

On March 11, 1875, Paul Bremond, railroad promoter and financier, secured a charter for the Houston East and West Texas Railway (HE&WT). This line was to run from Houston, through the piney woods of East Texas, and northeast to Shreveport, Louisiana. Construction began swiftly and slowly progressed northward. Bremond financed most of the construction until May 1878, when he sought outside financial help, securing $1,344,000 in bonds from the Union Trust Company of New York City.

The first survey through Shelby County had the rail route running through Buena Vista, or "Old Town," as it was soon to be known. Instead, a different route, three miles north, was selected. This route resulted in the new town of Timpson.

The early survey included two farm residences. One was known as the old Zack Booth home, located where Woodlawn Cemetery, Timpson's city cemetery, is now. A large two-story plantation home, owned by DeCalb Bryan and built prior to the Civil War, once stood where Timpson's Martin Luther King Park now stands. It was the only house in Timpson that sat "square with the world." Once Bryan's slaves were freed, the land was abandoned and it reverted to native vegetation, including pine trees.

Timpson was built on a plateau that was once a cornfield. Like all railroad towns, Timpson was laid out with the railroad, and not in the north-south pattern of most towns. Therefore, the streets in Timpson run at a 43-degree angle.

There was only one other farm home near the new town. Mark Blankenship owned a large log house a short distance north of the city limits on Rose Hill Road. It was here that town promoters and surveying crews ate before there were hotels and cafés. While Charles Noblet and his surveying crew were busily laying out the town, a construction crew was also busy opening the right-of-way and laying the track from Garrison, the last station south of Timpson.

While the steel had been laid and a few freight hauls had been made, it was not until May 1885 that the first passenger train came to Timpson. According to the *Nacogdoches News*, HE&WT would leave Nacogdoches at 8:00 a.m.—destination Timpson, Texas. Railroad officials and town promoters held a barbecue for the three passenger coaches and several flatcars of people, as well as those who came by wagon, horse, or buggy, to urge people to consider investing in or moving to the new town. Lots sold, and a rush to build was underway.

The one-mile-square town was named for HE&WT (Bremond's Road) executive Samuel Coulter Timpson, son-in-law of Paul Bremond. Within a year, approximately 1,000 citizens lived in Timpson, which became the county's major shipping point. By the census of 1890, five-year-old Timpson boasted a population of 1,200. Fifteen miles to the southeast, the county seat, Center—without a railroad connection—had a population of only 350.

Bremond's Road opened up East Texas to timber and its support industries. Later, it transported the large cotton and tomato crops to all parts of the nation. Without the railroad, the economy of the area might not have prospered as it did. When the cotton and tomato crops were gone, dairies, cattle, and then poultry came to the forefront. Agriculture has always been the major mainstay of the economy of Timpson and the surrounding communities.

It was not until after World War II that the population began to shift, moving to the larger cities to work to support the war, and then, as the veterans returned, to provide a way for them to support their families. Timpson was still an active city through the 1950s and early 1960s, boasting of banks, drugstores, hotels, cafés, theaters, leather shops, and all manner of mercantile stores. The city had a hospital, doctors, and a dentist. Saturdays were still "shopping days," when those in the county would come to town. They would shop, visit, and perhaps even participate in some kind of entertainment, such as the movies or going to the soda fountain for a treat.

A general decline of the downtown area in the 1970s and beyond resulted in some abandoned or empty buildings, unkempt premises, and closed businesses. Nevertheless, those whose families settled in and around Timpson over the years of its existence hold a great attachment to the area. Many who moved away return at retirement to again become a part of the community they love. Those who have stayed over the years continue to nurture and promote the area.

Timpson is showing signs of revival, with the natural gas industry beginning to boost the economy. Entrepreneurs and franchise businesses are discovering Timpson, and the city and the chamber of commerce are promoting growth. The population has leveled out at about 1,200, according to the 2010 census, but the future of Timpson looks promising again.

One

Railroad Boomtown

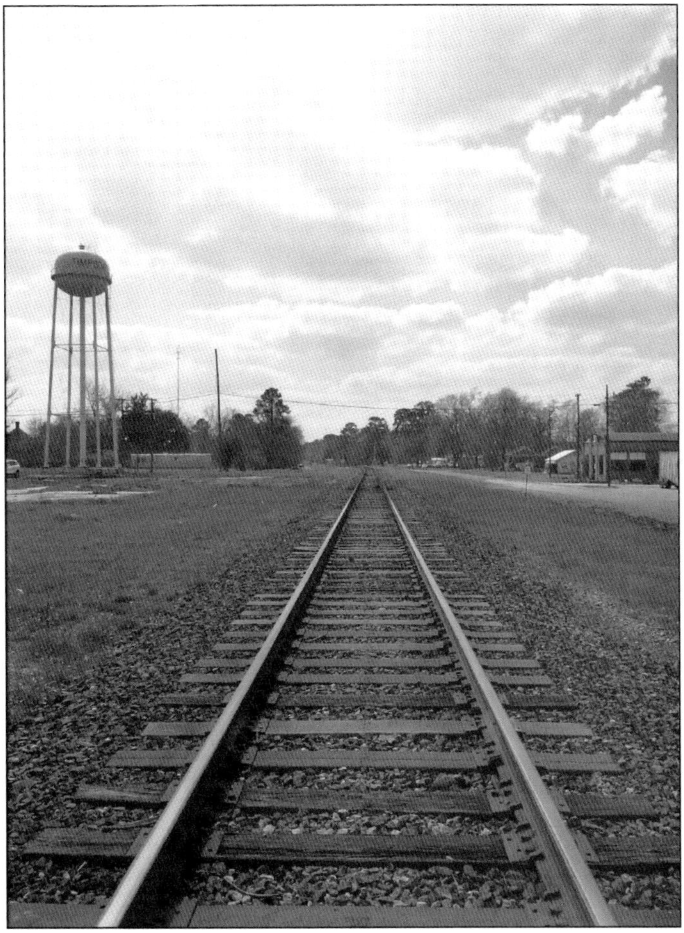

In May 1885, railroad officials and town promoters held a big barbecue beside the rails in front of the Cal Byran home. Surrounding dignitaries, country people, and neighboring merchants attended. The day was spent listening to addresses concerning the railroad and the advantages and possibilities of the new town. Maps were displayed and lots were bought and sold. This lot-selling project was the beginning of Timpson. (Photograph by Tempie Green Pike.)

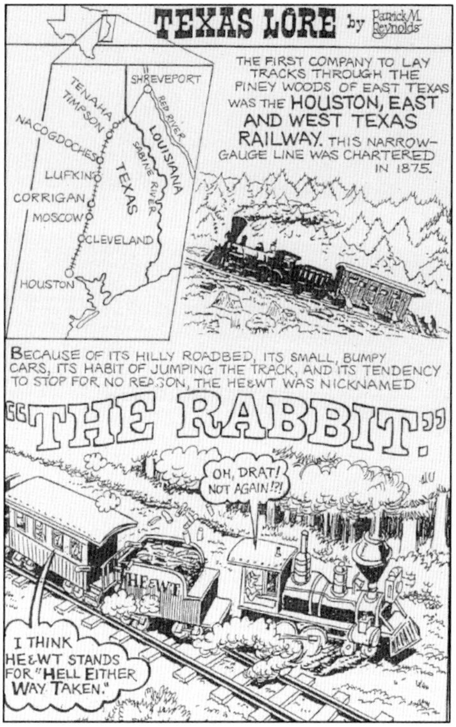

Author, illustrator, and cartoonist Patrick M. Reynolds chose "The Rabbit" as one of his topics for *Texas Lore*. Construction of the Houston East and West Texas Railway (HE&WT) began shortly after receiving a charter in 1875. Paul Bremond financed most of the construction, only securing outside financial help from Union Trust Company of New York City in 1878. The railroad went into receivership before it was finished. Bremond died on May 8, 1885, without seeing his railroad completed. (Courtesy of Patrick M. Reynolds.)

The HE&WT No. 344 engine is one example of the steam locomotives that came through Timpson during the city's infancy. This self-propelled vehicle was usually fueled by wood or coal. The fuel was burned to produce steam, which drove the engine. Both fuel and water supplies were carried with the locomotive, on the locomotive itself, or in wagons pulled behind. (DeGolyer Library, Southern Methodist University, Dallas, Texas, Ag1982.0232.)

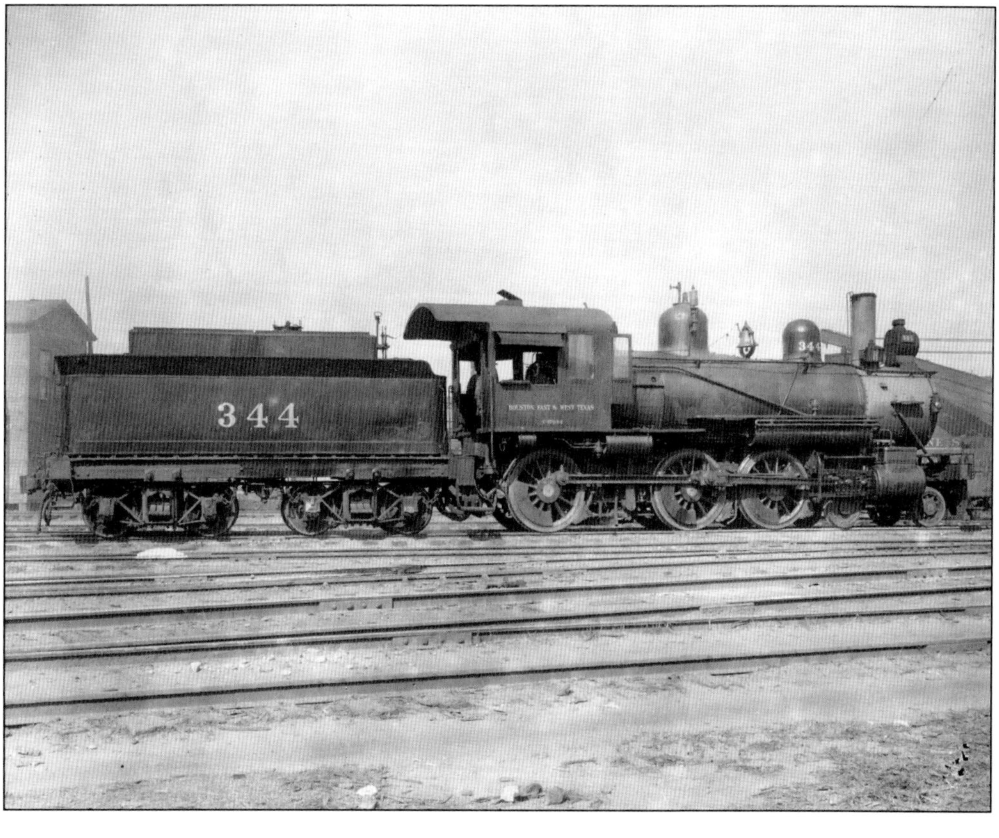

Timpson owes its inception to the railroad. From the time the first train came to Timpson, the town grew rapidly. This HE&WT Railway's December 1905 train schedule lists four trains a day traveling to and from Houston, Texas, to Shreveport, Louisiana. Of interest are dinner stops in Garrison for two trains, and the notation that Wells Fargo and Company Express operates on these lines. (Courtesy of TAGHS.)

HOUSTON EAST & WEST TEXAS RY.
HOUSTON & SHREVEPORT R. R.

EAST-BOUND				Effective Dec. 17, 1905		WEST-BOUND	
No. 5	No. 3	No. 1	Distance from Houston.	STATIONS	Distance from Shreveport	No. 2	No. 4
Houston Humble Special	Through Mixed	Houston Shreveport Passenger				Shreveport Houston Passenger	Through Mixed
A. M.	P. M.	A. M.				P. M.	P. M.
7 25	5 15			Lv. Galveston. . Ar		8 55	12 10
10 30	7 30	6 30	0.0	Lv‡ HOUSTON. Ar . . H.&T C. Depot . .	230.9	6 40	10 00
	f 8 11	f 6 58	9.8	. . . . Lock	221.1	f 6 13	f 9 28
11 30	8 32	7 12	17.7	. . . . Humble	213.2	5 55	9 08
	f 8 52	f 7 30	23.8	. . . . Japan	207.1	f 5 38	f 8 48
	9 08	7 43	28.9	. . . . New Caney . .	202.0	5 26	8 31
	f 9 35	f 8 05	37.2	. . . . Midline	193.7	f 5 05	8 05
	9 56	8 24	43.9	. . ‡Cleveland { Lv Ar	187.0	4 49	{ 7 43 7 23
	f10 11	f 8 39	49.1	. . . . Algie	181.8	f 4 35	f 7 07
	10 32	8 57	55.9	. . . ‡Shepherd . .	175.0	4 18	6 45
	f10 47	f 9 11	60.6	. . . . Urbana	170 3	f 4 04	f 6 28
	10 58	9 20	63.9	. . . . Goodrich	167.0	f 3 56	6 15
	f11 09	f 9 30	67.8	. . . . Lamont	163.1	f 3 46	f 6 00
	11 22	9 40	71.9	. . . ‡Livingston . . .	159.0	3 36	5 45
	f11 34	f 9 51	75.6	. . . . Marston	155.3	f 3 25	f 5 31
	11 46	10 02	79.9	. . . . Leggett	151.0	3 14	5 15
	12 11	10 25	87.8	. . . ‡Moscow . . .	143.1	f 2 52	4 46
	12 29	10 42	93.5	. . . ‡Corrigan . . .	137.4	2 36	4 28
	f12 47	10 56	99.3	. . . ‡Petersville . . .	131.6	f 2 22	f 4 10
	f 1 11	f11 15	106.3	. . . . Emporia	124.6	f 2 01	f 3 42
	f 1 14	f11 17	107.2	. . . . Diboll	123.7	f 2 02	f 3 39
	1 24	11 28	110.7	. . . . Burke	120.2	1 52	3 28
	1 48	11 50	118.7	Ar. ‡LUFKIN. . Lv	112 2	1 31	3 03
	1 53	11 50	118.7	Lv. ‡LUFKIN. . Ar	112.2	1 31	2 58
	f 2 26	f12 20	130.2	. . . . Lanana	100.7	f 1 03	f 2 26
	2 53	12 42	138.6	. . ‡Nacogdoches. . .	92.3	12 42	1 56
	f 3 16	f 1 03	144.1	. . . . Redfield	86.8	f12 23	f 1 32
	3 29	1 12	147.9	. . . . Appleby	83.0	f12 10	1 21
	f 3 39	f 1 19	150.4	. . . . Sterne	80.5	f12 02	f 1 10
	f 3 55	f 1 29	154.8	. . . . Fitze	76.1	f11 50	f12 57
	4 10	1 40	158.8	Ar . ‡Garrison. . Lv	72.1	11 40	12 43
	4 10	2 00	158.8	Lv . Garrison. . Ar	72.1	11 20	12 43
	f 4 24	f 2 11	163.0	. . . . Blair	67.9		f12 28
	4 37	2 21	167.2	. . . ‡Timpson . . .	63.7	10 58	12 15
	f 4 51	f 2 34	171.8	. . . . Bobo	59.1	f10 47	f12 01
	5 07	2 48	176.8	. . . †Tenaha	54.1	10 35	11 47
	f 5 22	f 2 59	180.9	. . . . Paxton	50.0	f10 24	f11 32
	5 43	3 16	188.3	. . . ‡Joaquin . . .	42.6	f10 09	11 12
	5 55	3 25	191.5	Ar‡LOG'SPORT. . Lv	39.4	10 00	11 00
	5 55	3 25	191.5	Lv LOGANSPORT Ar	39.4	10 00	11 00
	6 20	3 47	200.5	. . . Longstreet . . .	30.4	f 9 41	10 35
	6 35	4 02	207.4	. . . . Keachie	23.5	9 27	10 15
	f 6 52	f 4 13	212.4	. . . . Preston	18.5	f 9 16	f10 00
	f 7 09	f 4 26	218.5	. . . . Keithville . . .	12.4	f 9 04	f 9 45
	f 7 23	f 4 38	223.7	. . . . La Rosen . . .	7.2	f 8 53	f 9 29
	7 50	5 00	230.9	Ar . Shreveport. Lv . . ‡K. C. S. Depot . .	0.0	8 30	9 00
A. M.	A. M.	P. M.				A. M.	P. M.

Train No. 1, dinner at Garrison.
Train No. 2, dinner at Garrison.
Train No. 4, breakfast at Cleveland.
Wells, Fargo & Co., Express Operates on these lines.

f Flag Stop.
‡ Coupon Station.

"Riding the rails" took on a new meaning as workmen used handcars and other rail contraptions to get around. Thomas Jefferson Cammack came to Texas from Mississippi around 1884 to work on the railroad. He is shown here in front, with an unidentified man on the second bicycle-like vehicle. (Courtesy of Martha Peters Brothers.)

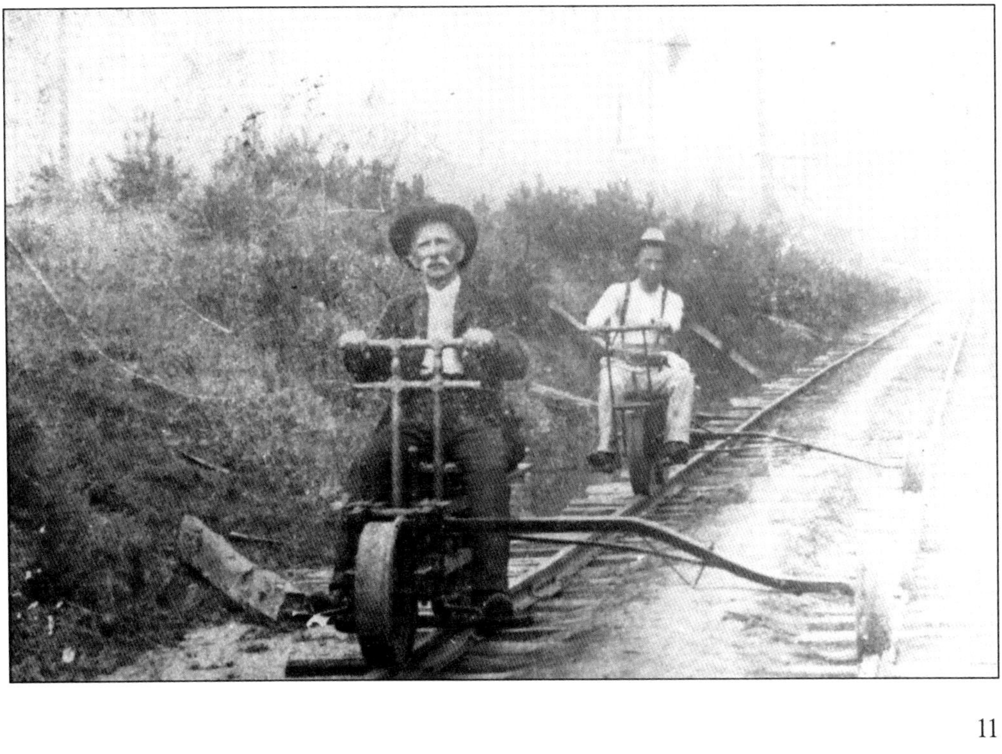

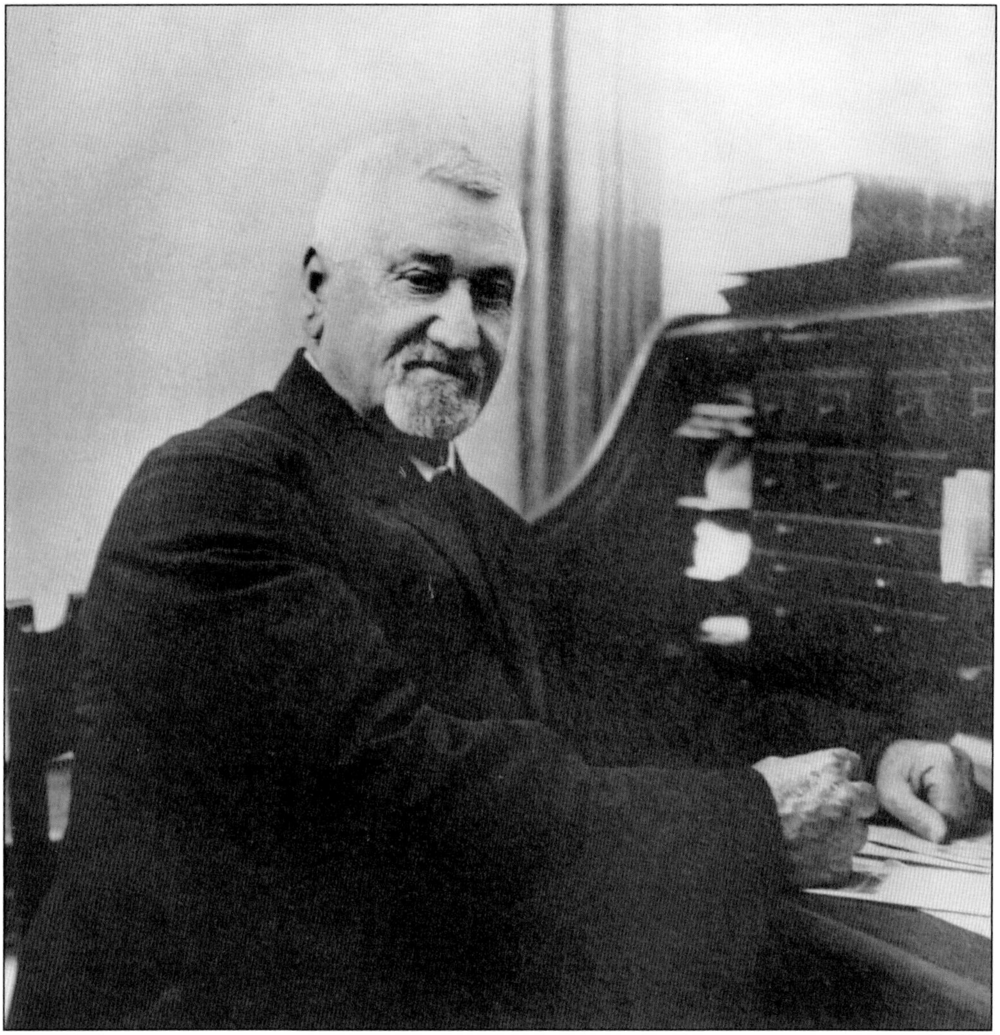

Thomas Smith Garrison was among the first to invest in the new town of Timpson. Called Captain Smith, he was already an established merchant, building contractor, saw miller and farmer at Caledonia since 1869. He built the first store in Timpson—a general merchandise store named Garrison and Avery—and made his first sale on August 19, 1885. Pat McLaughlin and T.J. Todd, also building stores, ran a close second and third. Garrison financed and helped manage the Texas and Gulf Railway from Timpson to Carthage, later selling it to the Santa Fe Railroad. Garrison was a director of the Timpson and Henderson Railway, which originally ran from Timpson to the Ragley Sawmill, in southwestern Panola County. He was chairman of the finance commission while serving as representative of the 25th Texas Legislature in 1897. In 1887, Garrison and T.C. Whiteside lent financial assistance to the building of a two-story lodge building for Timpson Masonic Lodge No. 437. Garrison was so identified with Timpson as to be called the "Father of Timpson" in *Texas and Texans* (1914 edition). (Courtesy of Timpson Masonic Lodge.)

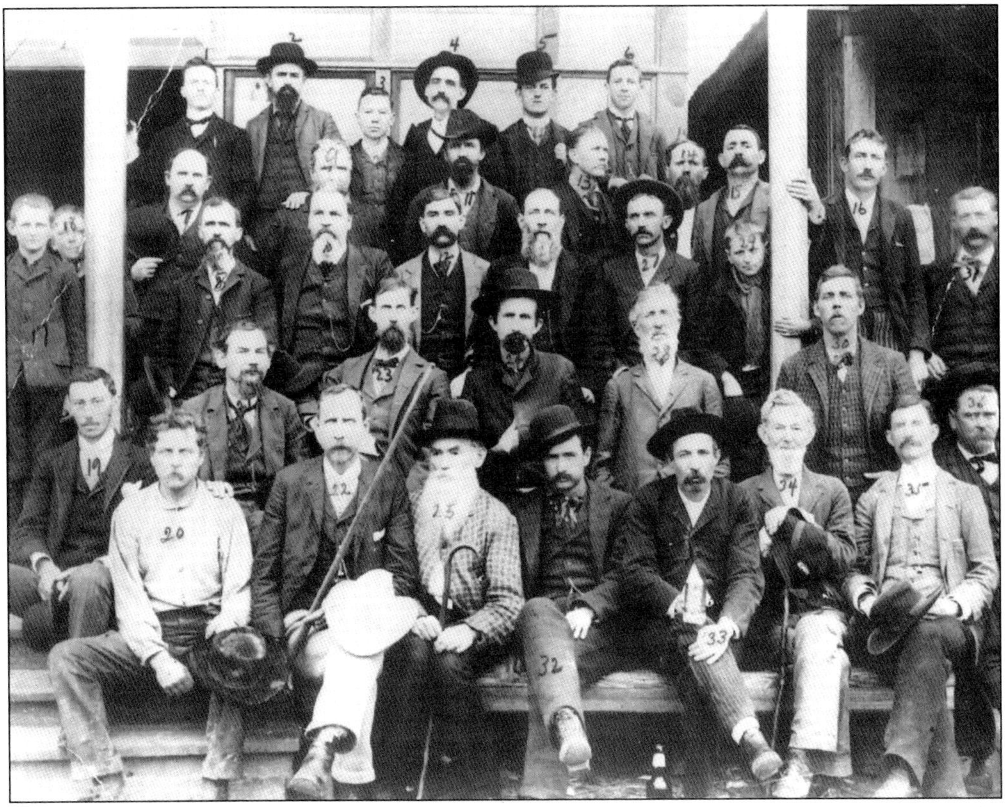

The Timpson Business League was formed in 1890 to promote the growth of the city. In 1909, the group published a pamphlet expounding on the modern utilities, businesses, schools, churches, and beautiful homes in Timpson, as well as the agricultural opportunities, and encouraged "industrious farmers" to settle here. This photograph was supposedly taken on the steps of the town's only saloon, located next door to R.T. Blair's store on Bremond Street. (Courtesy of TAGHS.)

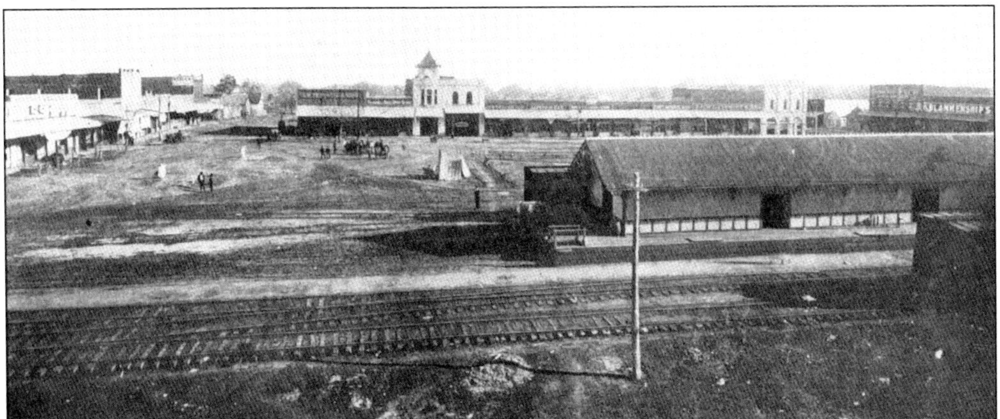

This partial view of the public square, taken between 1904 and 1909, shows the new Southern Pacific Depot in the foreground. By this time, there were several brick buildings; prominent among them were Blankenship's, on the west side of the square, and the R.T. Blair Building, on the east side of the square. The Cotton Belt Bank, with its cupola, sat near the middle of Front Street. (Courtesy of TAGHS.)

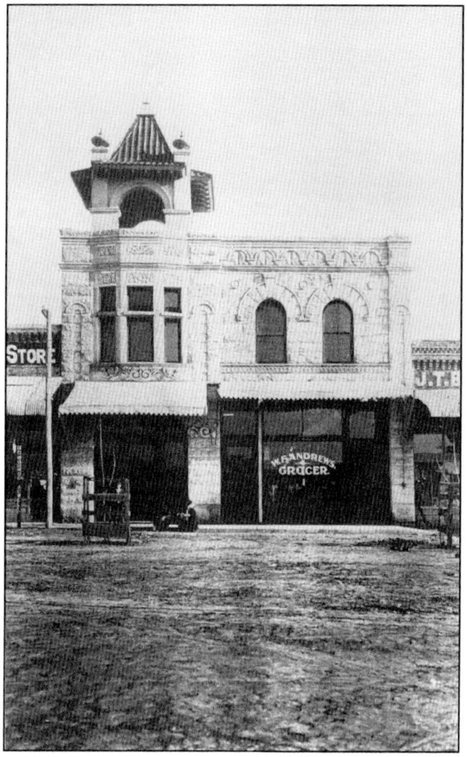

The Cotton Belt Bank, the oldest financial institution in Shelby County, is shown here on Front Street in 1909. Temple Doswell Smith chartered this bank in 1896; the architect was Alfred Giles of San Antonio. Temple D. Smith, W.G. Ragley, G.W. Trammell Jr., and cashier Stroud Kelly were the first officers. H.R. Fory was chairman of the first board of directors. (Courtesy of TAGHS.)

Built after Southern Pacific Railroad gained control of HE&WT in 1899, the depot exhibited the architectural trimmings associated with the Victorian era. It featured gingerbread trim and a white picket fence. Its stately appearance and size added to the feeling of permanence of the young city. Railroad agent H.R. Fory is shown in the foreground of this 1909 photograph. All others are unidentified. (Courtesy of TAGHS.)

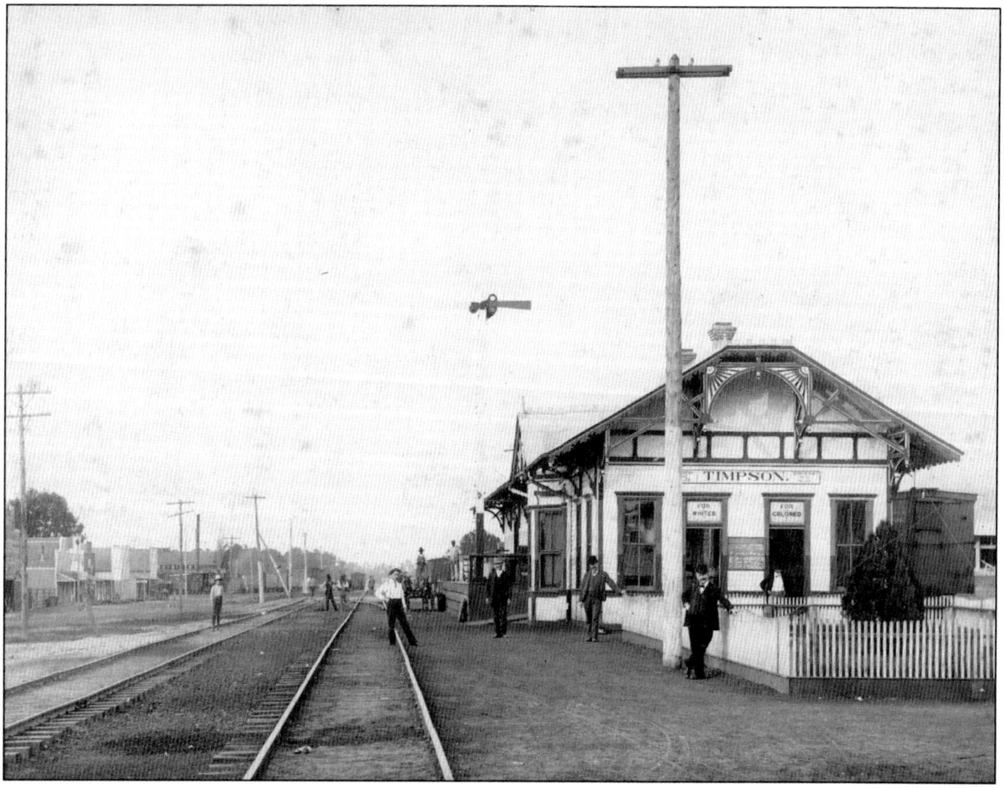

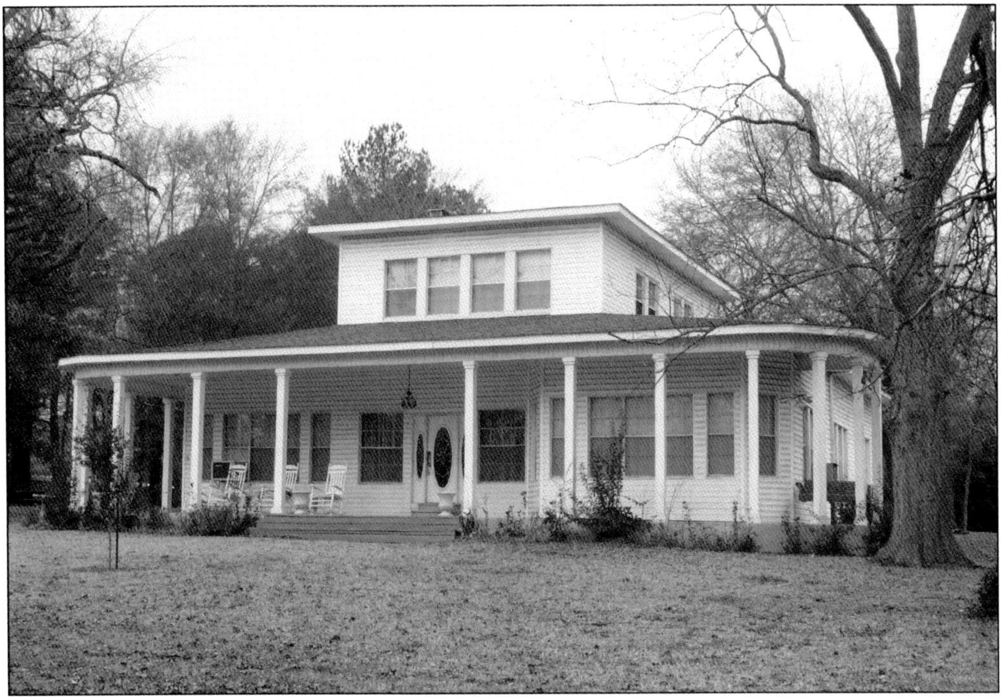

Thomas Jefferson Molloy and his wife, Miriam (Blair) Molloy, lived in this home on North Fourth Street, less than a block from her parents. Thomas Molloy began work with the *Timpson Times* at age 12, and in 1909 his name was placed on the masthead as business manager. In 1911, he and Sylvanus Winfrey bought the paper from Willie E. (Sampey) Ford and continued to publish the *Times* until December 1962. (Courtesy of TAGHS.)

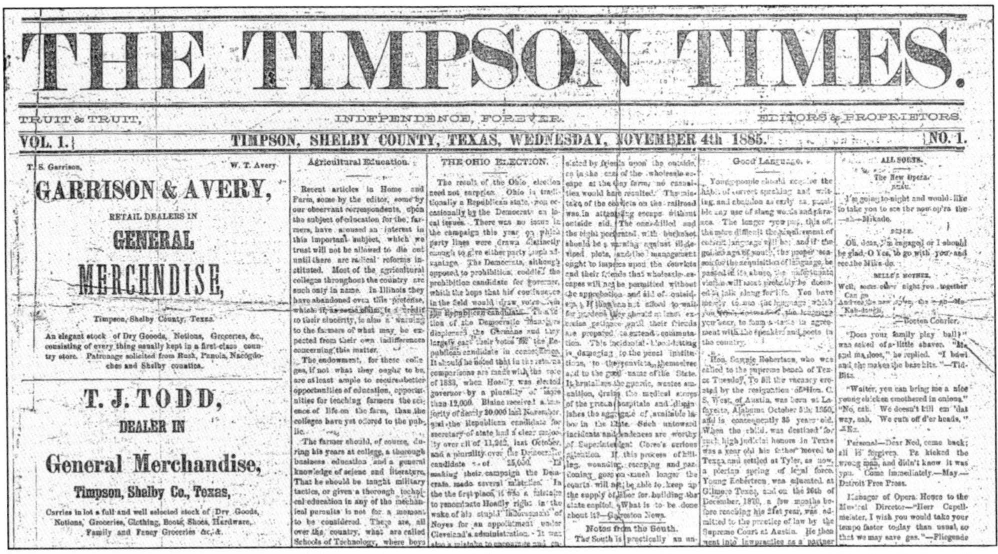

THE TIMPSON TIMES.

TRUIT & TRUIT, INDEPENDENCE, FOREVER. EDITORS & PROPRIETORS.

VOL. 1. TIMPSON, SHELBY COUNTY, TEXAS, WEDNESDAY, NOVEMBER 4th 1885. NO. 1.

T. S. Garrison, W. T. Avery

GARRISON & AVERY,

RETAIL DEALERS IN

GENERAL MERCHNDISE,

Timpson, Shelby County, Texas.

An elegant stock of Dry Goods, Notions, Groceries, &c., consisting of every thing usually kept in a first-class country store. Patronage solicited from Rusk, Panola, Nacogdoches and Shelby counties.

T. J. TODD,

DEALER IN

General Merchandise,

Timpson, Shelby Co., Texas,

Carries in lot a full and well selected stock of Dry Goods, Notions, Groceries, Clothing, Boots, Shoes, Hardware, Family and Fancy Groceries &c., &c.

Agricultural Education.

THE OHIO ELECTION.

Good Language.

ALL SORTS.

Notes from the South.

John Hays "Jack" Truitt and James Morgan Truitt, editors and proprietors, published the first edition of the *Timpson Times* on November 4, 1885. Jack also practiced law in Center, where he founded another newspaper, the *Champion*. Julia Phifer Truitt, James's wife, was associate editor and continued to publish the paper for about two years after her husband's murder. She would later be known for her short stories. (Courtesy of TAGHS.)

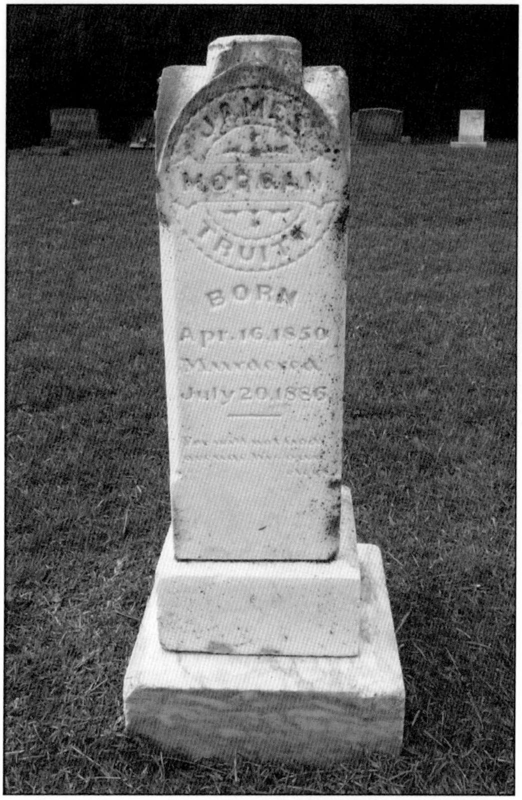

The first blood feud in East Texas, the Regulator-Moderator War, took place in and around Shelby County during the 1840s. Feuding became rife across Texas throughout the late 1800s, and in the first year of its existence Timpson was the site of vicious retribution. In Hood County, the Mitchell and Truitt families feuded in 1874 over a land dispute, and two of the Truitts were killed. The next year, Cooney Mitchell was legally hanged for the crime in Granbury, Texas. Cooney's son Bill Mitchell blamed Rev. James Morgan Truitt, a young minister whose testimony was key to the conviction. Truitt, born in Shelby County, brought his family to Timpson about September 1885. Reverend Truitt's life was cut short in the early evening hours of July 20, 1886, when Bill Mitchell fired a bullet through his head at point-blank range, with his wife, Julia, and their young daughter Hallie looking on. Buried in Timpson's new cemetery, Truitt's gravestone proclaimed that he was "MURDERED." (Courtesy of TAGHS.)

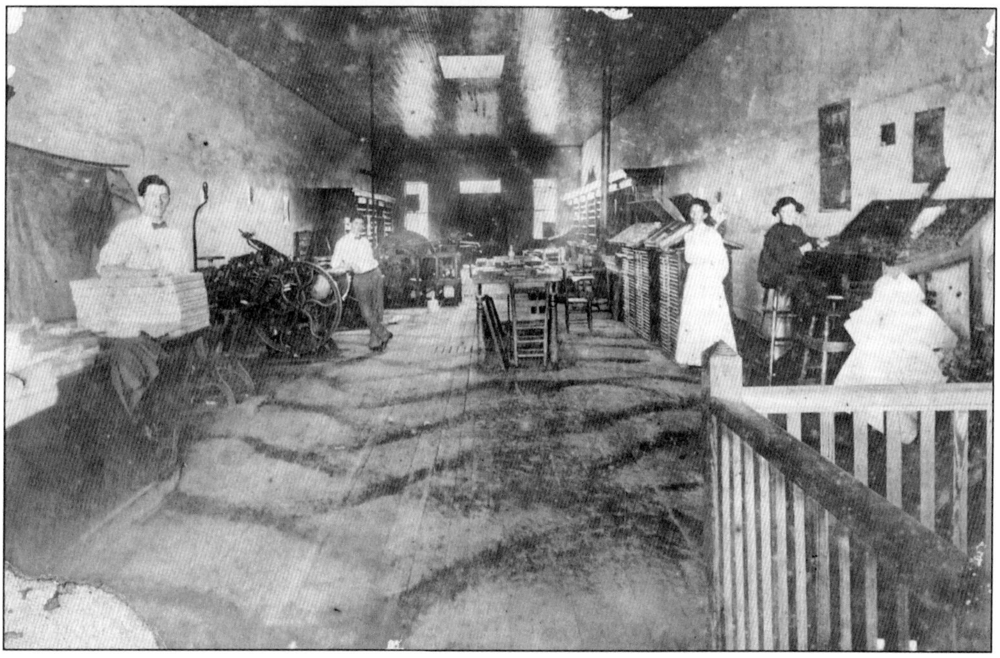

Syl Winfrey and Tom Molloy become owners of the *Timpson Times* in 1911 and operated it as a daily and weekly until 1945, then as a weekly until 1962, when it was sold to Rex and Luna Bell. At the time of this early 1900s photograph, all type was set by hand. (Courtesy of TAGHS.)

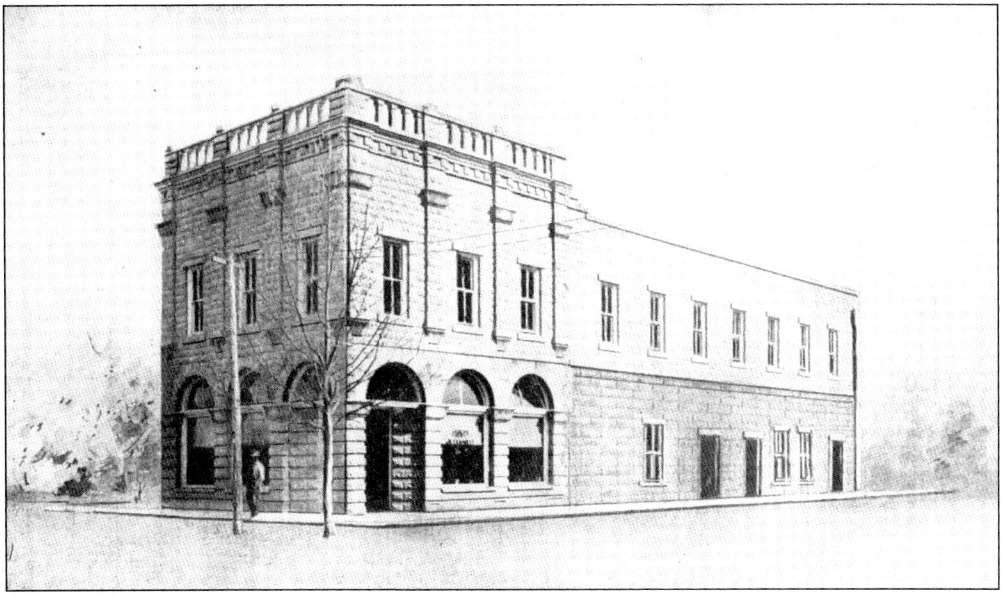

The classic limestone building on the corner of Main and Jacob Streets held the first national bank chartered in Shelby County, called the First National Bank. In 1909, it became a state bank known as the Guaranty State Bank, and later the Guaranty Bond Bank. Timpson's two banks merged in 1939, taking the name of one and the location of the other, and becoming the Cotton Belt State Bank. (Courtesy of TAGHS.)

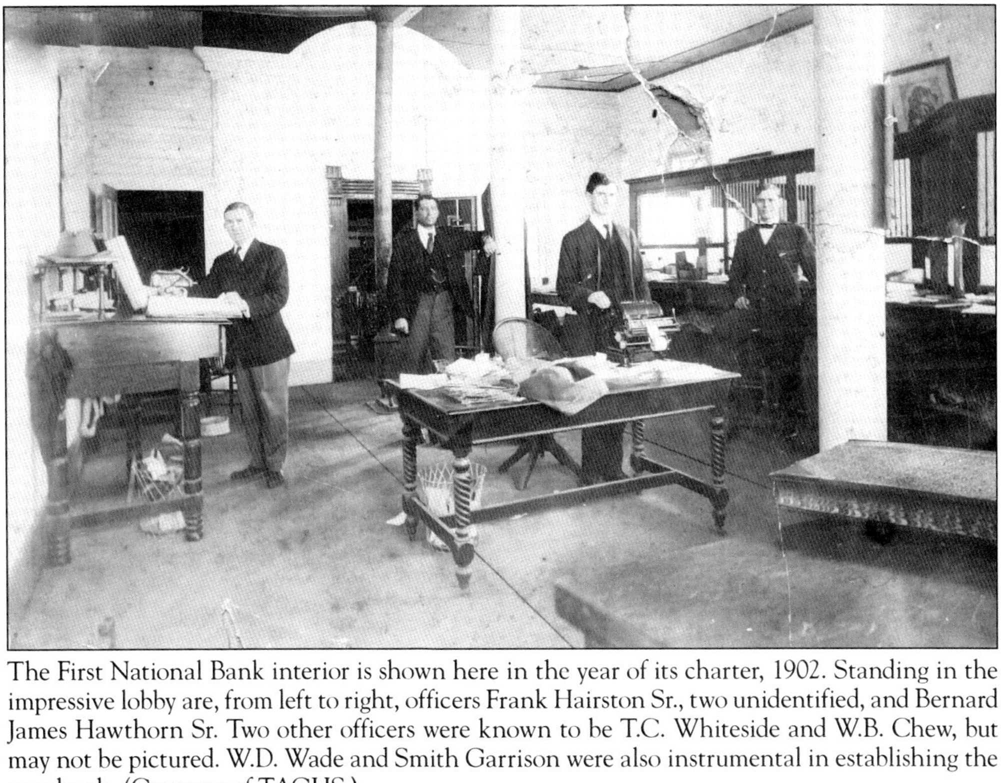

The First National Bank interior is shown here in the year of its charter, 1902. Standing in the impressive lobby are, from left to right, officers Frank Hairston Sr., two unidentified, and Bernard James Hawthorn Sr. Two other officers were known to be T.C. Whiteside and W.B. Chew, but may not be pictured. W.D. Wade and Smith Garrison were also instrumental in establishing the new bank. (Courtesy of TAGHS.)

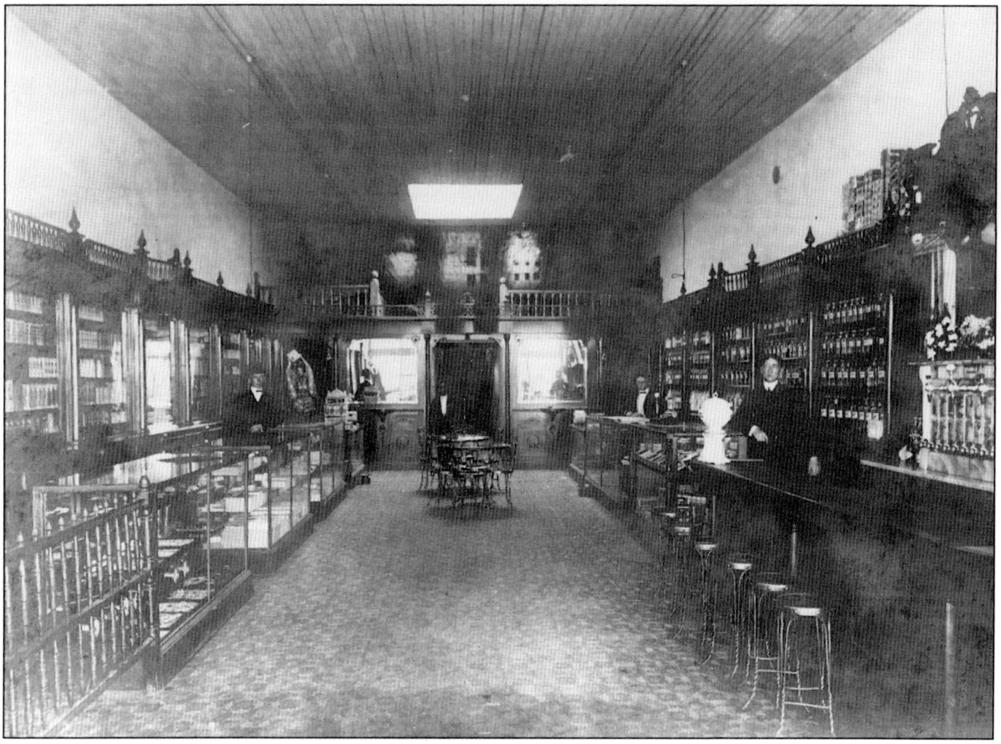

Dr. John Burgamy Bussey moved his medical practice from Buena Vista, Texas, to Timpson after February 1886, and opened Bussey Drug Store on Plaza (Front) Street. The store served as a base for his medical practice and contained a prescription department, a soda fountain, and, later, a place for his son John to indulge his interest in phonographs and radios. (Courtesy of TAGHS.)

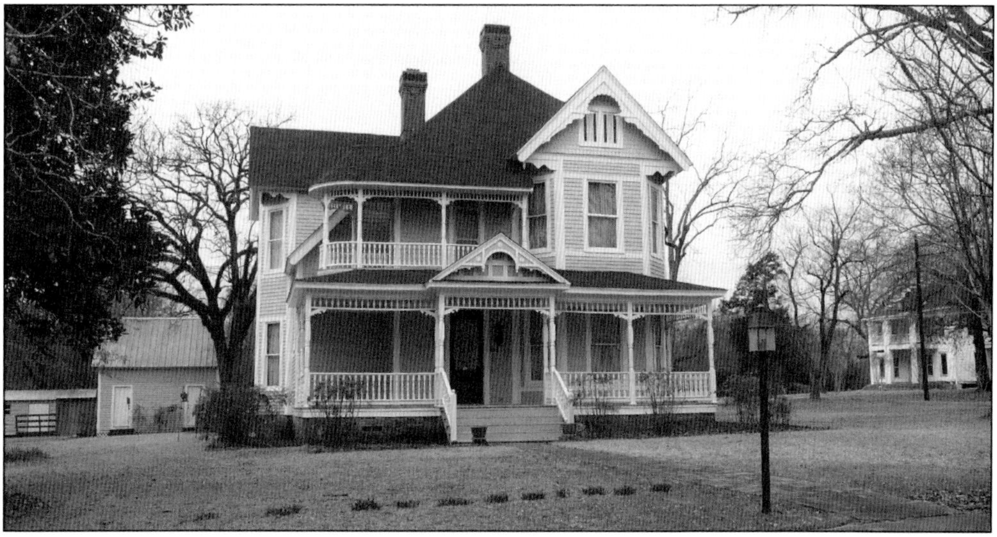

Dr. John Burgamy Bussey and Frances Rebecca (Rather) Bussey built this Victorian-style home at the corner of Jacob and North Fourth Streets in 1886. In the background at right is the R.T. Blair home. Bussey graduated from the University of Louisville, in Kentucky, in 1859, and then served as a southern Civil War surgeon. He began his medical practice in Shelbyville, Texas, later moving to Buena Vista.

Dr. Edgar Butts Clements is shown at the time of his graduation from Memphis Hospital Medical School in Memphis, Tennessee, in 1885. He was the first doctor to locate in the new town of Timpson, sometime before November 1885. His office was located in T.J. Todd's General Merchandise Store on the corner of Front and Jacob Streets. He later relocated to Trammell's Drug Store. (Courtesy of Nannette C. Johnston.)

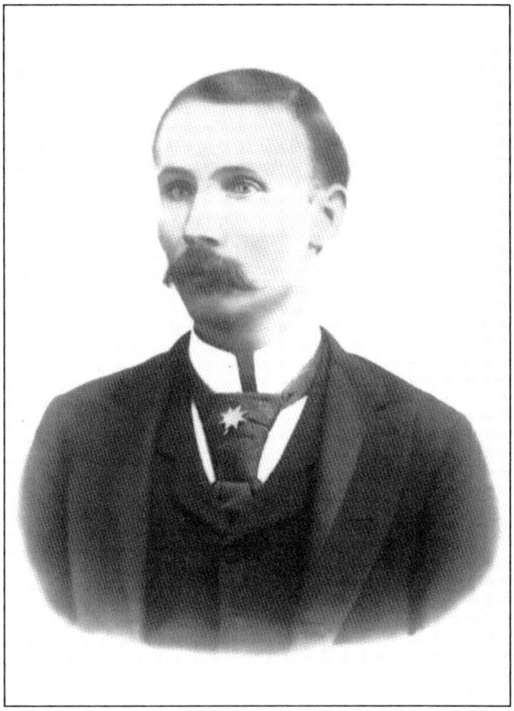

Thomas Jefferson Clements, his wife, Harriett Elizabeth, and their five children came to Texas in the late 1860s from Marion County, Georgia. Clements was elected Justice of the Peace for Precinct 7 (Timpson) in November 1888 and served until October 1911. Clements is shown here in 1908 with his son Dr. Edgar Butts Clements' family; seated second from left (second row), after his daughter Mollie. (Courtesy of Nannette C. Johnston.)

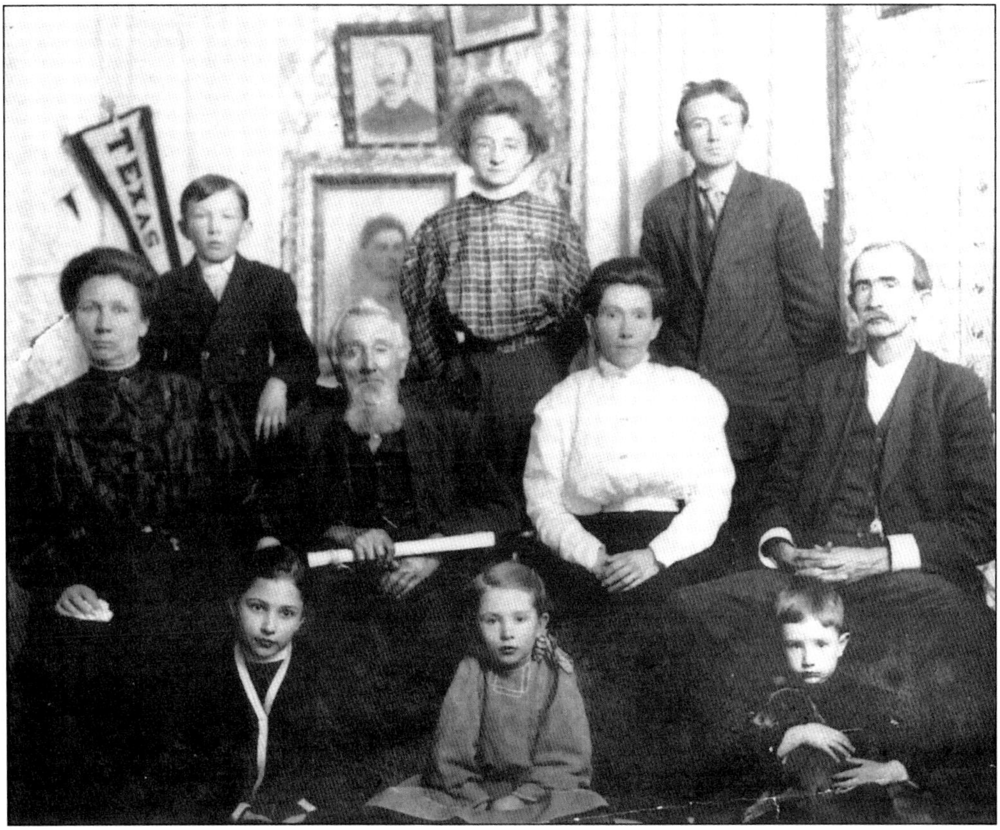

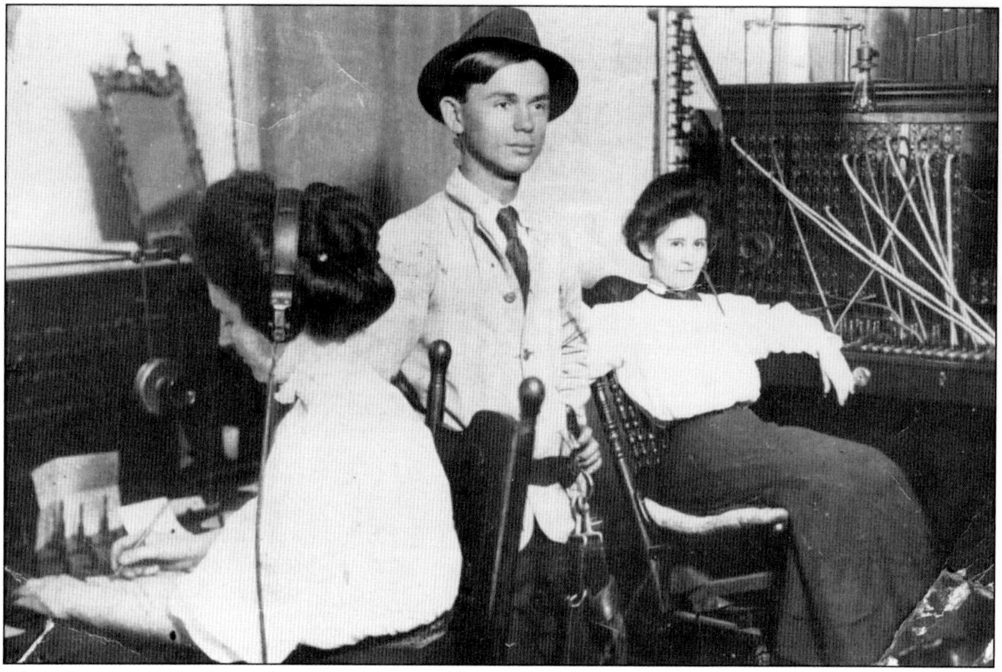

The Timpson telephone franchise was sold to John B. Bussey and Howard R. Fory in 1898, 11 years after its invention. Known as the Timpson Telephone Company, it was located in a wooden building on property owned by John Bussey on the north side of the railroad, near the present-day Quick Stop. Employees are thought to be, from left to right, Ella Octavia Vawter, Clyde Haden, and Mollie Wagon. (Courtesy of TAGHS.)

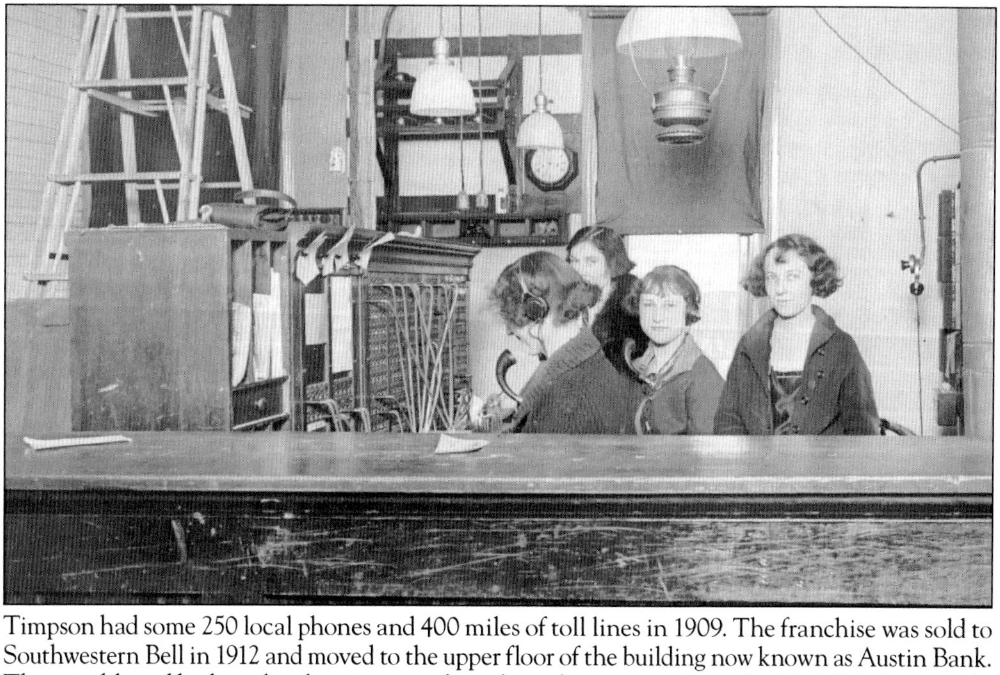

Timpson had some 250 local phones and 400 miles of toll lines in 1909. The franchise was sold to Southwestern Bell in 1912 and moved to the upper floor of the building now known as Austin Bank. The switchboard had two local positions and two long-distance positions. In this 1924 photograph, the only person to be identified is Oma Allen, on the far right. (Courtesy of TAGHS.)

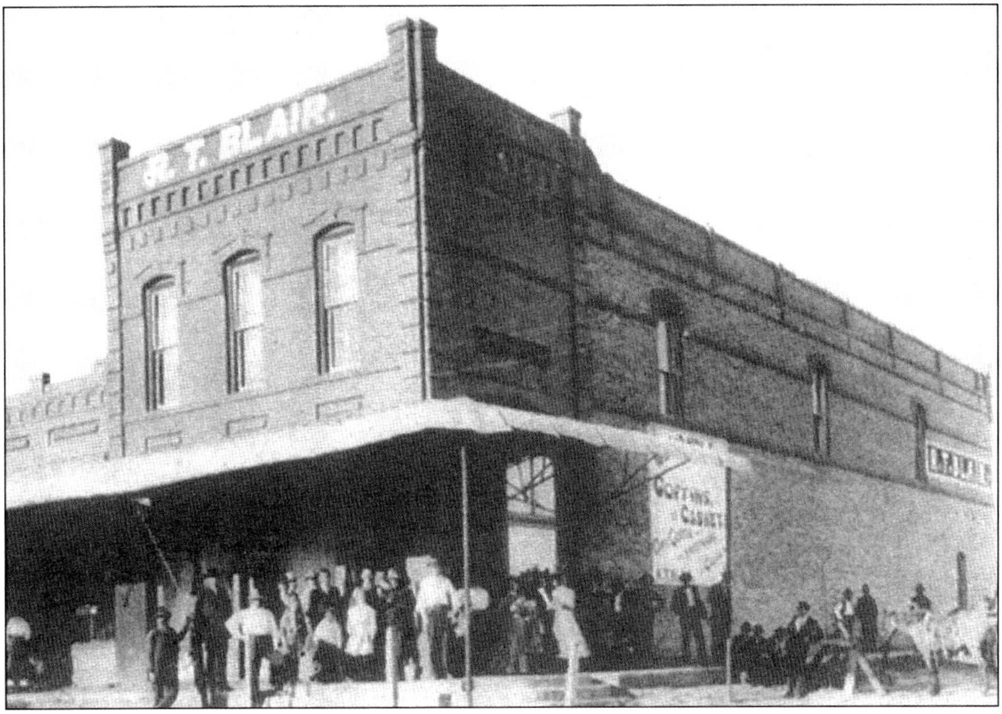

The R.T. Blair Store, built in 1904, was located in a large two-story brick building on the corner of Bremond and South First Streets. The store is shown on a typical Saturday in the early 1900s, as people came to town to shop. There were hitching posts for horses, buggies, and wagons beside the building. Blair liked to sit in his cowhide-bottom straight chair in the back doorway to speak to everyone who passed by. (Courtesy of TAGHS.)

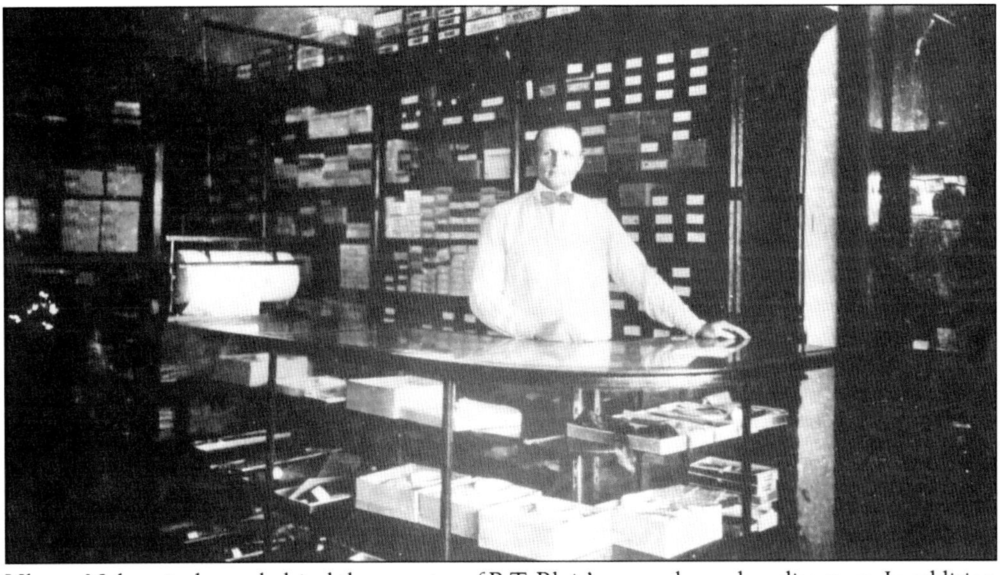

Ulysses Nelson is shown behind the counter of R.T. Blair's general merchandise store. In addition to a complete line of groceries, clothing, and other supplies, Blair sold buggies, horse collars, halters, reins, and other items for horses and buggies. It is said that he kept the buggies upstairs. (Courtesy of TAGHS.)

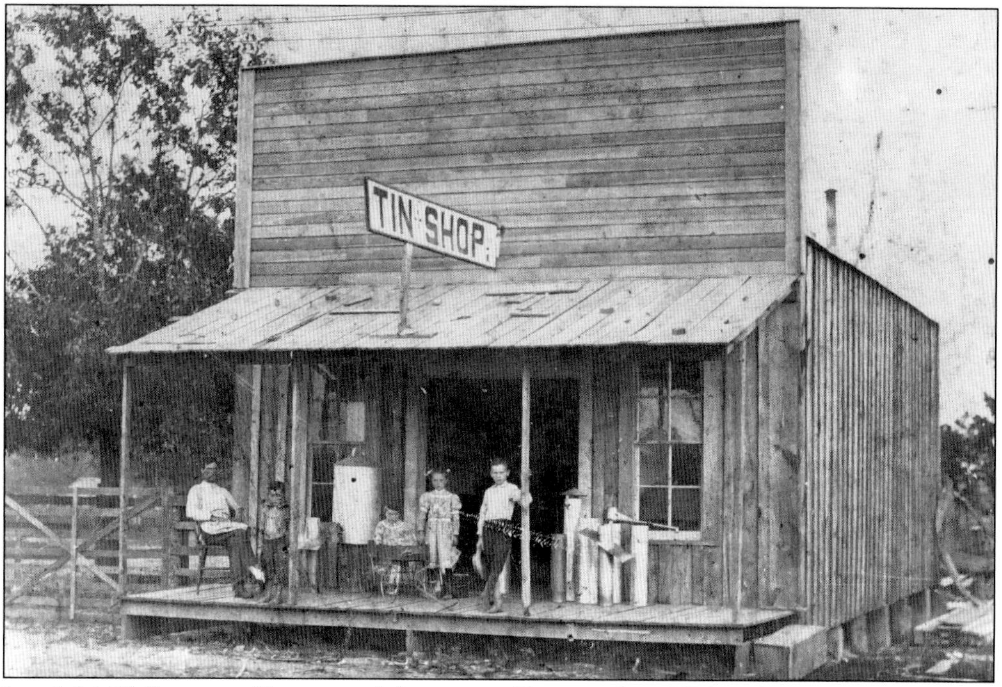

Joseph McClellan moved his tinsmith business to Timpson from Walnut Springs, Texas, in 1900 or 1901. This 1903 Tin Shop was located on South First Street, on lot 29 (now Austin Street). In the tin shop, McClellan made cisterns, roofing, gutters, stovepipe, flues, pipe for mills, milk cans, etc. Shown here are, from left to right, Joseph McClellan and his children Brownlow, Lyle, Thelma, and Aubrey. (Courtesy of Tom McClellan.)

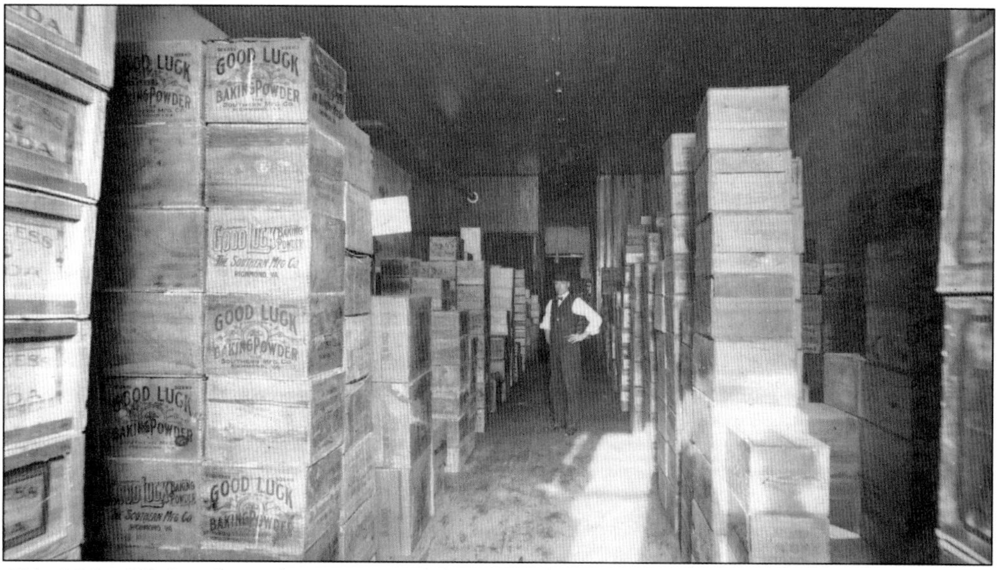

Alfred John Wigley, shown here, managed the Nacogdoches Grocery Company wholesale grocery and general merchandise warehouse in Timpson for more than 20 years. The company was founded in May 1902 by a group of Nacogdoches businessmen who erected a large two-story brick building in Nacogdoches along the HE&WT and Sabine railroad tracks. Their trade territory covered 11 counties in East Texas. (Courtesy of Martha Wigley Wheeler.)

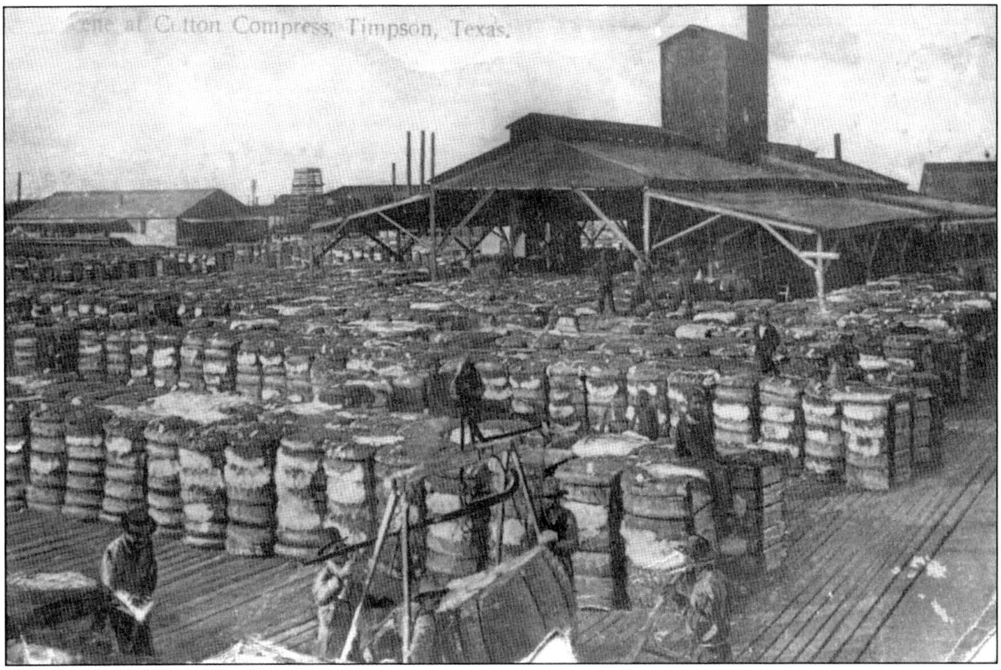

The Timpson Compress Company was organized and built by Fort Worth businessman Tom B. Owens in 1903. Timpson businessmen T.P. Rutherford, Deason Hairston, R.T. Blair, John Wood, and J.E. Blankenship were part of the early venture. H.R. Fory was the first president and manager. The first year 28,000 bales were pressed. The business moved to Harlingen, Texas, in 1947. (Courtesy of Lou Nell Billingsley.)

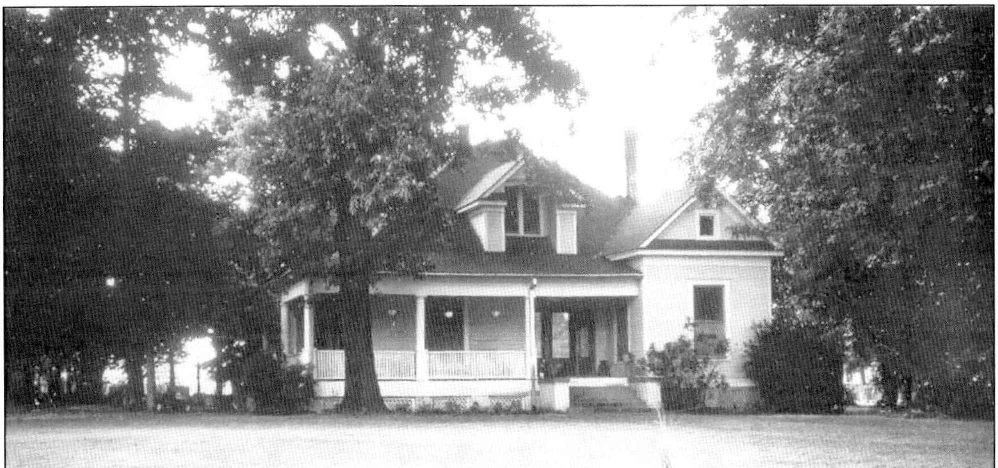

The Howard R. and Martha (Monkhouse) Fory home was built in 1898 from lumber planed at Johns and Fory Lumber Company in Timpson. Fory later bought the Timpson Handle Factory, where the interior trim was made. The home, located on South Second Street, was purchased by Ted and Kathleen Taylor in 1971, after Martha Fory's death at the age of 97. The home was destroyed by fire in 1982. (Courtesy of Kathleen Taylor.)

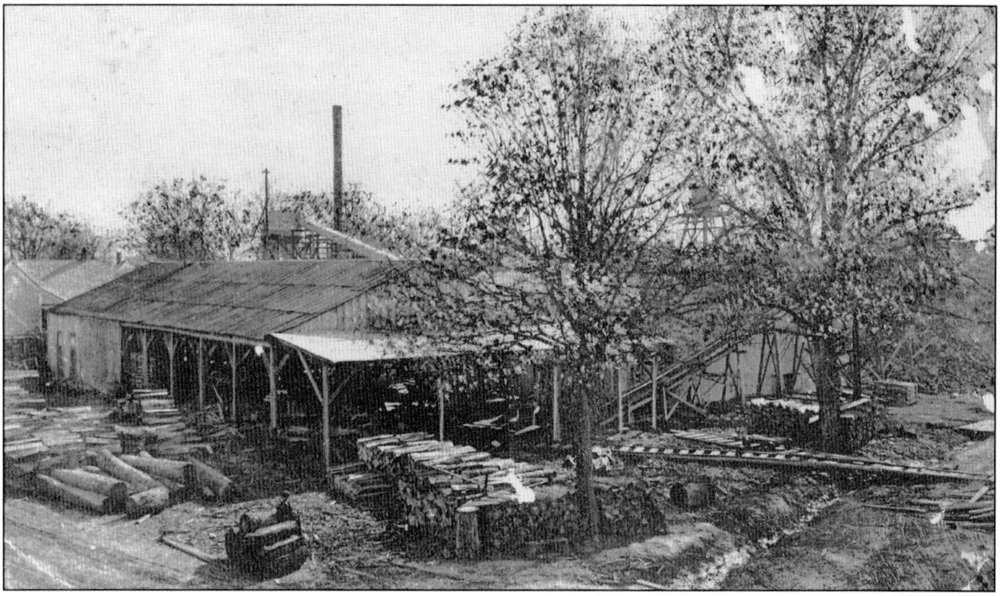

The Timpson Handle Company (above) was built around 1905 and was then purchased and completely reconstructed by H.R. Fory in the fall of 1906. Fory was the president and general manager. The factory manufactured cant hook, ax, adze, pick, sledge, hatchet, hammer, and mining tool handles of hickory with the finest grain and elasticity. Thirty-five men and boys were employed, making 300 dozen handles a day. The handles were sent throughout the United States and to several foreign countries. In 1908, the Texas State Fair and the Louisiana State Fair awarded the Timpson Handle Company the first premium for the best display of manufactured handles. In 1912, the mill burned and was never rebuilt. During this same period of time, Timpson had two planer mills and a stave factory. (Courtesy of TAGHS.)

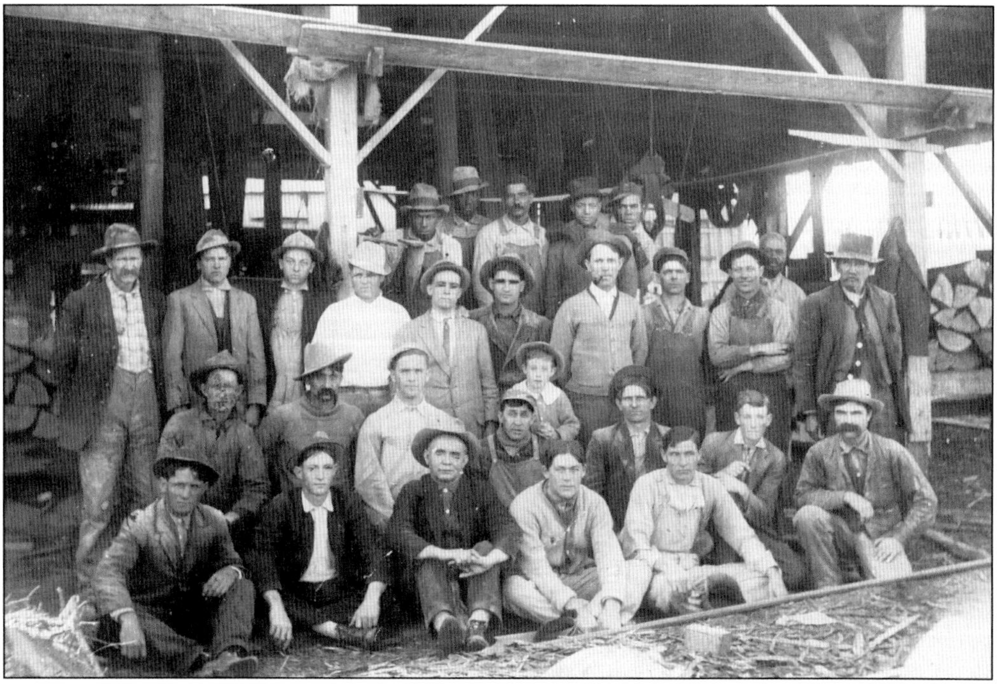

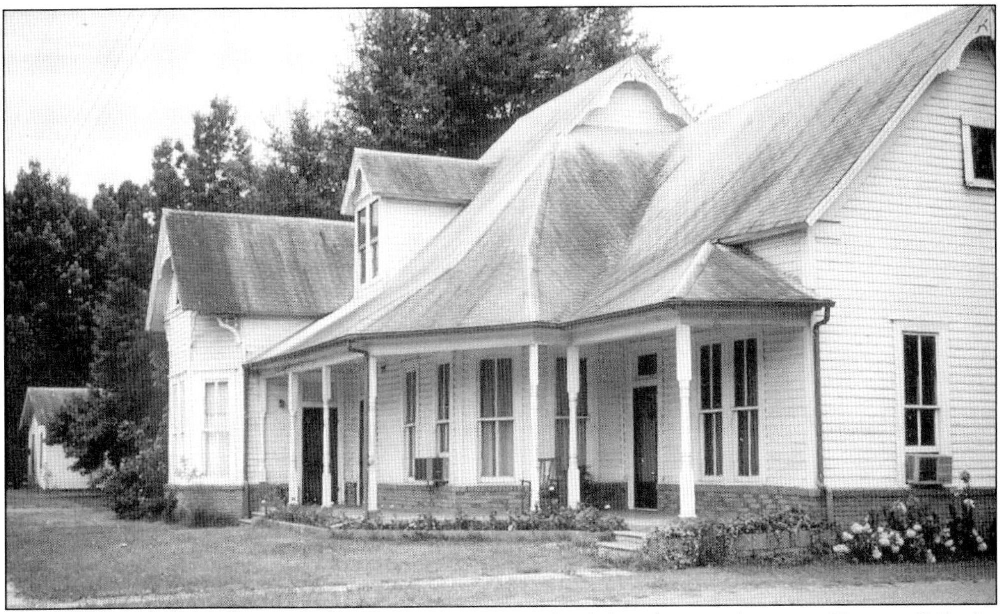

This home, located on US 59 and Prairie Street, was built by Thomas Augustus Trammell Sr. for his bride, Hallie Emma (Burns) Trammell, around 1896. Trammell was the co-owner of Trammell and Sons Hardware on Bremond Street. Trammell was only 39 years old when he died. His wife remained in the home and raised her four children alone. (Courtesy of TAGHS.)

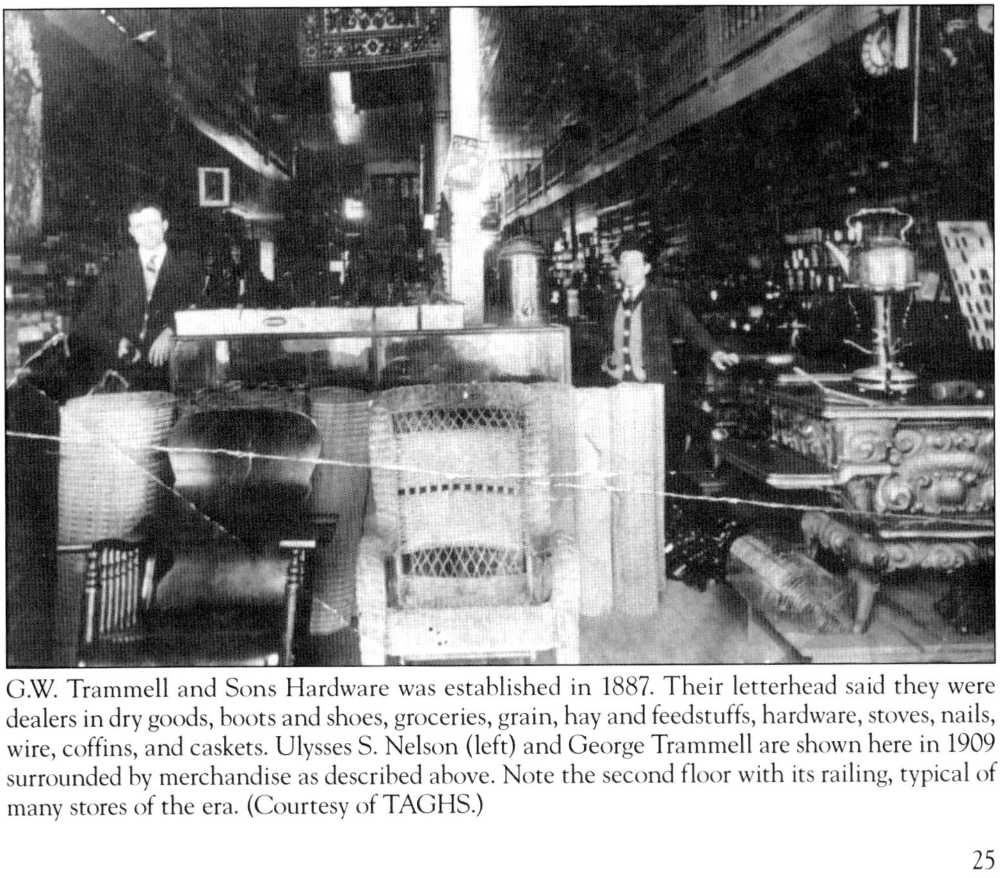

G.W. Trammell and Sons Hardware was established in 1887. Their letterhead said they were dealers in dry goods, boots and shoes, groceries, grain, hay and feedstuffs, hardware, stoves, nails, wire, coffins, and caskets. Ulysses S. Nelson (left) and George Trammell are shown here in 1909 surrounded by merchandise as described above. Note the second floor with its railing, typical of many stores of the era. (Courtesy of TAGHS.)

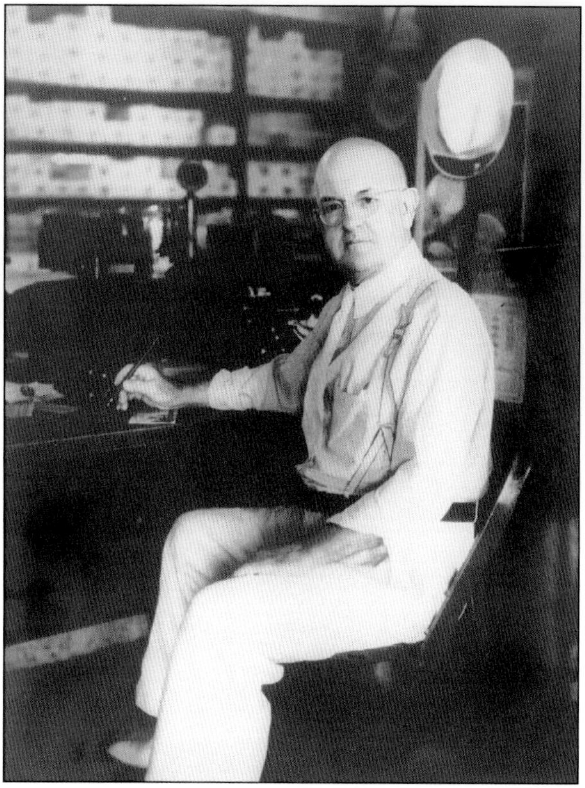

J.E. Blankenship was a young entrepreneur, selling apples to railroad workers before the railroad reached Timpson in 1885. Then in 1890, at age 18, he built his first general merchandise store. The small frame building carried his name, Blankenship's. In 1898, he built a large brick building on Jacob Street and remained in this location until his death in 1965. Blankenship was often seen at his desk. (Courtesy of TAGHS.)

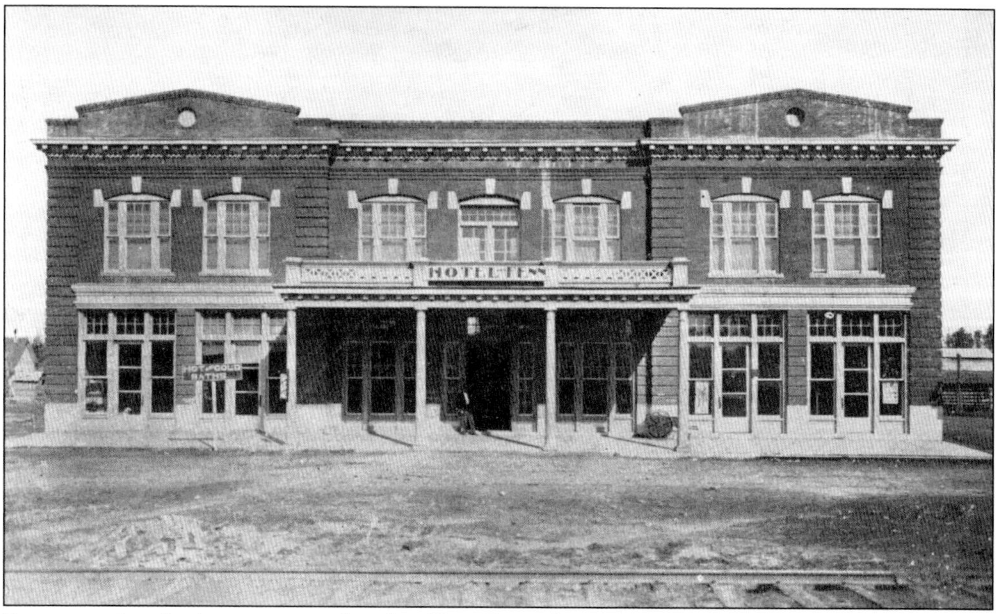

Recognized as the largest, nicest hotel in East Texas for many years, the Blankenship Hotel was a favorite stopping place for railroad men and traveling salesmen. Built in 1904, it was owned or managed by Lenora Fenn, J.M. Weaver, and Evie (Burns) Motley before becoming the Blankenship Hotel in 1929. Located on Railroad Avenue, it faced the depot. The hotel was demolished in 1960. (Courtesy of TAGHS.)

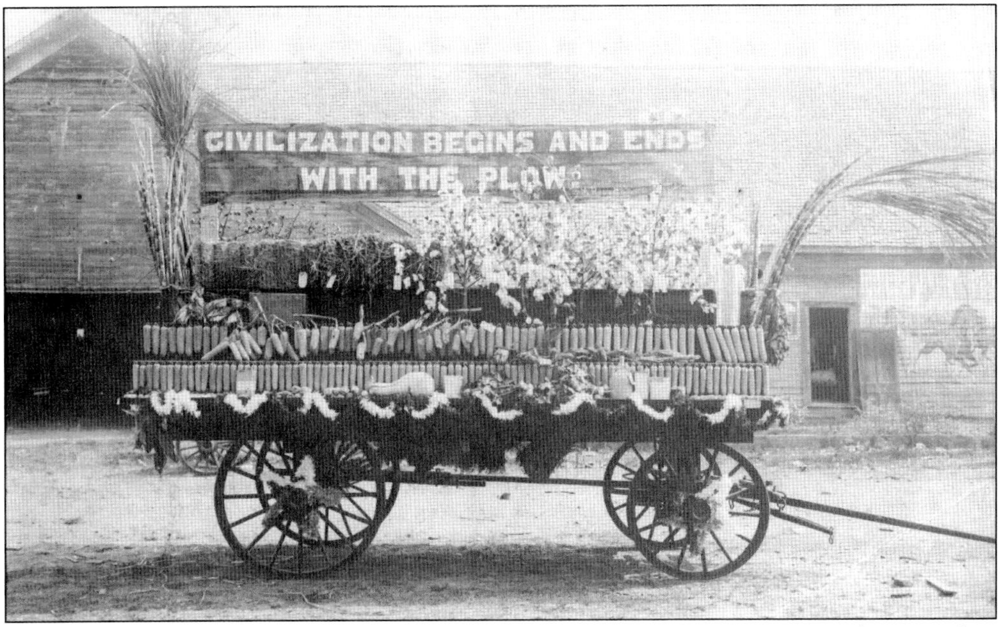

This wagon, laden with produce, was exhibited at the Louisiana State Fair in early November, around 1912. Shreveport was a market for agricultural items produced in East Texas, and Timpson and the surrounding communities attended the fair to view new equipment and learn new techniques for an improved way of life. Products included sugar cane, corn, cotton bolls on the stalk, bales of hay, and squash. (Courtesy of TAGHS.)

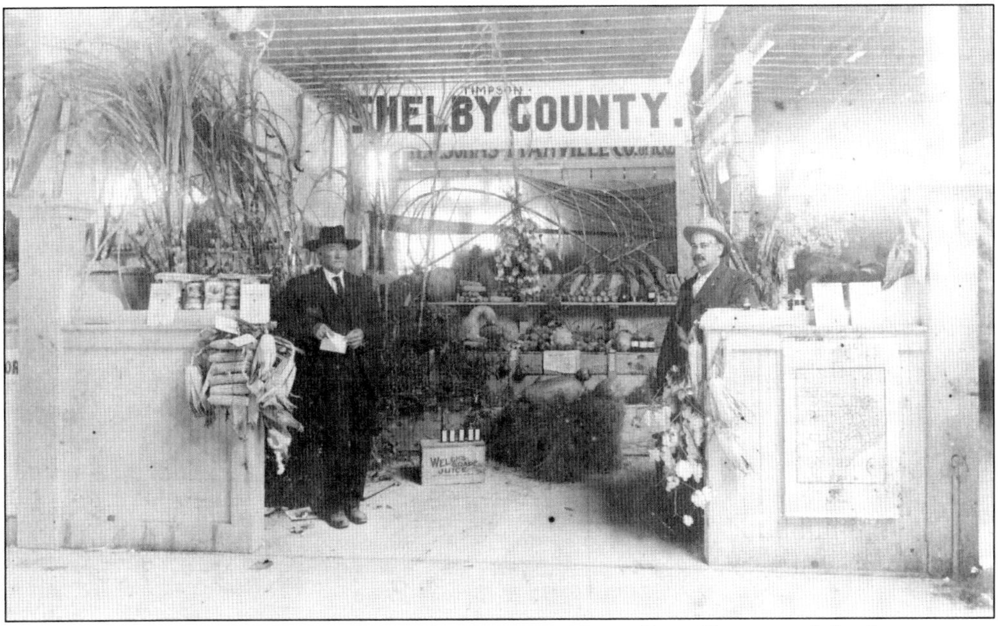

Most likely, this fair booth was also at the Louisiana State Fair. Shreveport's leading citizens founded the fair in 1906 to assist in developing the agricultural and industrial resources of the area. Upon close inspection, the two unidentified men in the photograph had the 1909 Timpson Business League's publication, "Timpson," ready to hand out to prospective Timpson citizens. Additional products shown were tobacco and canned peaches. (Courtesy of TAGHS.)

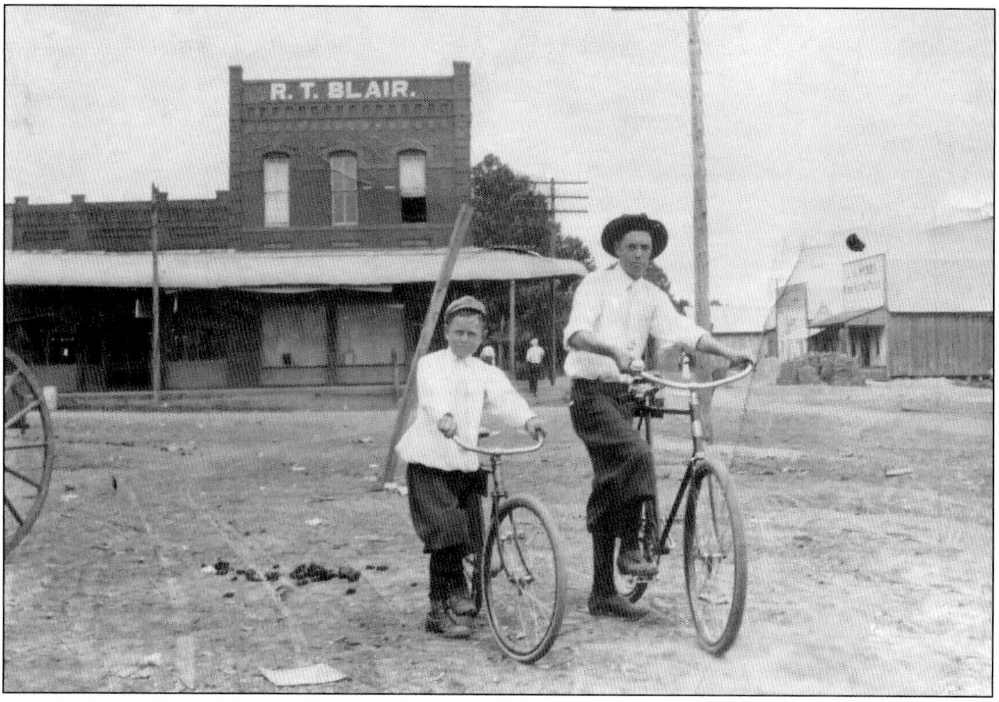

Gus (left) and Burns Trammell, sons of T.A. and Emma Trammell, are shown in 1910 or 1911 in front of the R.T. Blair store. The streets were as yet unpaved, and many people still traveled by horse and buggy, mule and wagon, or, if in the city, bicycles. In the background at right are wooden stores, one of which reads "J.A. Moses, ? Boots Feed." (Courtesy of Mary Alice Hooper Largent.)

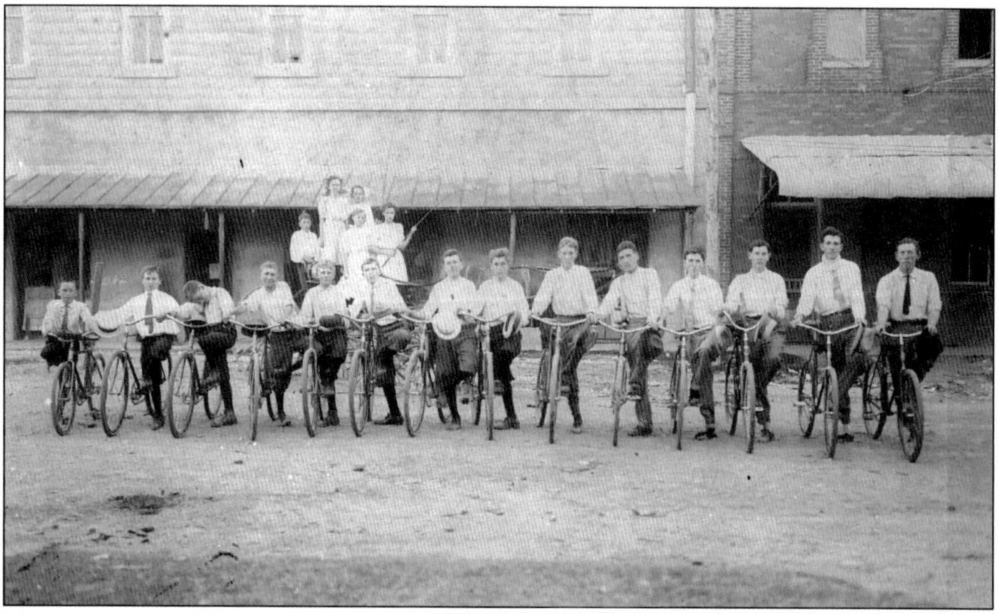

The young town of Timpson had a variety of activities to involve and entertain its citizens. The bicycle race through the streets of Timpson was a popular event. These young racers pose with their feet on the pedals and their hands on the handlebars. All are holding hats to shield their eyes. (Courtesy of TAGHS.)

Victor Alcide Hebert was a sales representative for Southern Drug Company of Houston, living in hotels and traveling a large East Texas territory. Coming to Timpson in 1905, Victor and his wife, Alice Vivian, and son Edmond moved into their first home on South Second Street in Timpson, next to SoSo Park. Hebert chose Timpson because railroads connected from all directions. He retired in 1944. (Courtesy of Glenda Hebert Watters.)

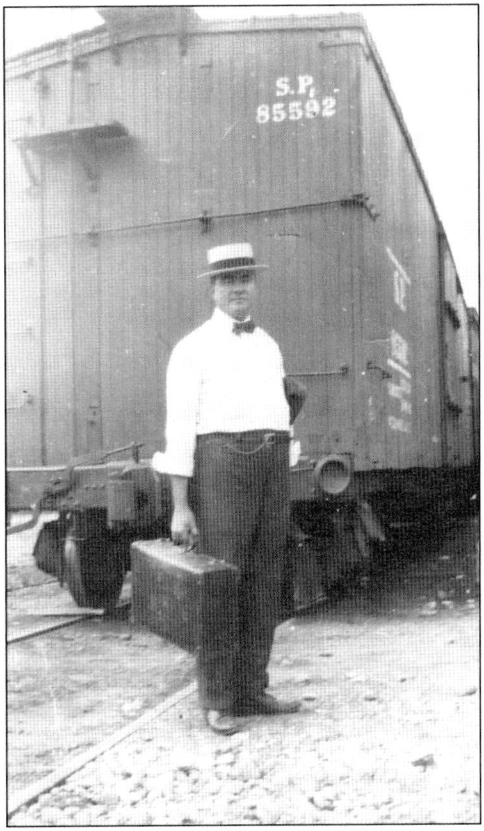

The Timpson Concert Band is shown here on April 23, 1909. It gained wide recognition in deep East Texas during the 1920s and 1930s while under the directorship of Clifford E. Busey. At its peak, there were 25–30 members. Early directors included John David Ford, Howell L. Walker, Floyd Elija Matthews (from 1913 to 1916), and Clifford E. Busey (from sometime after 1916 to 1934). (Courtesy of TAGHS.)

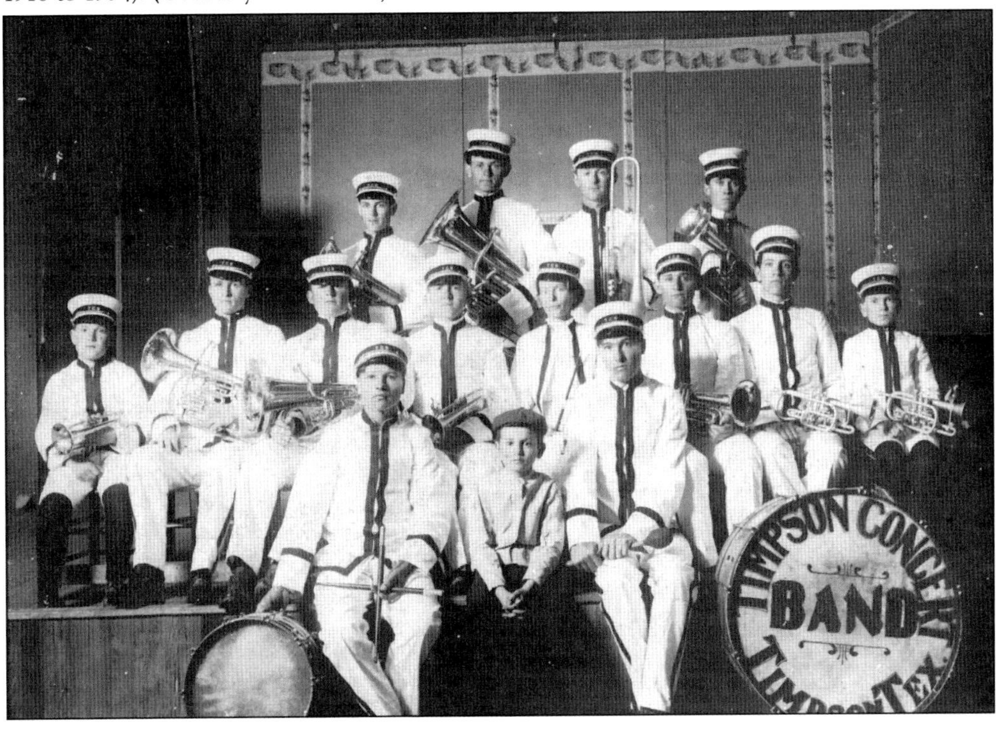

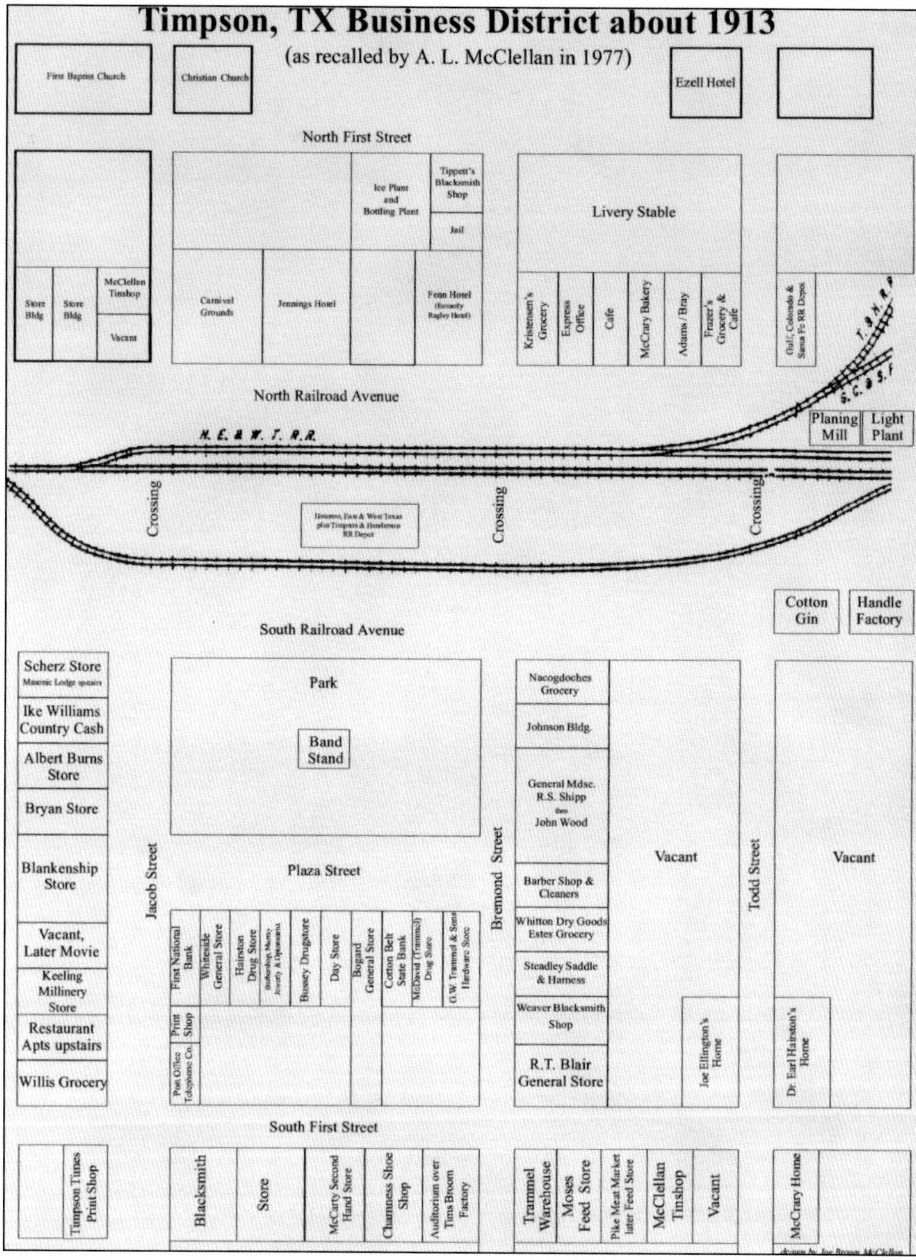

Charles Noblet, the railroad surveyor, was also responsible for laying out the city of Timpson. It was laid out parallel with the railroad, at 43 degrees off north. The city was surveyed at one square mile, then subdivided into commercial and residential lots and blocks. Major streets were named for railroad officials, stockholders, and early settlers. The city itself was named for Samuel Coulter Timpson, railroad executive and son-in-law of Paul Bremond, founder of the HE&WT Railway. Bremond and Jacob Streets were named for railroad stockholders, and Todd and McLaughlin Streets were named for early settlers. Joe Brown McClellan drew this 1913 map, as recalled by A.L. McClellan in 1977. Lynn Alexander converted the hand-drawn map to this computerized drawing in 2002. Upon close inspection, three hotels, two banks, three drugstores, three cafés, and numerous other businesses can be identified. (Courtesy of TAGHS.)

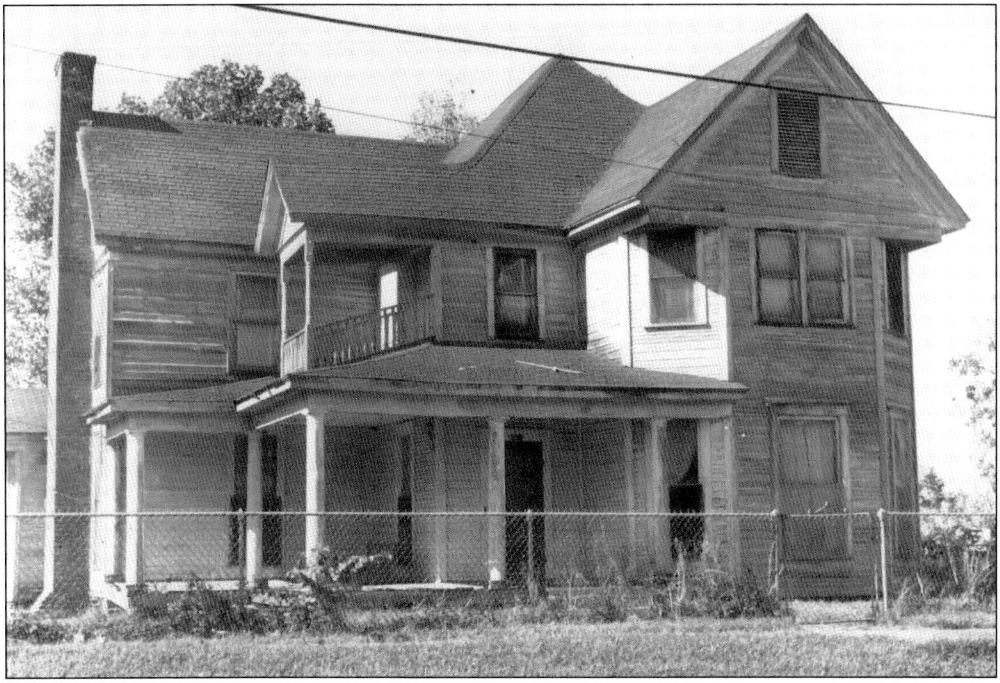

The "old" Albert F. Bryan home was located across from Timpson High School on South First Street (Bear Drive). Bryan built this house for his bride, Onie Freeman, in 1887. They lived there until 1898, when Bryan built a grand Victorian home on Washington and South First Streets. Bryan sold the original home above to Moultrey Brown, a sawmill engineer. It was torn down in the 1980s. (Courtesy of TAGHS.)

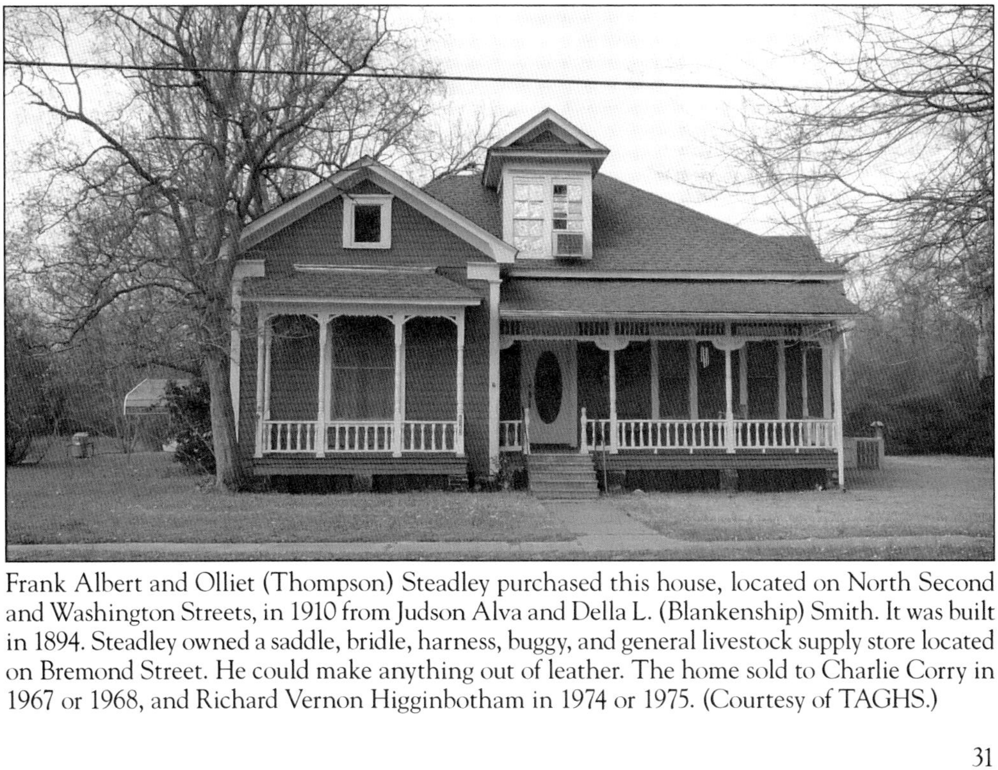

Frank Albert and Olliet (Thompson) Steadley purchased this house, located on North Second and Washington Streets, in 1910 from Judson Alva and Della L. (Blankenship) Smith. It was built in 1894. Steadley owned a saddle, bridle, harness, buggy, and general livestock supply store located on Bremond Street. He could make anything out of leather. The home sold to Charlie Corry in 1967 or 1968, and Richard Vernon Higginbotham in 1974 or 1975. (Courtesy of TAGHS.)

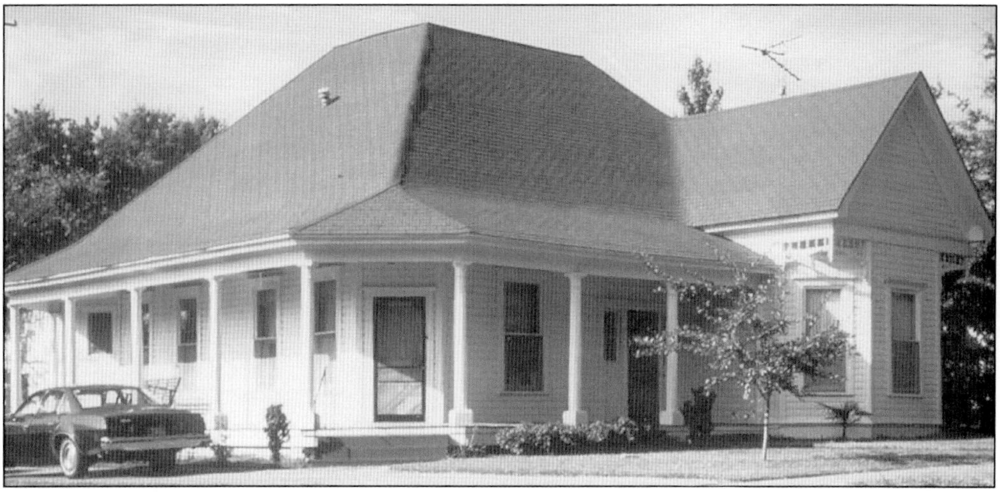

William J. "Bill" Walker brought his family to Timpson before 1910. He and his wife, Nancy L. (Graham) Walker, moved into this home on what is now Bear Drive. The home was built in the late 1800s. Walker taught school and was later admitted to the bar. He was also a traveling salesman, broker, jobber, and an insurance agent. Nancy Walker was also an insurance agent. (Courtesy of TAGHS.)

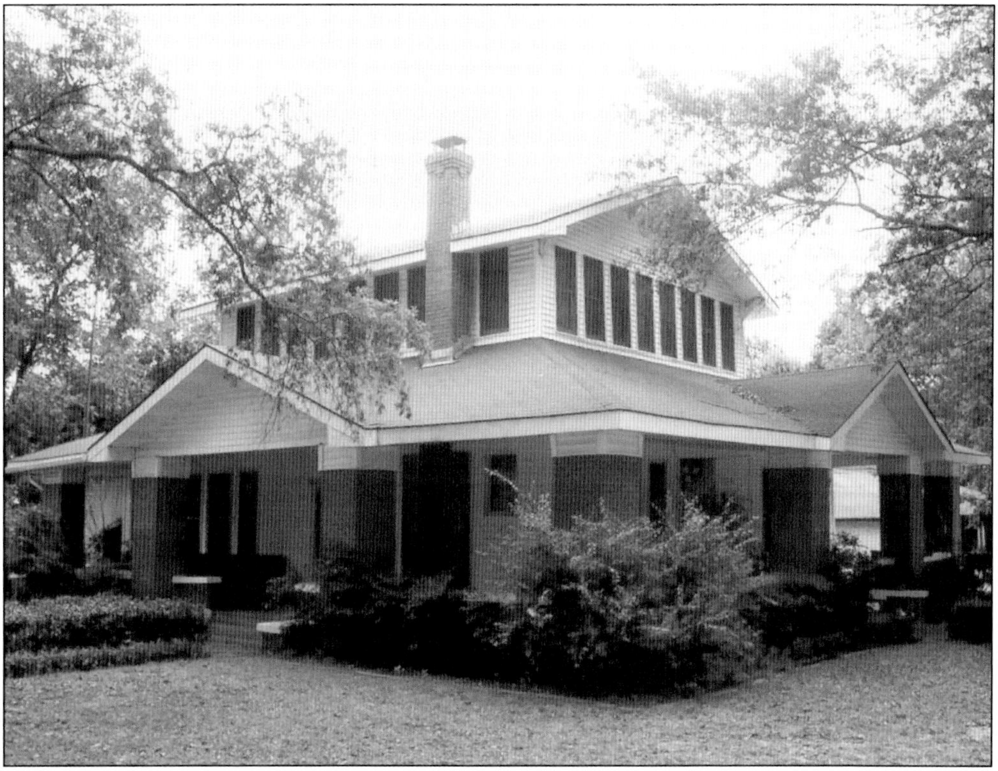

This home, located on South First Street, was occupied by Dr. George Earl Hairston and his wife, Ollie May (McClendon) Hairston. Hairston was a dentist in Timpson for many years, and he and his wife were the parents of three children. Mina McClendon, a sister of Mrs. Hairston, made her home with them and became a teacher in Timpson. (Courtesy of TAGHS.)

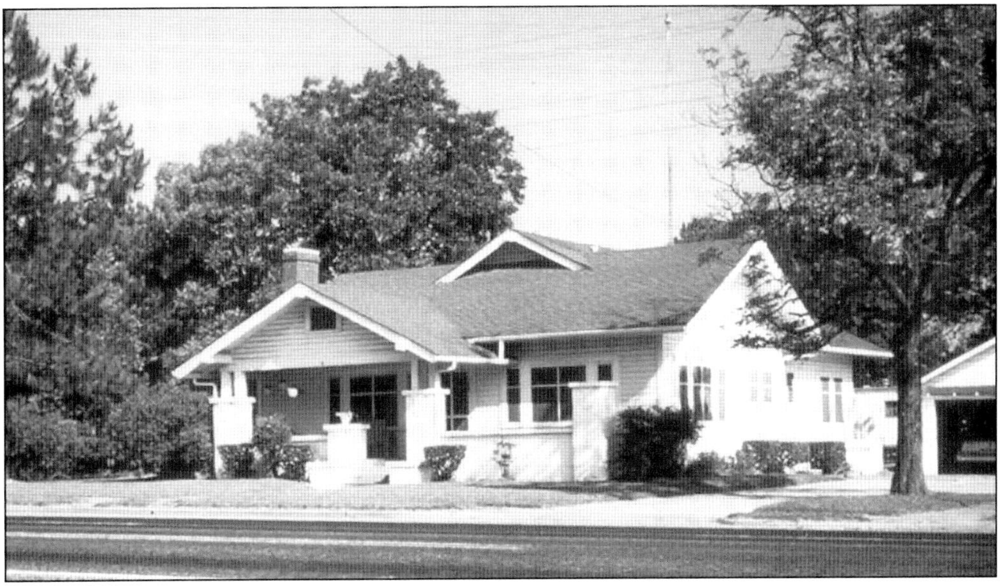

Albert Franklin and Myra Euginia (Blankenship) Burns built this home around 1917. It is located at Highway 59 and Washington Street. Burns owned a mercantile store on Bremond Street, where his wife and three daughters, Maydelle, Evie Ruth, and Doris, worked. Each daughter earned a master's degree and became a schoolteacher. The home was deeded to the Timpson Area Genealogical and Heritage Society when the estate was settled. (Courtesy of TAGHS.)

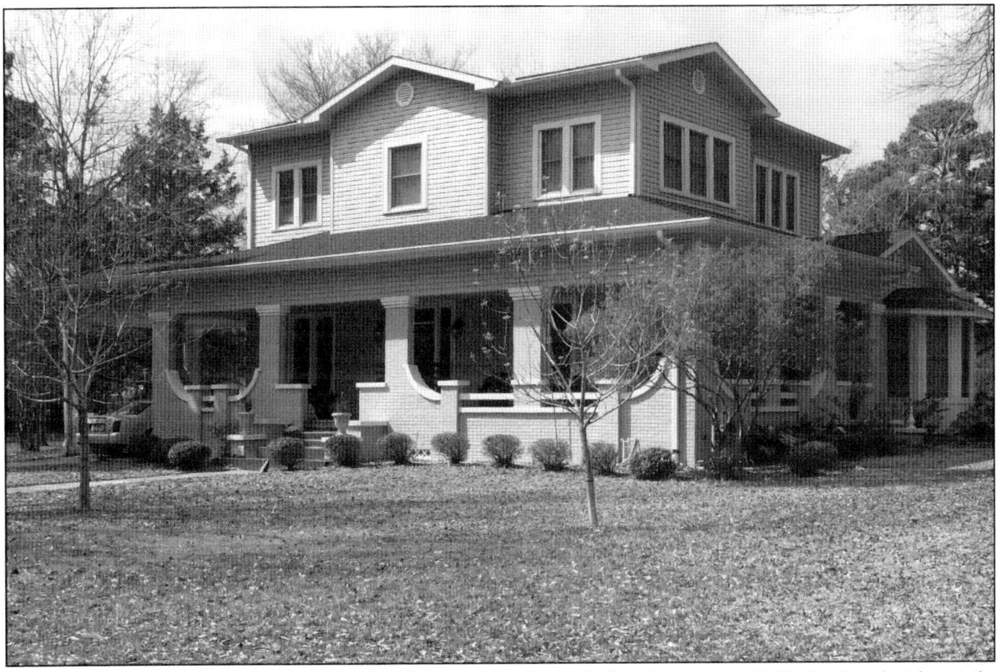

Trammell Pitts Rutherford, a cotton buyer, purchased this home in 1899 for his bride, Ada Clementine Whiteside, from out-of-state stockholders of the HE&WT Railway. It was located at the corner of South First and Washington Streets. After Ada's death in 1914, the home was completely remodeled. It began as a two-story dogtrot style and became a modern home. Rutherford married Nellie Meador in 1917. (Courtesy of TAGHS.)

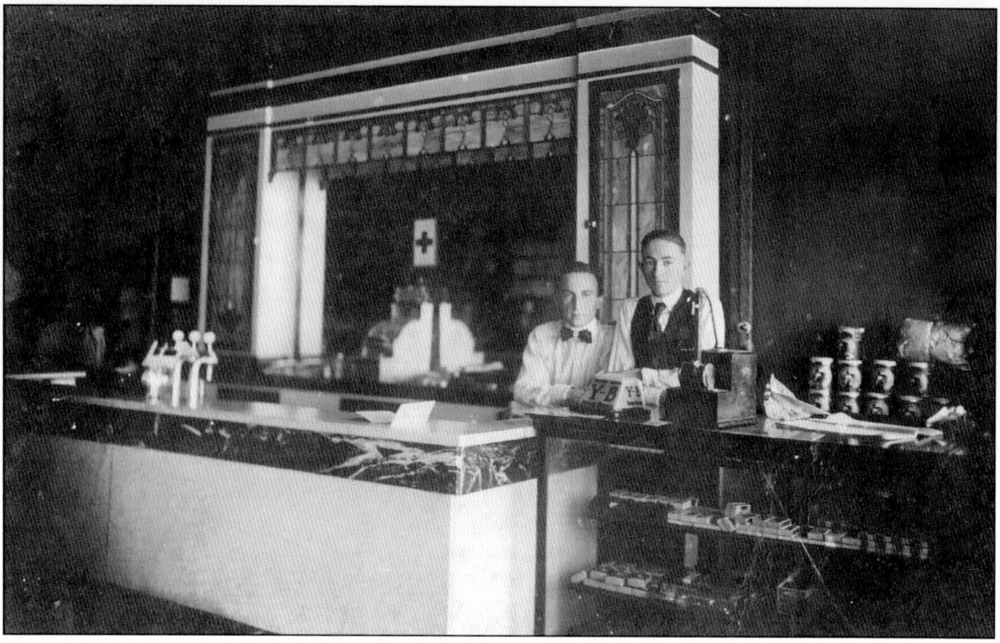

Grover C. McDavid purchased this store, located on Front Street, from Trammel Brothers Drug Store before 1919 and renamed it McDavid's Drug. It had a large soda fountain where Dewey McClung (left) and Charles Wigley prepared favorite treats for customers. McDavid was the pharmacist. His store also served as the bus station in Timpson, staying open from 7:30 a.m. to 10:07 p.m., and on Sundays, for the convenience of the bus passengers. (Courtesy of Martha Wigley Wheeler.)

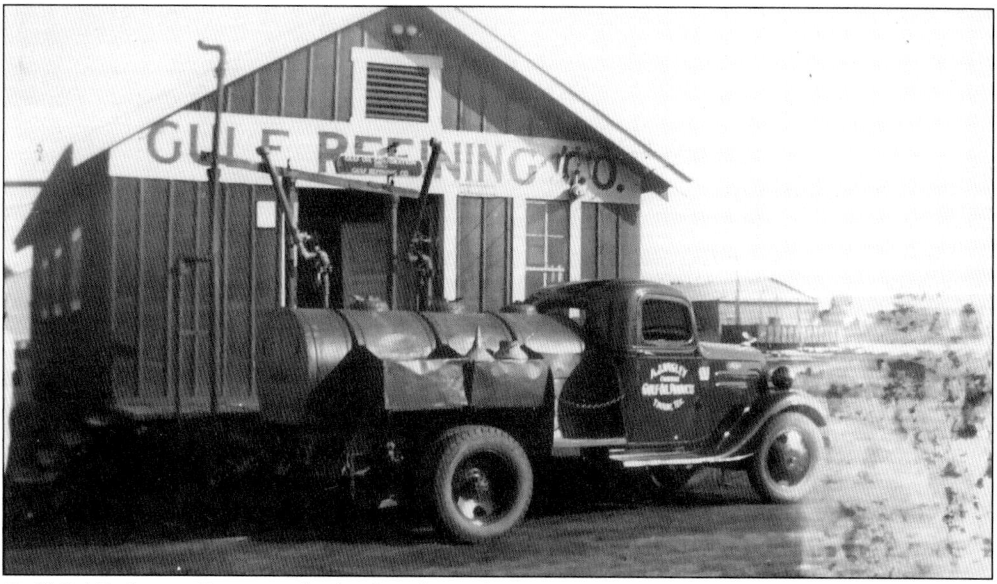

Gulf Oil Refining Company had a distributorship in Timpson as early as 1929. For many years, F. Ollie B. Johnson was the consignee, but he left in 1935 to become district field supervisor for the company in Corpus Christi, Texas. Alfred John Wigley was consignee at the time of this photograph. After Wigley's death, in 1940, D.A. McClung, a local cotton buyer, took over the distributorship. (Courtesy of Martha Wigley Wheeler.)

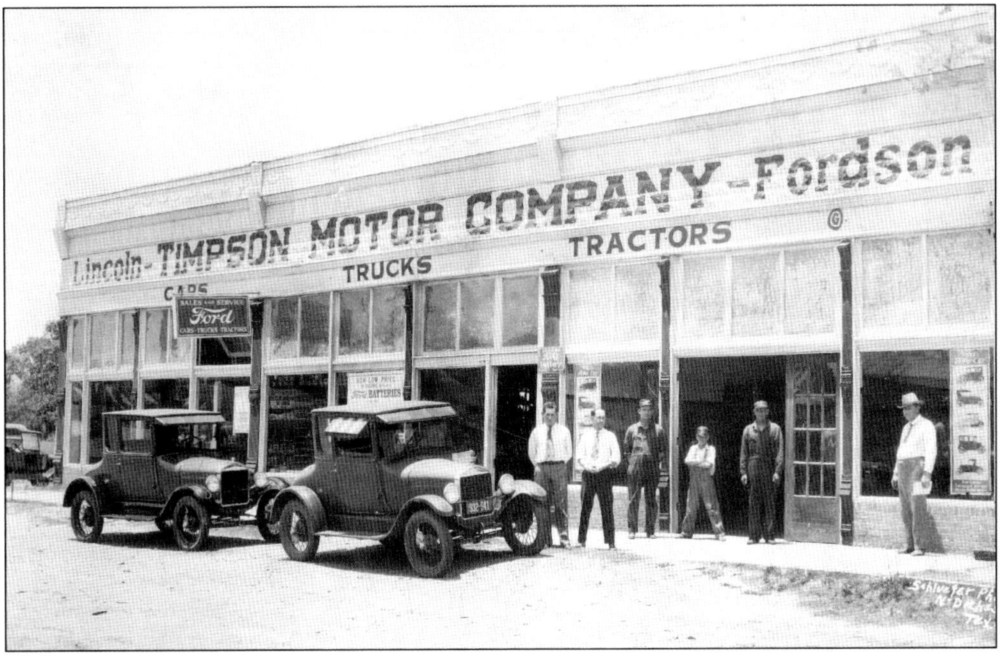

One of the oldest automobile dealerships in Timpson was the Timpson Motor Company, located on Railroad Avenue. In this 1920s photograph, Arris A. Beck, second from left, is selling Ford and Lincoln automobiles and Ford trucks and tractors. Byron Smith is on the far right; all others are unidentified. The company later moved to the corner of Bremond and South First Streets and was known as the Ford Motor Company. (Courtesy of TAGHS.)

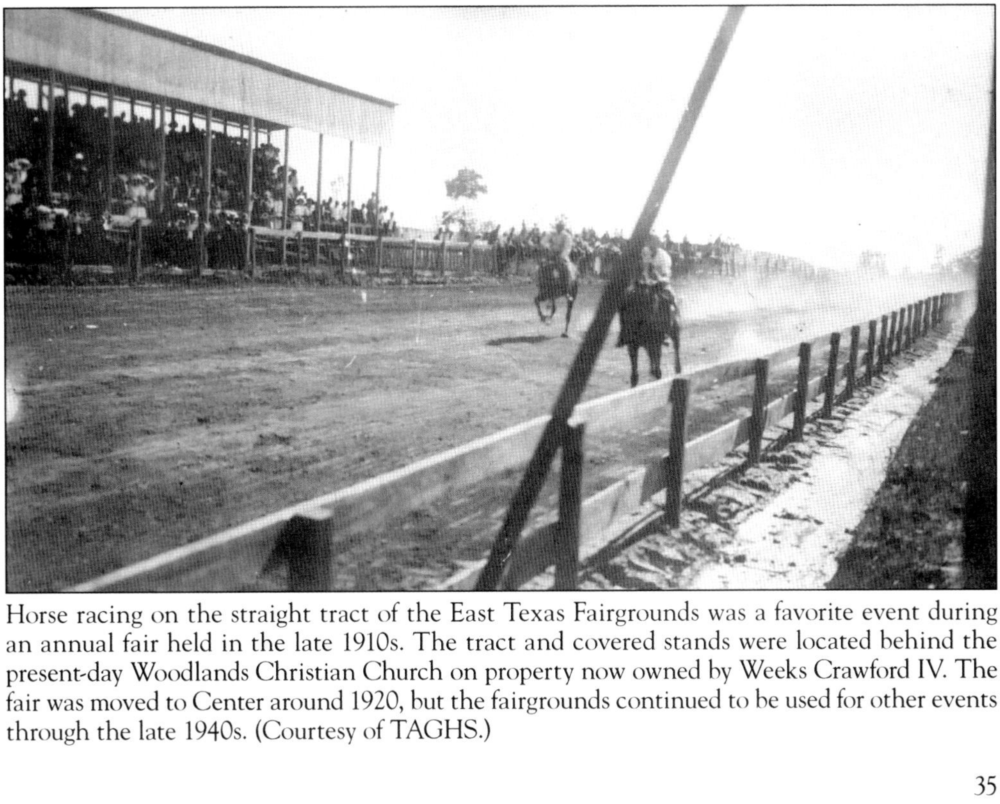
Horse racing on the straight tract of the East Texas Fairgrounds was a favorite event during an annual fair held in the late 1910s. The tract and covered stands were located behind the present-day Woodlands Christian Church on property now owned by Weeks Crawford IV. The fair was moved to Center around 1920, but the fairgrounds continued to be used for other events through the late 1940s. (Courtesy of TAGHS.)

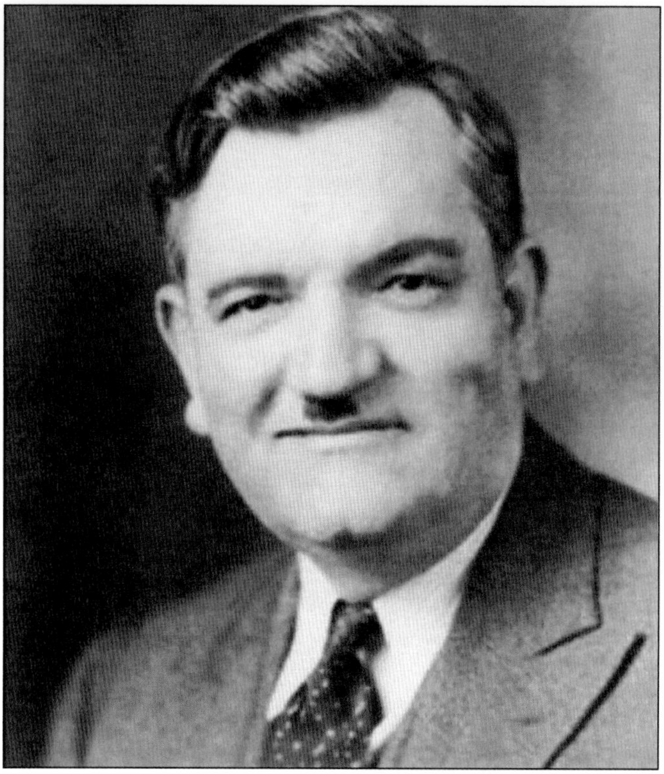

Virgil Oliver Stamps was born in Upshur County, Texas. He attended the singing school of Richard M. Morgan in 1907, and later began teaching music. In 1919, Stamps, his wife, Addie, and their two children moved to Timpson, near his family. He established a music store and taught music in Timpson, and was a field representative for the James D. Vaughan Music Company. Virgil Stamps died in 1940. (Courtesy of Will Stamps.)

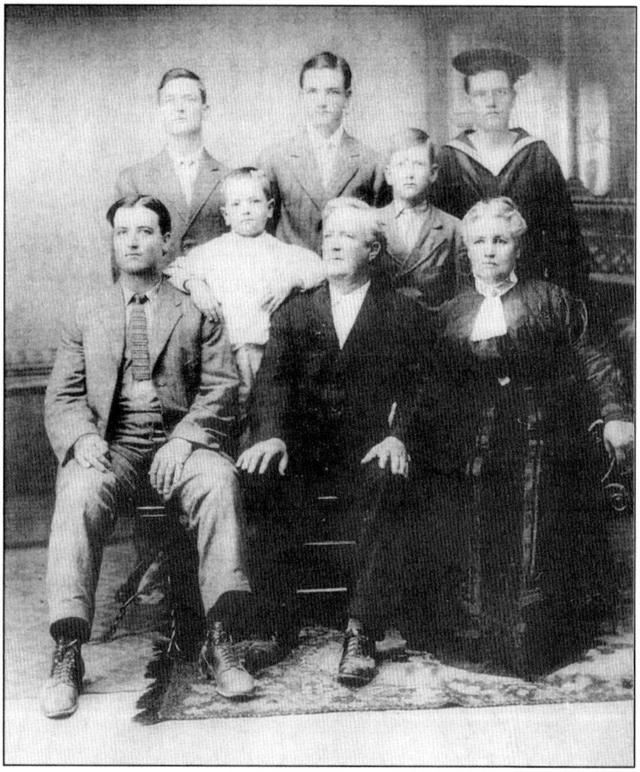

William Oscar Stamps and his wife, Florence Corinne Rosser, with their 16-year-old son, Fred, moved to Timpson in 1917 from Ore City. W.O. bought a grocery store, and the whole family was here by 1920. The oldest son, Charlie, was a veterinarian. V.O. established a music store and taught music. Fred Stamps married Amy Stilley, a Timpson girl, on November 5, 1922. (Courtesy of Will Stamps.)

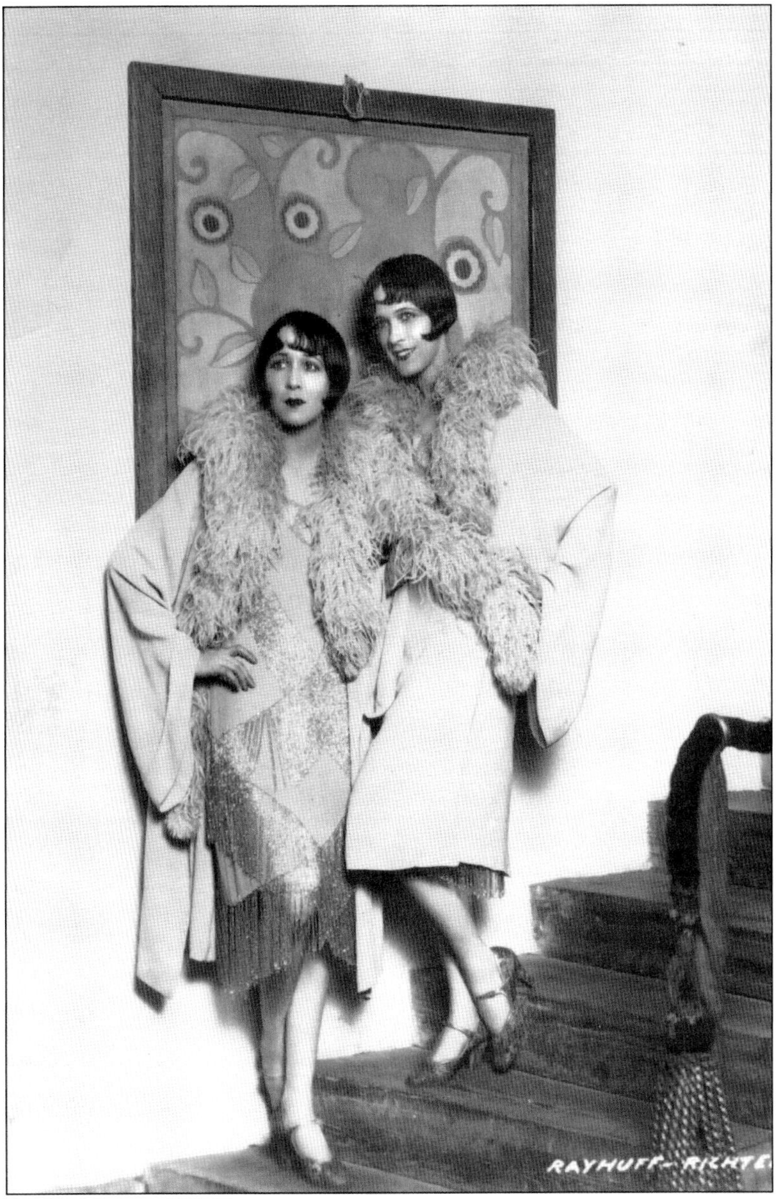

Velma (left) and Thelma Connor, the "Connor Twins," are shown during their time as performers in the Ziegfeld Follies. Born on December 1, 1904, to John Wesley Conner and Alice Cornelia (Hartsfield) Conner, the twins began singing and dancing at an early age. The family moved to Houston before 1910, where the twins were discovered by Gus Edwards (known as "The Star Maker"). They first appeared on stage in *When Shall We Meet Again*, with Gus Edward's Revue, in 1921. The twins' next stop was the Ziegfeld Follies, where they achieved brilliant success, touring Europe and the United States. They were a singing and dancing act for 25 years, playing the Globe Theatre in London in 1928 and 1929. The twins appeared together in the 1932 film *Million Dollar Baby*. During World War II, they entertained American troops with USO camp shows. Velma Connor also appeared in a string of 18 Western movies. While visiting their parents in Timpson in 1932, they performed, to much acclaim, before two large audiences at the Victory Theatre. (Courtesy of Jan Magness Barrett.)

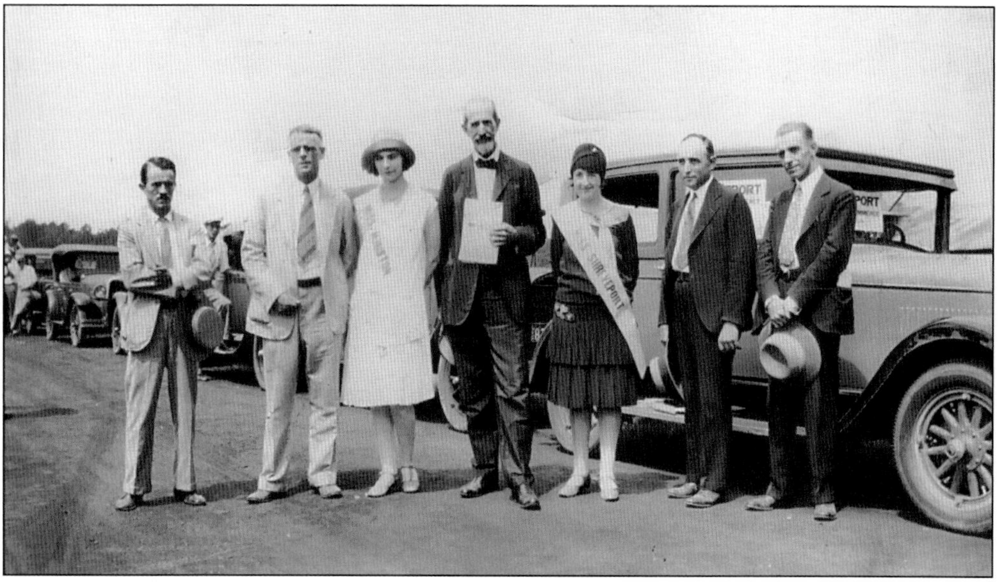

Prominent Houston and Shreveport citizens came to Timpson in 1924 to participate in the celebration of the Houston-Shreveport Airline Association organized for the building of Highway 35 (later US 59). They are, from left to right, a staff correspondent from the *Post Dispatch*, W.G. Jones of Motor League, and Jewita Jones, all of Houston; Col. M.F. Witherspoon, unidentified, Vernon Boast, and R.G. Morgan, all of Shreveport. (Courtesy of TAGHS.)

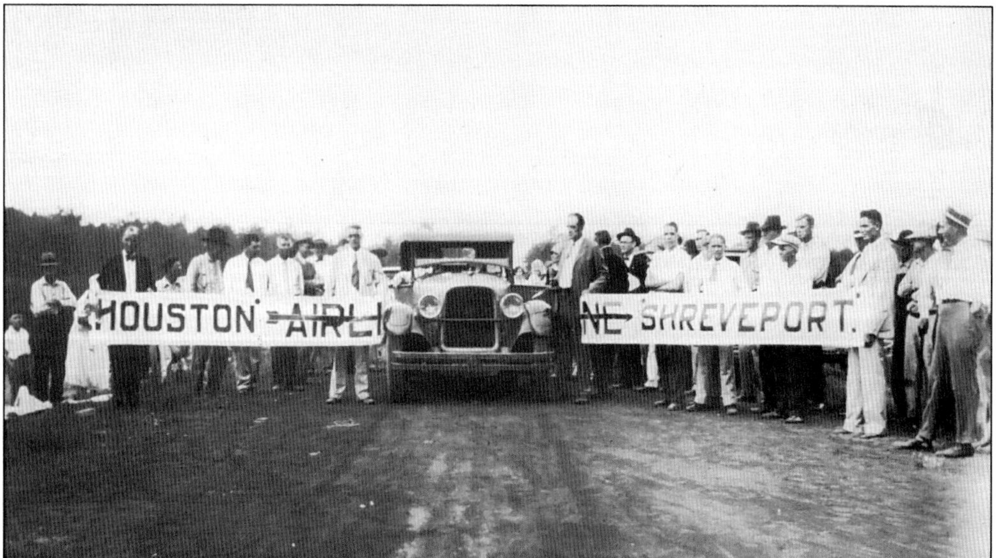

Highway 35 began as a hodgepodge of country dirt roads connecting the towns between Houston and Shreveport. In the early 1920s, it was an established route, although impassable at points, with some gravel improvements. By July 1926, the state highway commission began granting federal and state aid toward its improvement. The Houston-Shreveport Airline Association, headed by J.R. Nichols, was formed at Timpson to support this effort. (Courtesy of TAGHS.)

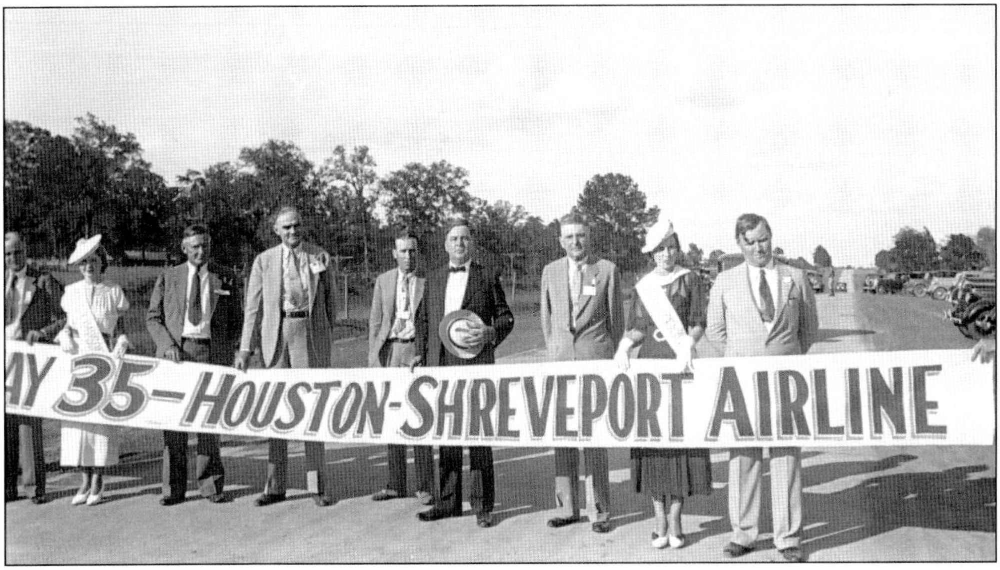

Shown at the ribbon cutting for the opening of Highway 35 in Timpson in 1935 are, from left to right, Deason Hairston (mayor of Timpson), Verna Smith (Miss Timpson), unidentified highway official, Gebb Gilcreast (highway engineer), unidentified official, John Wood (in dark suit holding hat), T.E. Huffman, highway official, unidentified (Miss Tenaha), and Dave McNeill (mayor of Tenaha). (Courtesy of TAGHS.)

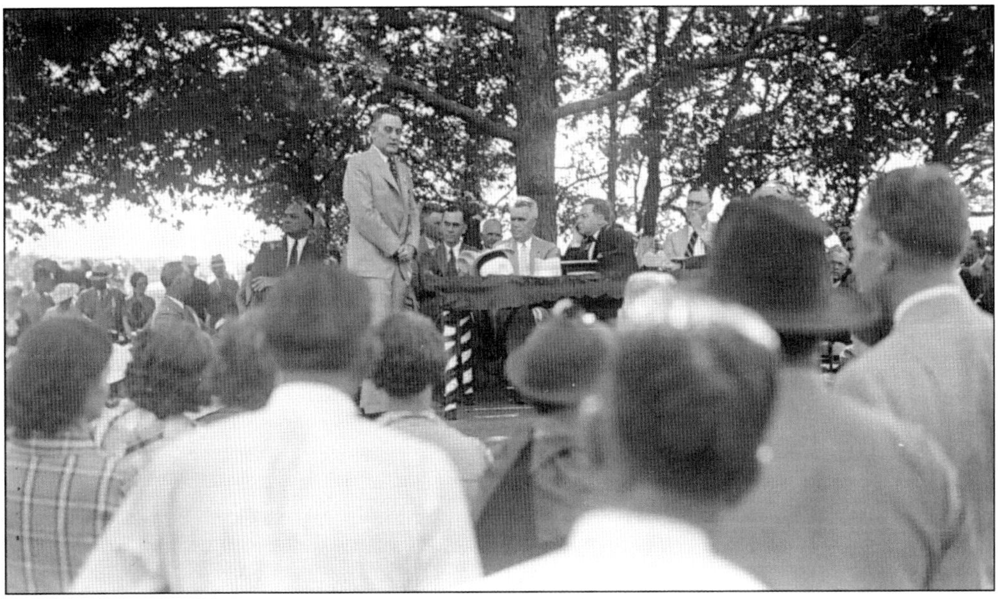

It was not until the mid-1930s that Highway 35 got its biggest improvement, when John Wood, local merchant and chairman of the State Highway Commission, gained approval to concrete the entire route. Festivities to celebrate the opening of Highway 35 were held in Bobo, beside Green's Lake, in 1935. Seated at the table behind the speaker are, from left to right, Edmond Hebert, unidentified, John Wood, and unidentified. (Courtesy of TAGHS.)

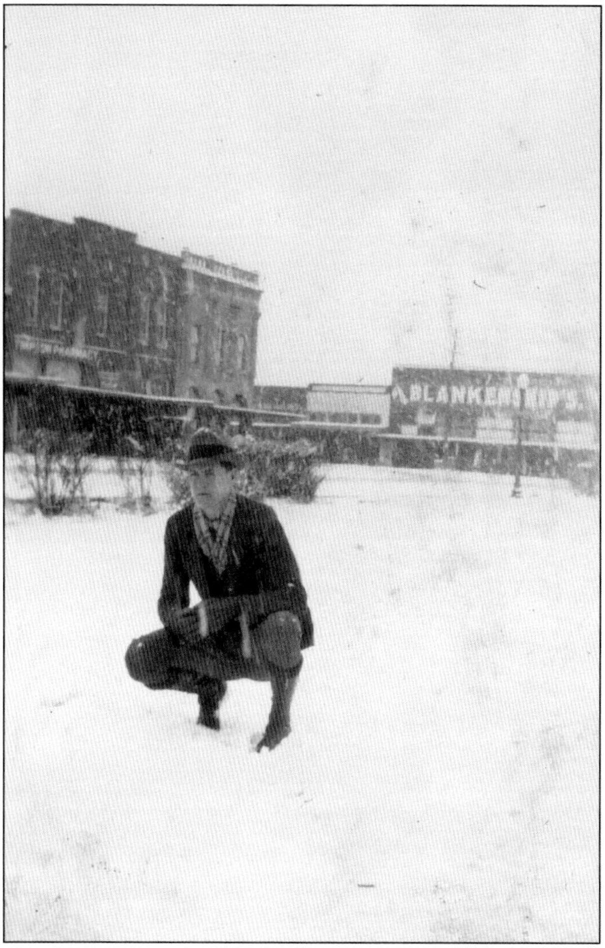

Clinton McClellan is crouched down in the snow of Park Plaza around the late 1920s or early 1930s. Clinton was born in Timpson in 1906 and graduated from Timpson High School in 1928. In the street scene behind him are, from left to right, businesses Timpson Pharmacy, unidentified, Guaranty Bond State Bank (at this time), and across Jacob Street is Blankenship's general merchandise store. (Courtesy of Tom McClellan.)

By the early 1920s, Park Plaza had a paved sidewalk and streetlights on the Main Street side of the park. It also had a covered gazebo on the east side of the park, and the beginnings of ornamental hedges along Main Street. In this photograph, the city was filled with people and vehicles, possibly for a political rally or the ever-popular band concert. (Courtesy of TAGHS.)

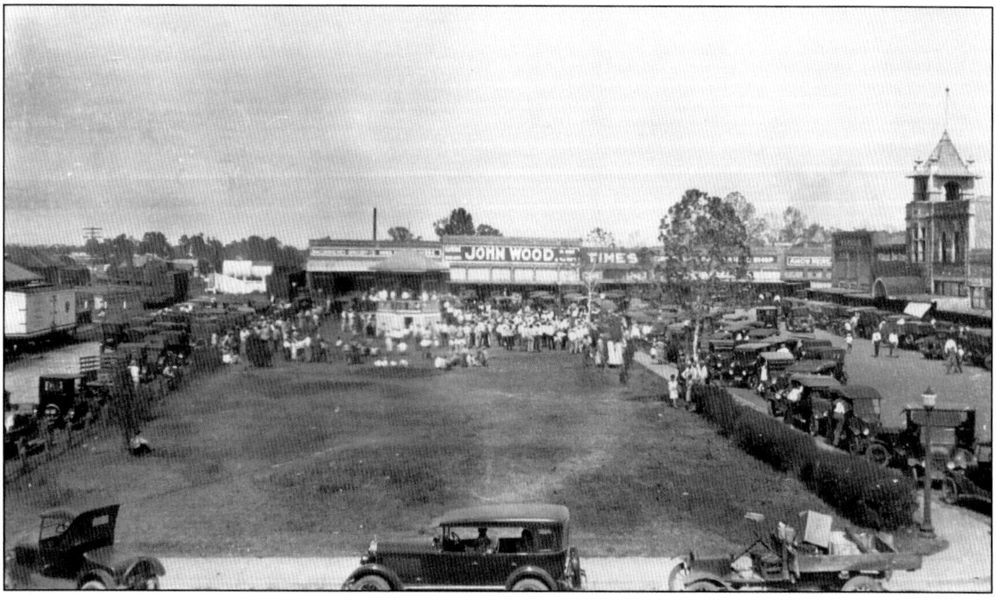

Two

That Old-Time Religion

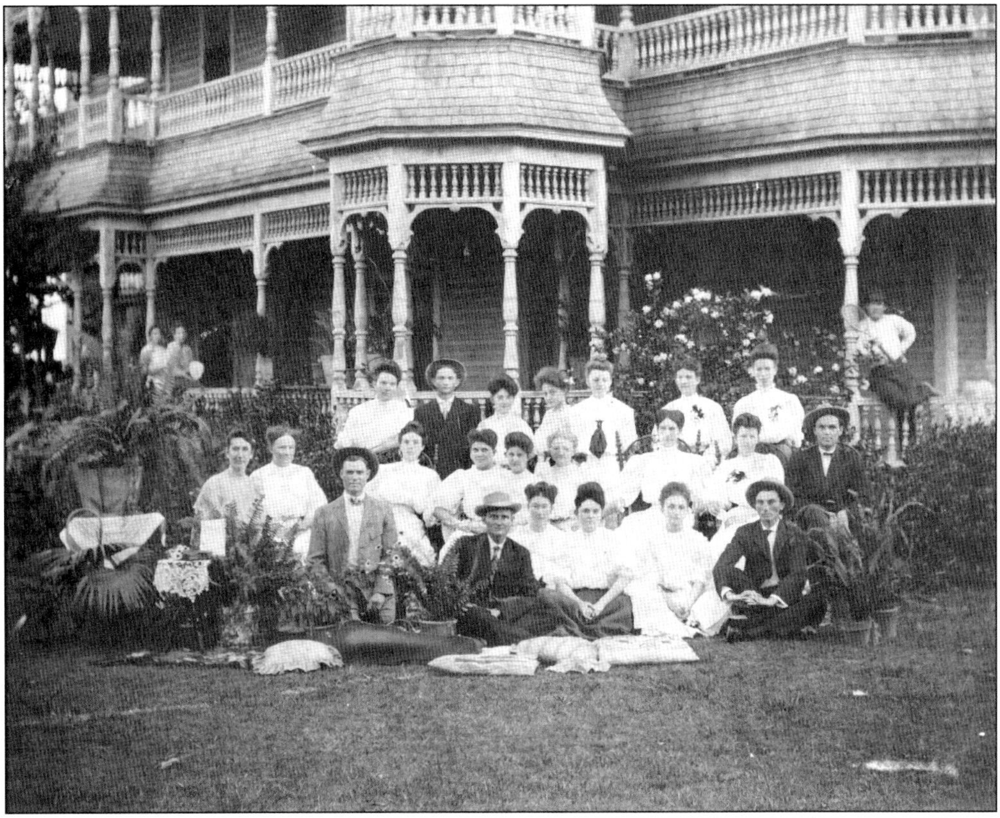

Adele Sanford, daughter of Thomas Smith Garrison, hosted a Sunday school party in 1903 for this group from the Timpson Methodist Church. The lovely Victorian home in the background was built by Charles Eugene Sanford in 1897 and occupied by his family until around 1906. The house was later used as a hospital before being sold to Frank Whiteside. It burned in the 1950s. (Courtesy of First United Methodist Church.)

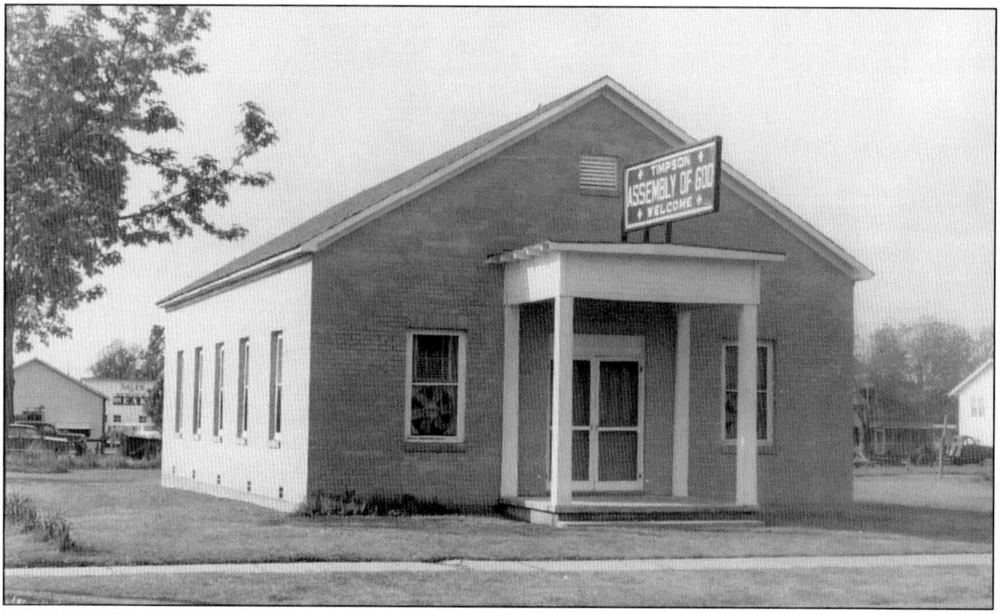

The First Assembly of God Church was founded in 1937 under the leadership of Sister Pearl Collins, meeting first in the Ruben Molloy tomato shed, and then in the Whitton building for six years. The church bought lots on Highway 59 at Houston Street from Willie Tyer and son Leonard Tyer in 1940. In 1943, the first church building was finished (above). This building was remodeled in 1971 to add an educational wing, restrooms, nursery, and foyer. As it continued to grow, the church needed more room and bought the three lots directly behind it in 1980. With a seating capacity of 400, the new sanctuary was completed in 1981. (Courtesy of TAGHS.)

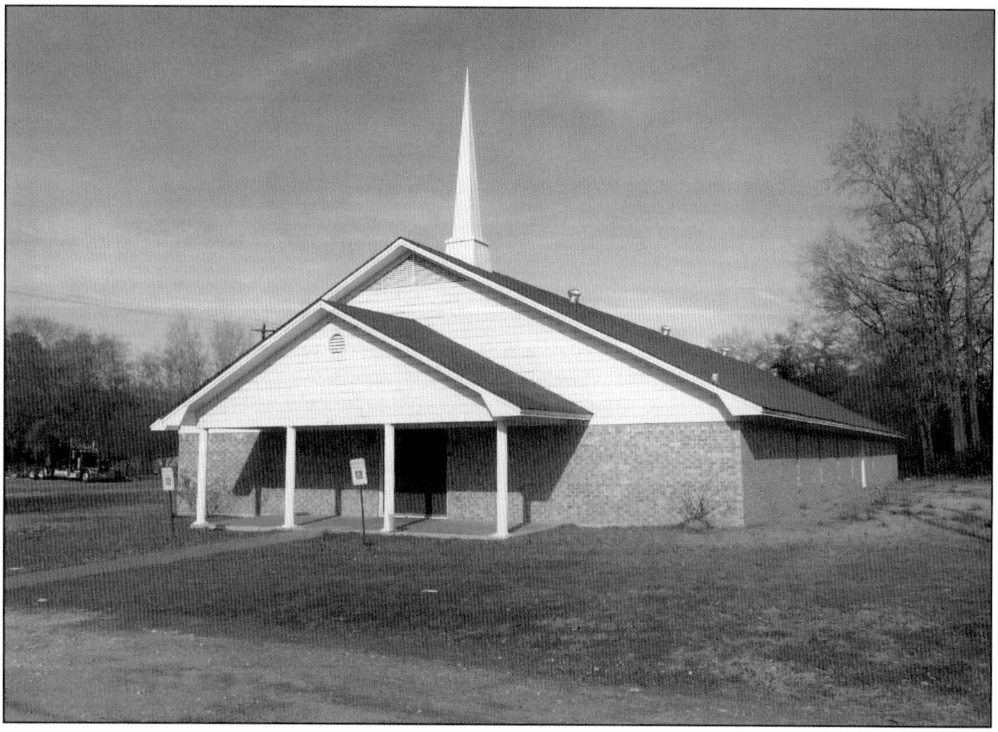

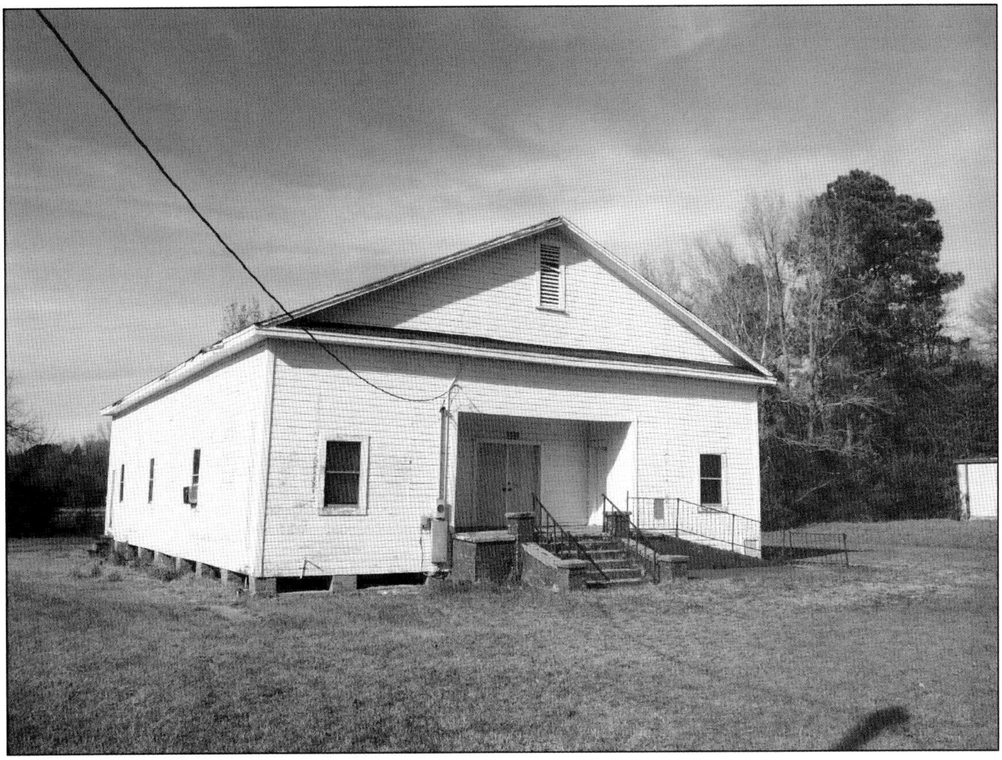

L.H. Weaver purchased a 10-acre lot in 1889, selling it to the East Legion C.M.E. Church trustees. It is not known where the congregation first met, but in 1915 the church was built near Railroad Avenue. G.W. Griffin was the first pastor. Individual members donated a small amount each week toward construction. By 1916, there were 163 members and it was one of the leading colored Methodist churches in this area. (Courtesy of TAGHS.)

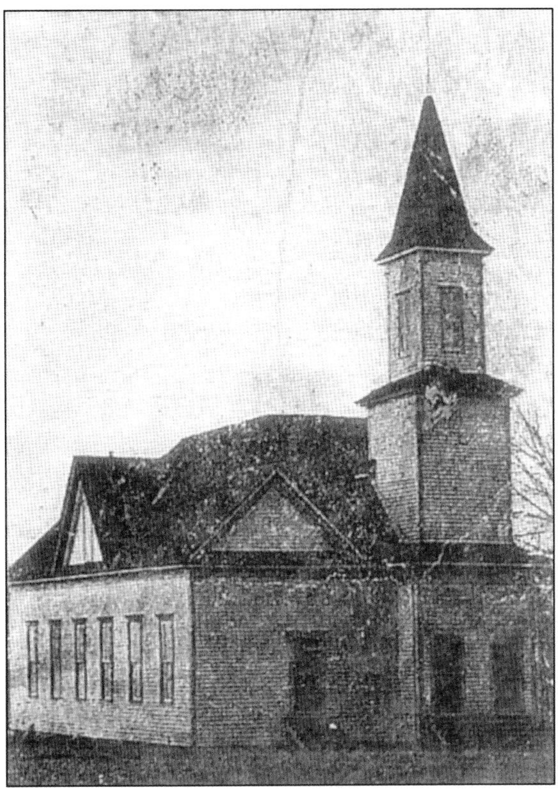

The Baptists moved into their first church building in Timpson in 1889. It was a wooden structure with a large belfry adorning the roof. It was built on property deeded to J.B. Bussey, trustee of the church, in July 1886 by the railroad town site company. Rev. W.F. Alford was the first pastor of the new First Baptist Church. (Courtesy of First Baptist Church.)

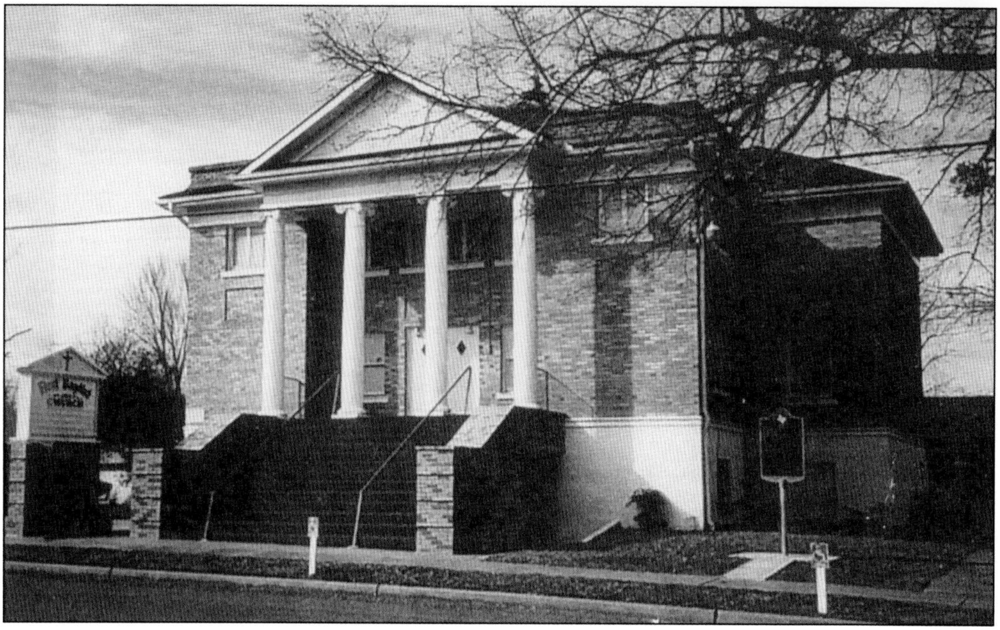

The First Baptist Church was called the North Side Baptist Church between 1902 and 1954. A beautiful two-story brick building with a classical entry portico was erected in 1917. The structure included a kitchen, a large assembly room, and Sunday school rooms in the basement. The basement was the favorite site of many meetings, meals, showers, and receptions. In 1961, an educational building was added. (Courtesy of First Baptist Church.)

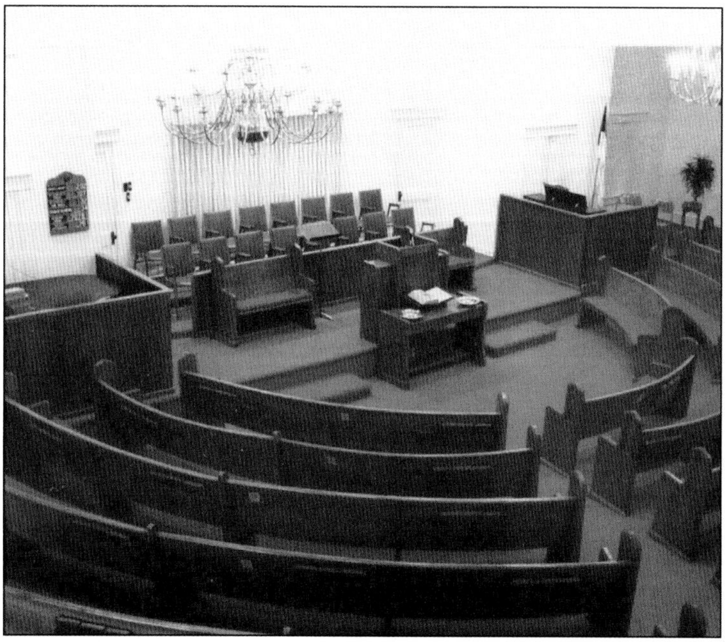

The main-floor sanctuary of the First Baptist Church was designed in an amphitheater (or rising gallery) style, with a ceiling almost three stories above the pulpit area. The ceiling was later adorned with beautiful chandeliers. Many services, baptisms, and weddings were held here. In 1939, the congregation numbered 485 members. (Courtesy of First Baptist Church.)

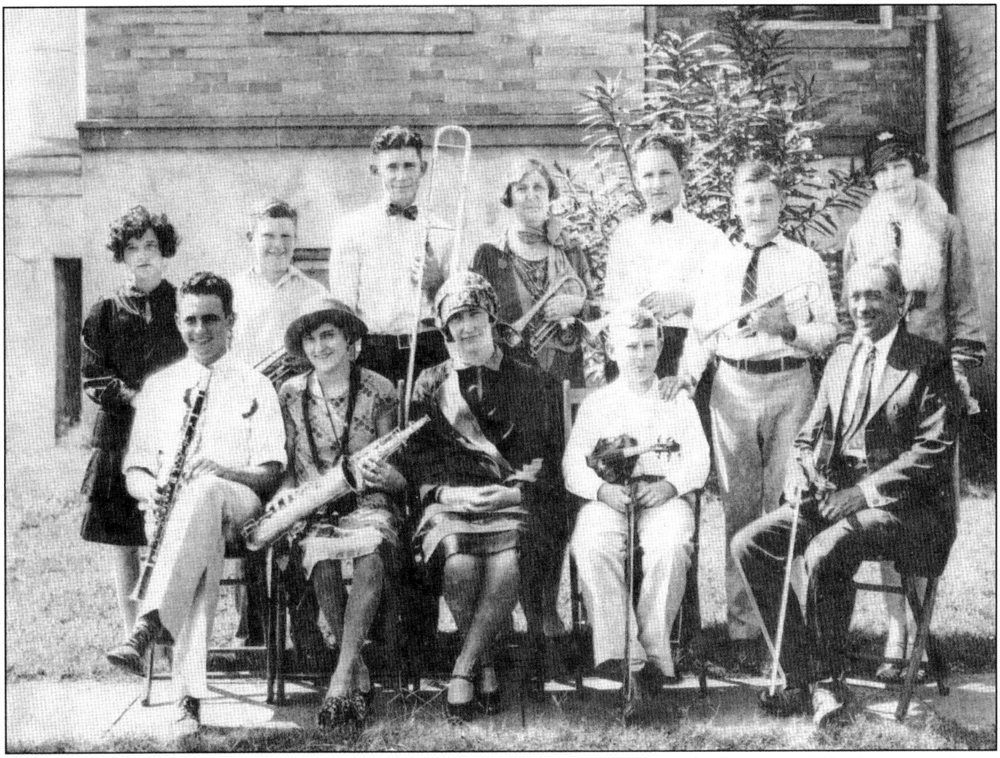

The First Baptist Church Orchestra is shown here around 1926, with director C.E. Busey, in front of the church on North Second Street. The musicians are, from left to right, (seated) Judson Smith, Ernestine Gathright, Louise Rutherford, Pat Byrn, and Clifford E. Busey; (standing) Margaret Willis, William Bussey, Espy Wedgeworth, Pearl Busey, Frank K. Bussey Jr., Kavanaugh Francis, and Ben Jean Nelson. (Courtesy of First Baptist Church.)

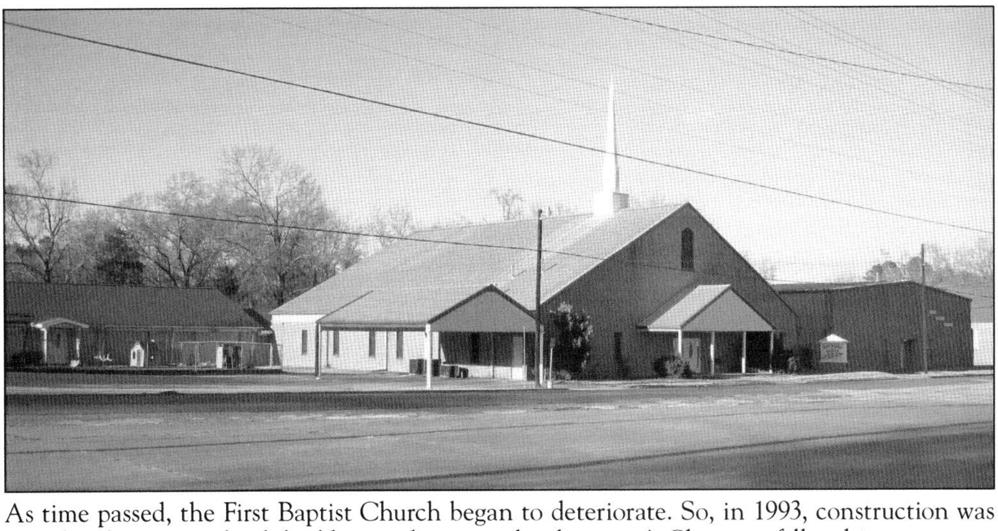

As time passed, the First Baptist Church began to deteriorate. So, in 1993, construction was completed on a new brick building with a street-level entry. A Christian fellowship center was also constructed parallel to the main church building. It was located on property donated by Mary Ruth Green McKibben, daughter of Joe and Ruth Blankenship Green. (Photograph by Sandra Bush Brownlow.)

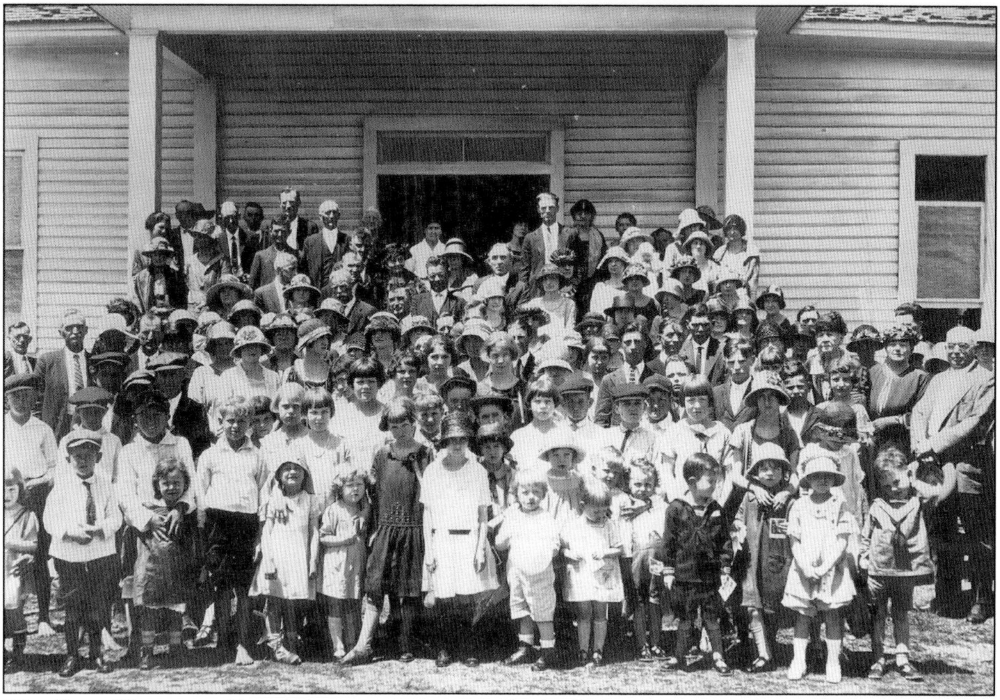

The First Christian Church began services in the hall above Duke's Saloon in 1886. Within the year, a wooden church was built on the corner of North First and Jacob Streets. The charter families were Weaver, Day, Duke, Haden, Herrington, Booth, Brinson, McLemore, Childress, and Hardy. Many members assemble in front of the church in 1920. The church was bricked and completely remodeled in 1964. (Courtesy of TAGHS.)

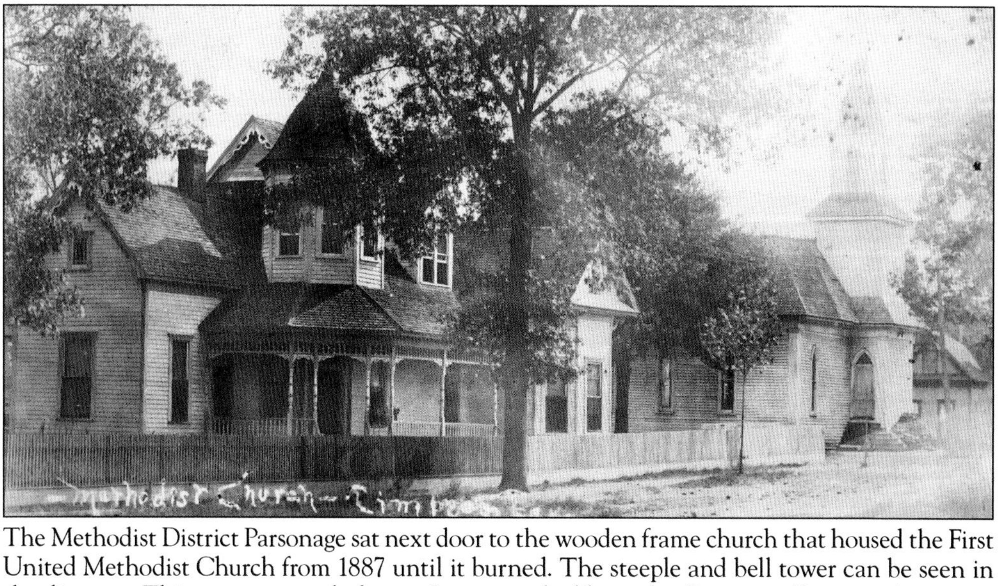

The Methodist District Parsonage sat next door to the wooden frame church that housed the First United Methodist Church from 1887 until it burned. The steeple and bell tower can be seen in the distance. This copy was made from a 2¢ postcard addressed to Jeannette Ramsey. A note on the card said "Christmas 1907." (Courtesy of the Timpson First United Methodist Church.)

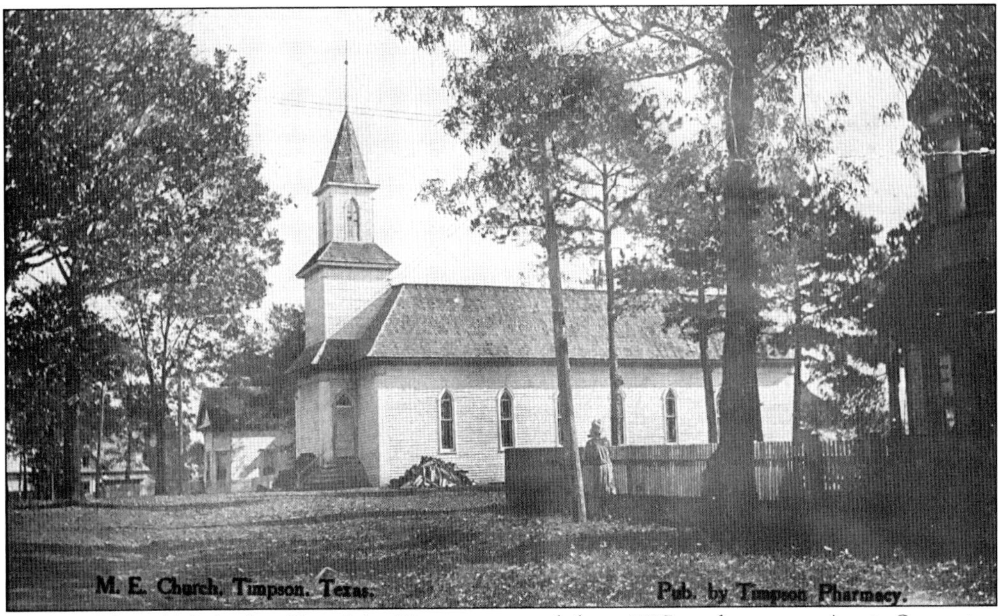

The First United Methodist Church building was erected about 1887 on the current Austin Street site, and used until 1908, when it was destroyed by fire. The deed for the land, bought from R.F. Kellum, is dated September 29, 1886. T.S. Garrison, S.C. Kelly, and H.S. Ross signed the deed, as trustees of the M.E. Church, South. (Courtesy of the Timpson First United Methodist Church.)

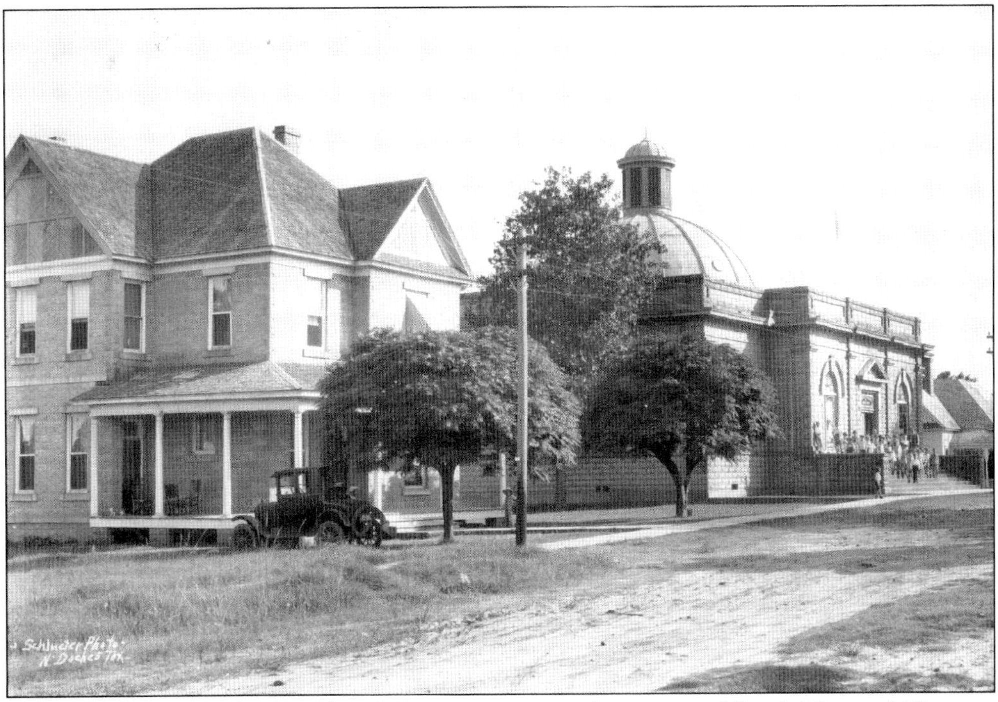

The First United Methodist Church Parsonage sat on the corner of South First and Timpson Streets. Beside it is the second building to house the First United Methodist Church. It was built in 1909 of cement blocks and featured a domed roof and ceiling and stained-glass windows. (Courtesy of the Timpson First United Methodist Church.)

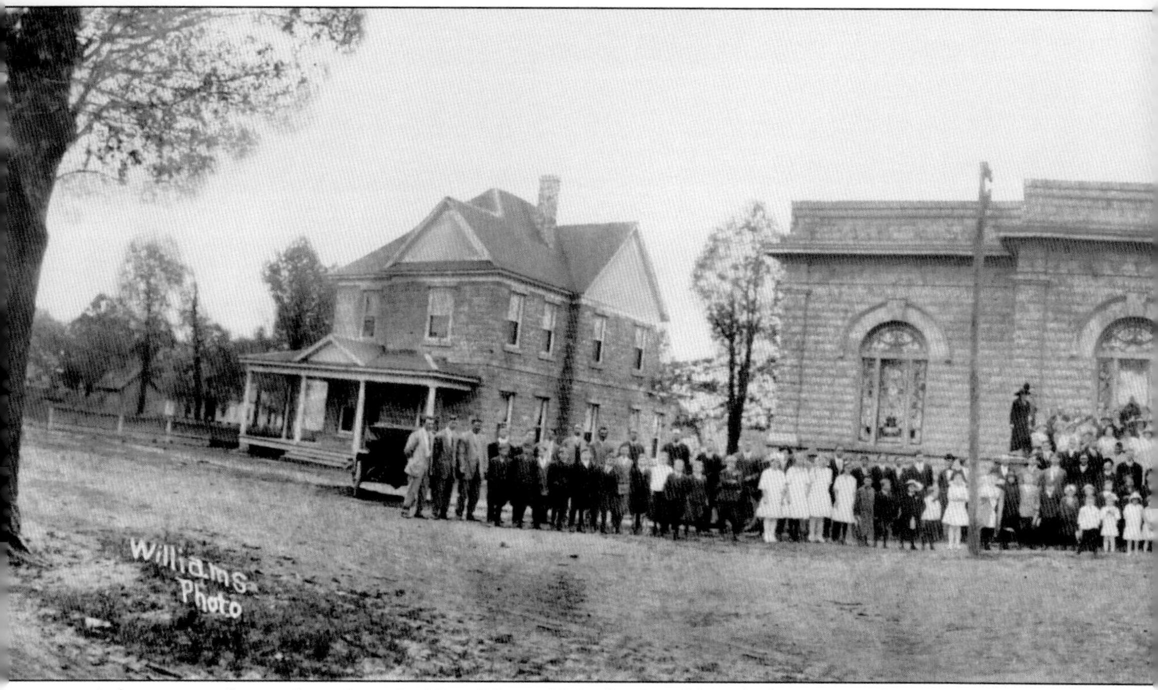

A large crowd is gathered at the First United Methodist Church for a special occasion, possibly Easter services or some district-wide event. The First United Methodist Church built its second building from cement blocks made on site by T.S. Garrison and his crew. The cornerstone of the $10,000 building was laid on May 8, 1909. Dr. G.C. Rankin, of Dallas, arrived that day on the Texas and Gulf Railroad to officiate at the laying of the cornerstone. The church was built with

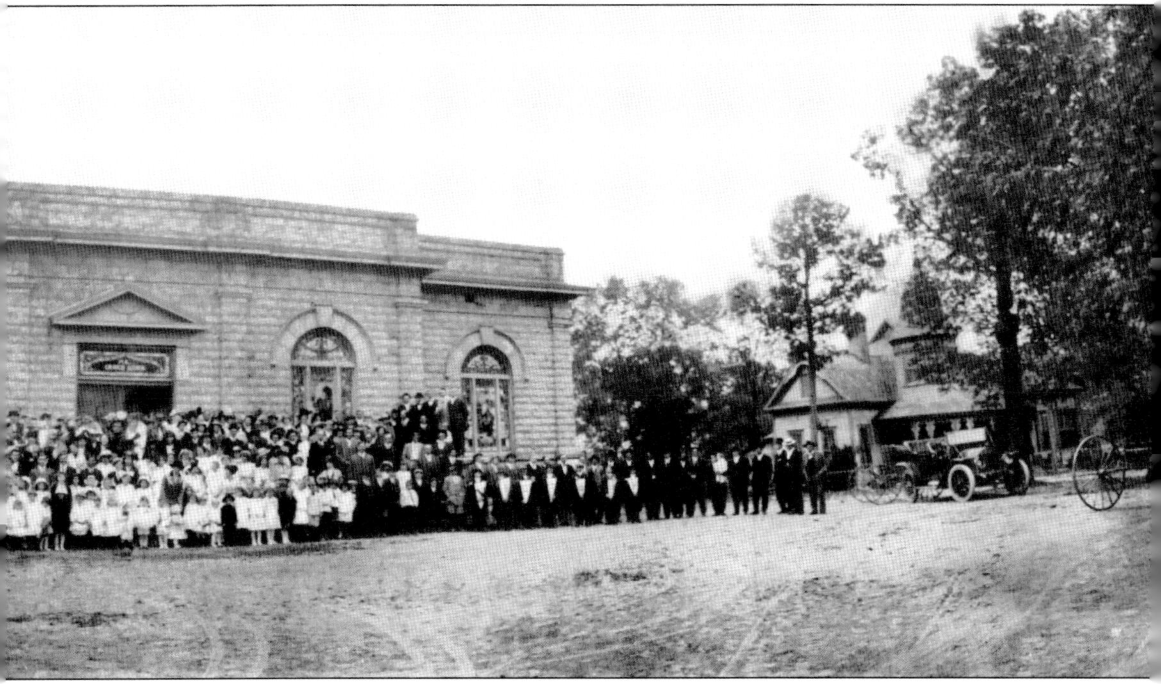

a domed roof that is not visible in this photograph. After 40 years, the building was torn down in 1949 because of structural problems. The large two-story home beside the church (left) was the church parsonage. The automobile dates this photograph to the late 1910s or early 1920s. (Courtesy of the Timpson First United Methodist Church.)

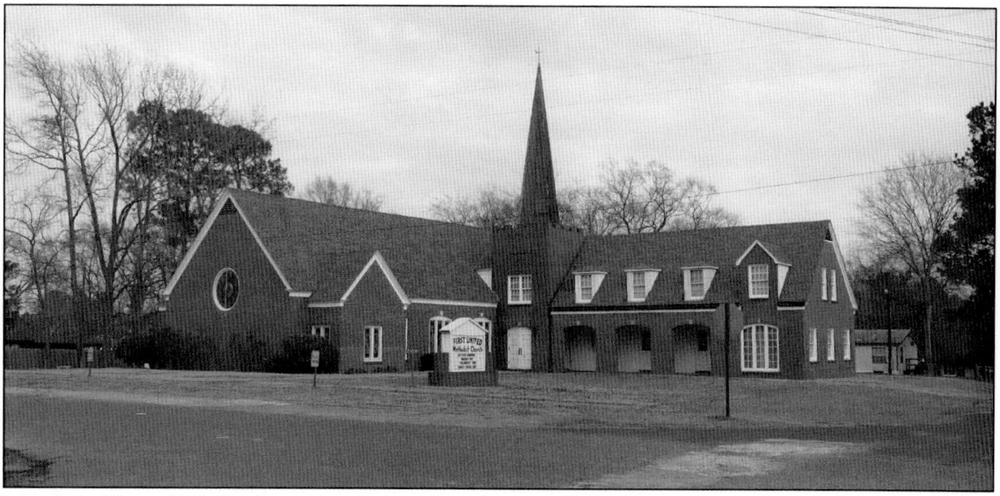

The First United Methodist Church stands today as it did on its consecration day, May 14, 1950. A lighted sign, given in memory of Albert F. Burns, a faithful member for 40 years, identifies the church. The light shines through the stained-glass windows that were saved from their last church, and the melodious organ and chimes still call the faithful to worship. (Courtesy of the Timpson First United Methodist Church.)

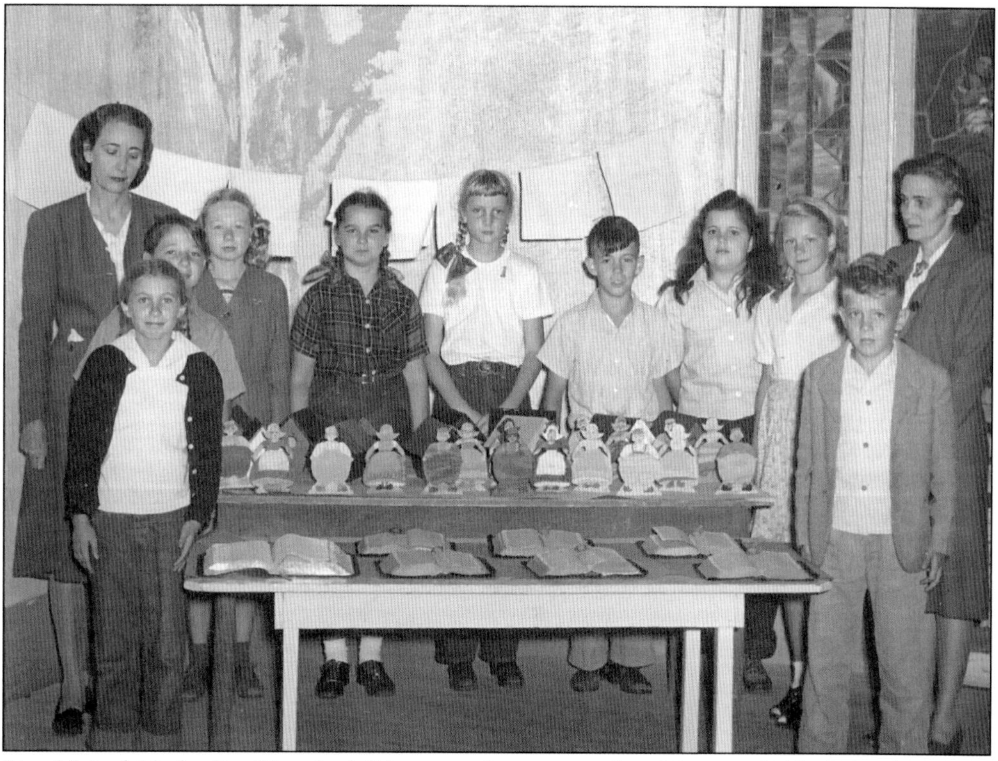

First United Methodist Church children are shown attending Vacation Bible School in 1948. Pictured here are, from left to right, Louise Hebert, Martha Boucher, Jack Dent, Betty Hawthorn, Shirley Hartley, Glenda Hebert, Paul Wendell Amos, Ada Mac Crawford, unidentified, Philip Amos, and Mrs. Tot Taylor. Bibles are displayed on the first row, and Dutch figures and birdhouses made by the students are on the second row. (Courtesy of Martha Wigley Wheeler.)

Looking over some sheet music in 1909, representing three generations are, from left to right, Geraldine Howell Hooper; Ellen Hill Buffon, her grandmother; and Irene Buffon Howell, her mother. Geraldine was born in Iowa, moved to Wyoming, and then California. She met her future husband, John Brinson Hooper (from Timpson), at her aunt's rooming house. They moved to the Rose Hill Community in Timpson, where they remained for over 50 years. Geraldine died in 1997 at age 95. (Courtesy of Marian Hooper Bodiford.)

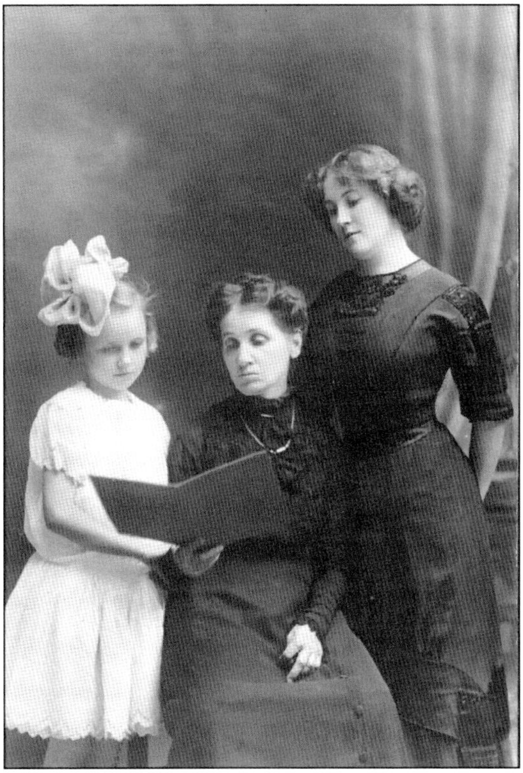

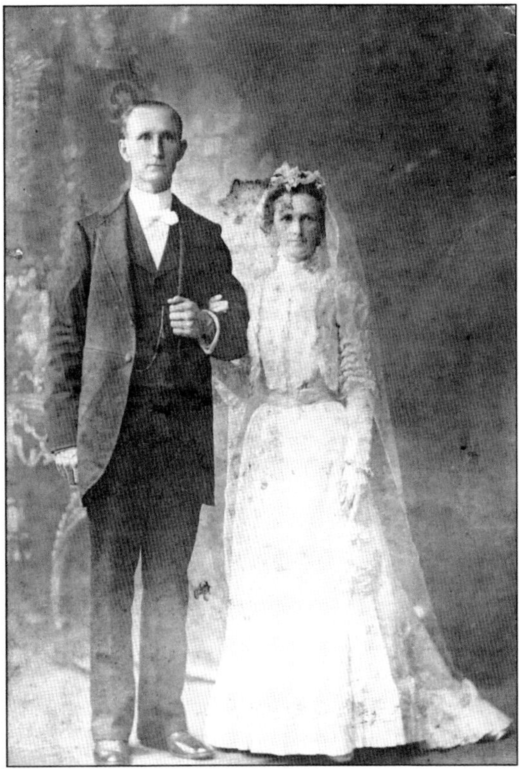

Elbert Newton Weaver (left) and Nellie Sophronia Wallace are shown here on June 3, 1900, in their wedding finery. Weaver was born in Center, Texas, on October 28, 1869, to George and Harriet Woolwine Weaver. He grew up and was educated in Timpson. He became a bookkeeper, then a merchant in Timpson. In the 1920s, Weaver relocated his family to California. He died on May 16, 1942, in Los Angeles, California. (Courtesy of TAGHS.)

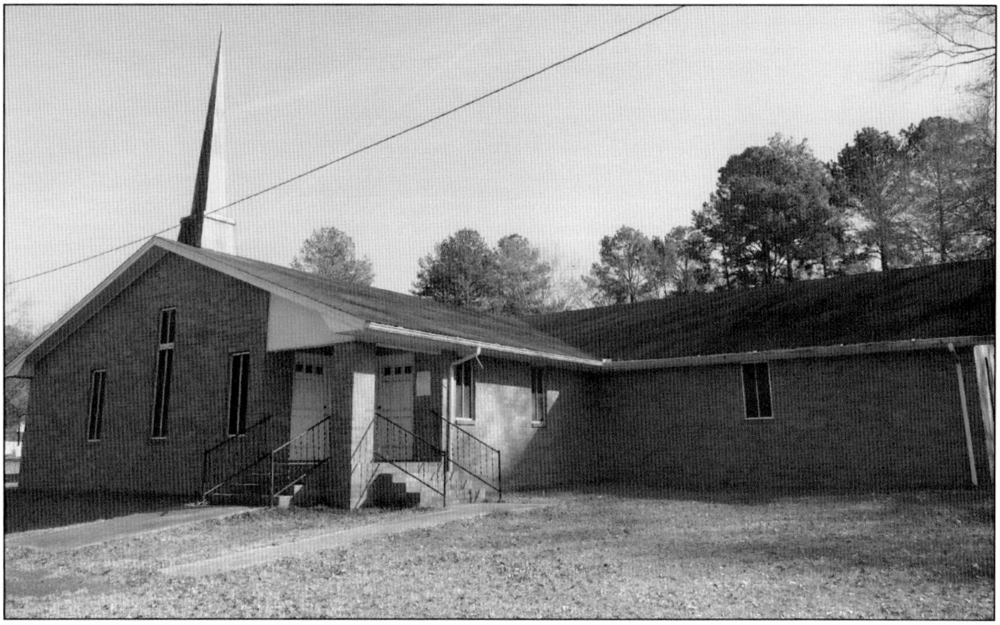

Smyrna Missionary Baptist Church was organized by a white minister and turned over to its black members before 1866. Until about 1900, it served as both church and school. The church has moved several times. In November 1983, the church building and all contents were destroyed by fire. A new building was constructed in 1984 on FM 947 and continues to serve the members today. (Courtesy of TAGHS.)

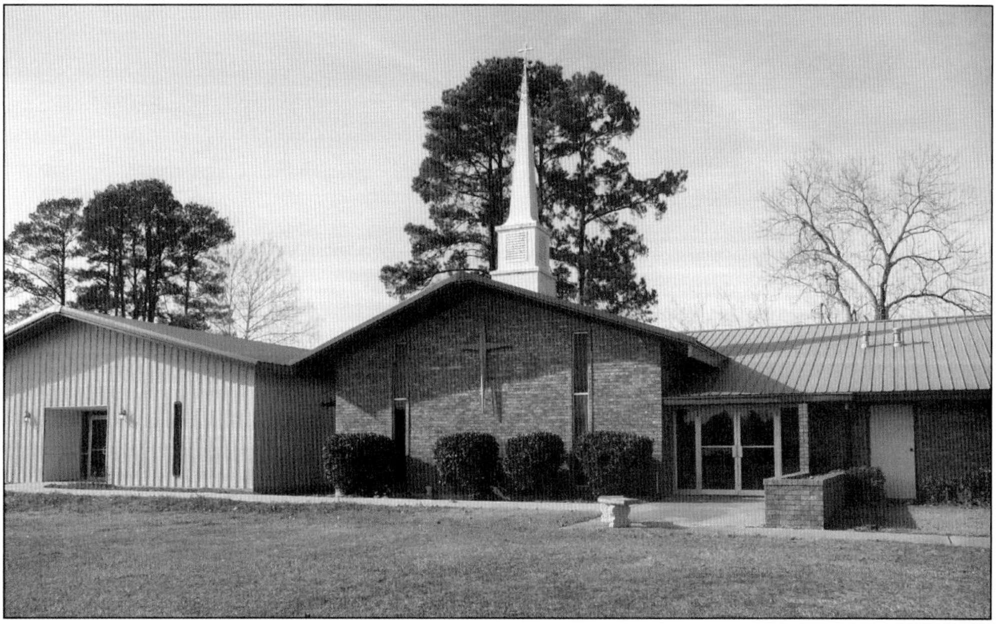

The Woodland Christian Church was established in 1972 through the efforts of five dedicated men: Donald Amos, Tom Amos, Travis Billingsley, Butch Trala, and H.G. Wolcott. A two-acre tract of land on US 59 and US 84 was purchased. Brother Bob Cox held the church's first revival in April 1972 and his son, Brother Billy Cox, became the first pastor. The current pastor is Brother Roy Platt. (Courtesy of TAGHS.)

Three

SCHOOL DAYS

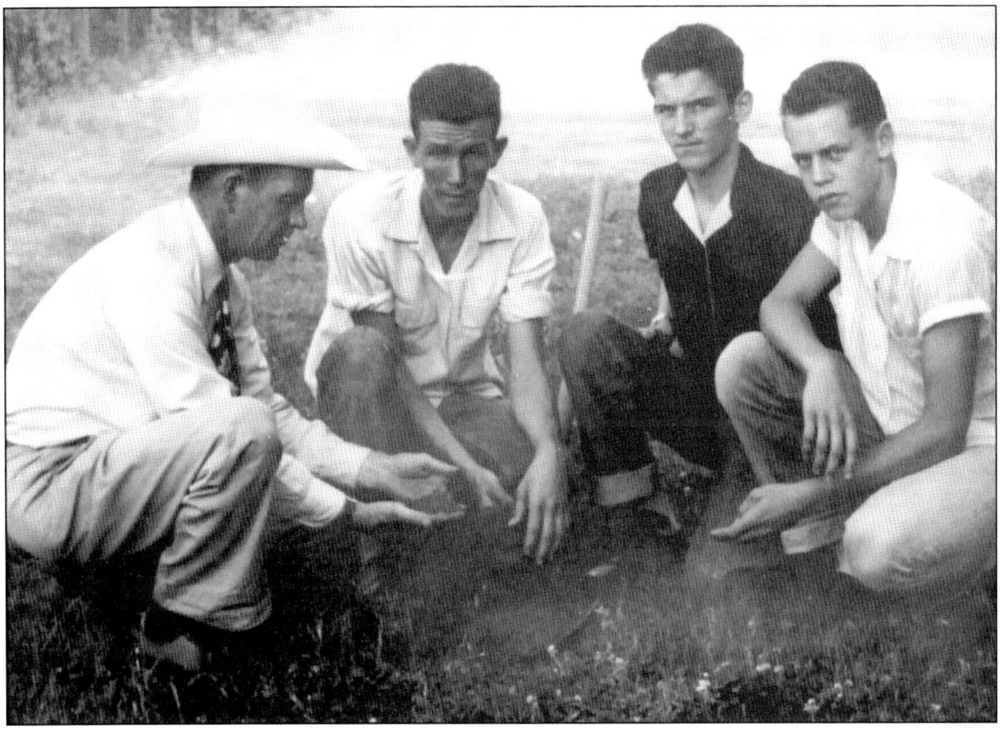

Cecil Wharton, Timpson High School agriculture teacher, uses a field trip to teach students one of many lessons. Shown here in 1956, they study soil conditions and how to take a soil sample. From left to right, the students are Willie Herndon, Lester Hughes, and Robert Pate. (Courtesy of Helen Woodfin Pate.)

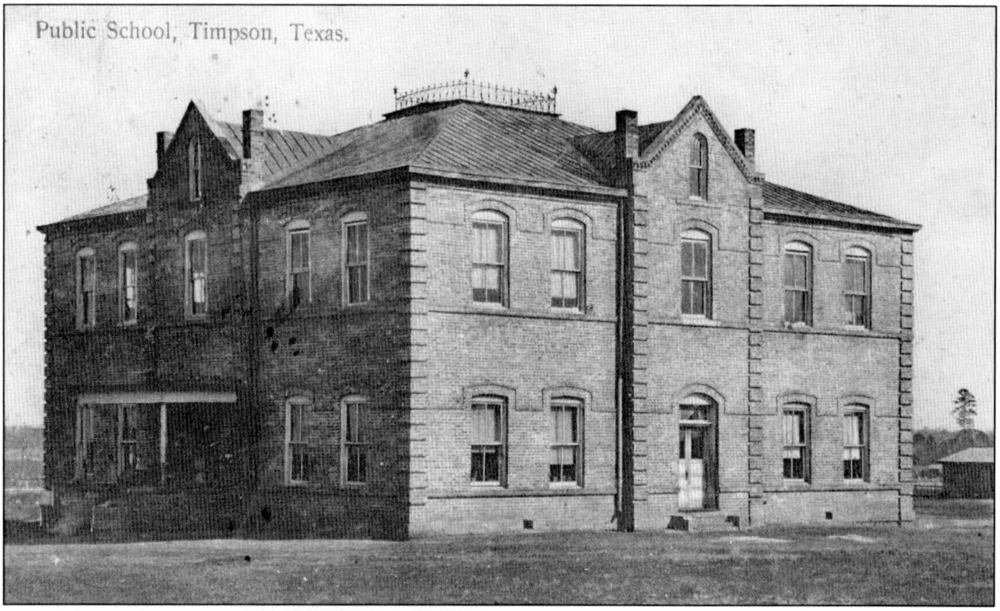

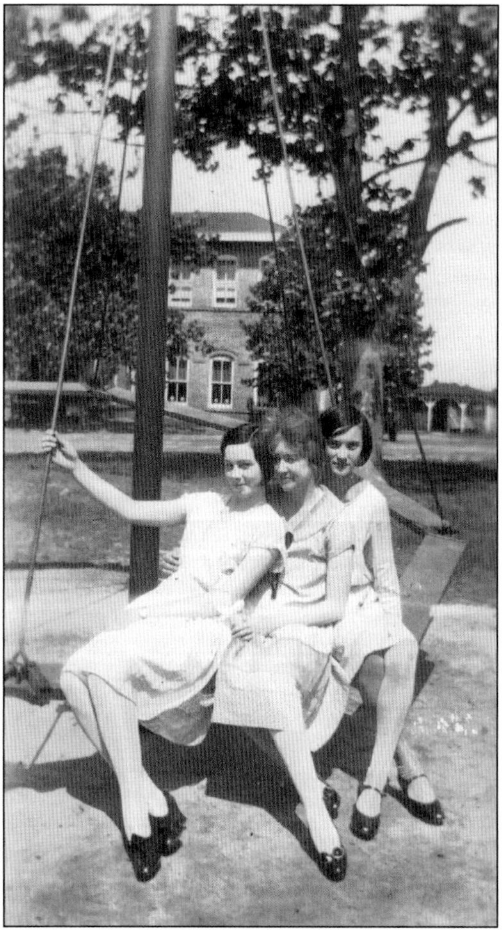

After Timpson's first two-story wooden school building burned in 1899, students met in the Methodist church. In 1901, voters passed a bond to build a new school. The two-story, eight-room brick building was built on the site of the present school campus on Bear Drive. First classes were held in the fall of 1902. In 1910, eight more rooms were added, one of which was an auditorium/ study hall. (Courtesy of TAGHS.)

Posing on the merry-go-round in front of the old two-story Timpson High School are cousins Claryce Hairgrove (left), Lura Hairgrove (center), and Emma Hairgrove. At this time, in the late 1920s and early 1930s, the school had outdoor restrooms. The attractive building seen in the back right of the photograph housed both girls' and boys' facilities. (Courtesy of Martha Peters Brothers.)

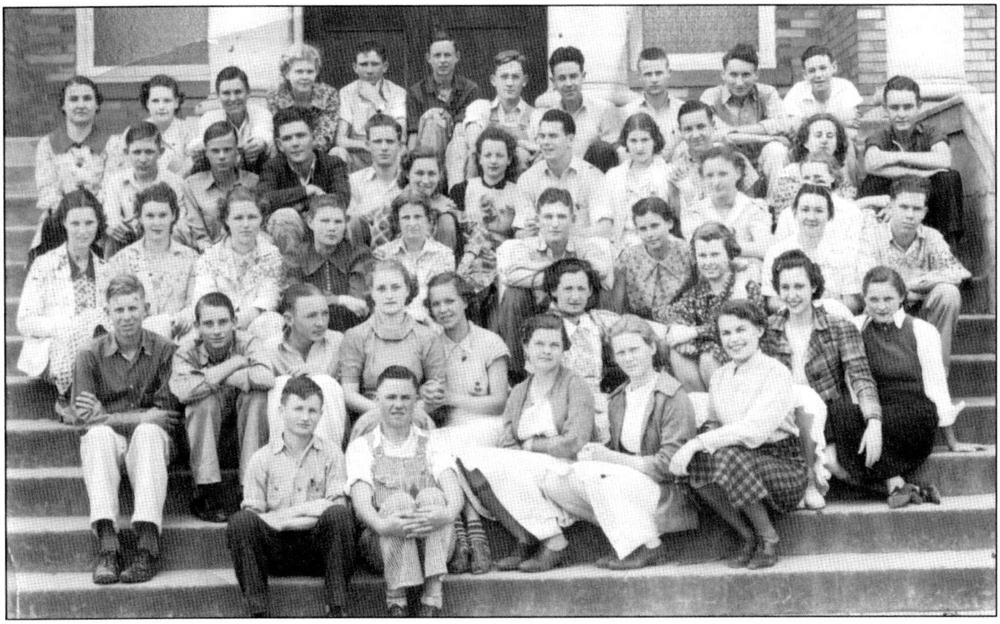

Once again, in the spring of 1937, Timpson School was destroyed by fire. Beginning in the fall of 1937, high school students met at the First Baptist Church (nicknamed "Baylor"), and elementary students met at the First United Methodist Church (nicknamed "SMU"), the armory (nicknamed "A&M"), The First Christian Church (nicknamed "TCU"), and individual homes. The class of 1938 is shown here on the steps of the First Baptist Church. (Courtesy of TAGHS.)

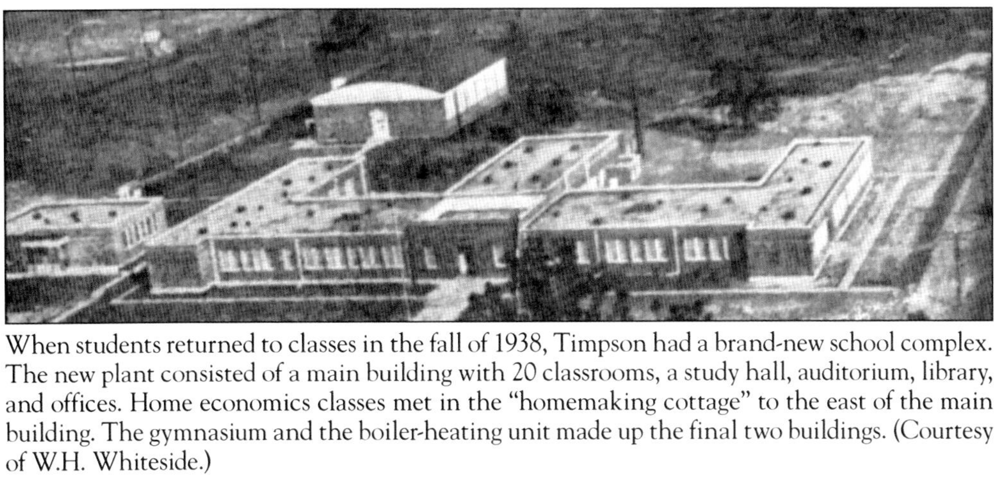

When students returned to classes in the fall of 1938, Timpson had a brand-new school complex. The new plant consisted of a main building with 20 classrooms, a study hall, auditorium, library, and offices. Home economics classes met in the "homemaking cottage" to the east of the main building. The gymnasium and the boiler-heating unit made up the final two buildings. (Courtesy of W.H. Whiteside.)

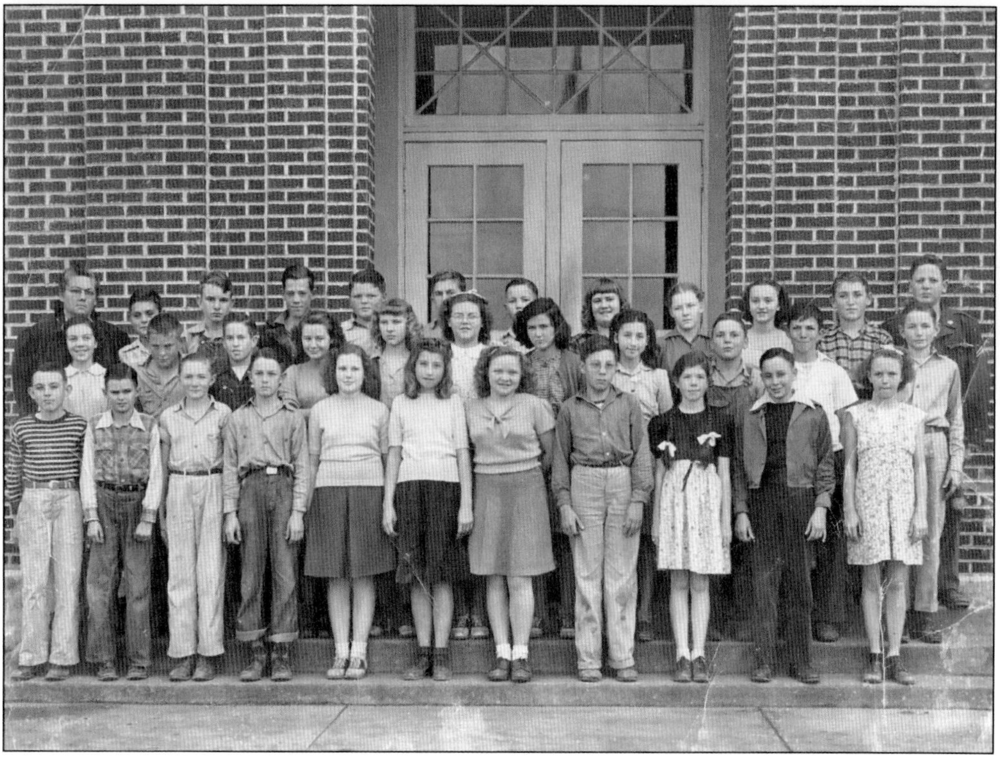

In 1946 or 1947, these seventh-grade students find appearance to be important. They have outgrown the playground and have only one year left before high school. Note that the boys have tucked-in shirts and belts. Girls wear skirts, blouses, and saddle oxfords with socks. One lad foreshadows the rolled-up jeans of the 1950s. (Courtesy of TAGHS.)

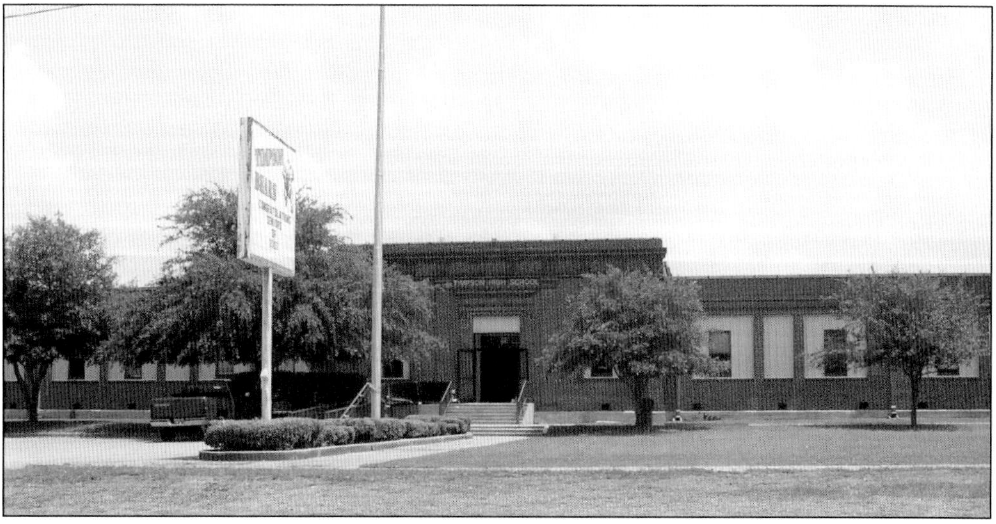

In 1988, the entire school underwent a major remodeling. The old elementary buildings, cafeteria, and band hall were torn down and replaced. A new middle school complex and a new gymnasium were built. This 2002 photograph shows the exterior remodeling, but the design of the original building remained intact. Recently, a new roof was added, changing the roofline over the entrance. (Courtesy of TAGHS.)

John A. Alexander was one of several principals to provide leadership to the Timpson Colored School, also known as Timpson North Campus. Others were Jim Jones, Albert Hooper, J.H. Rowe, E.D. Benton, J.I. Wallace, and M.B. Davis (1912). Others were A.L. Turner (1913–1922), M.W. Harris (1922–1929), and Alexander (1929–1969). When Alexander retired and the Timpson schools were integrated, the Timpson North campus was closed. (Courtesy of Charles E. Tatum.)

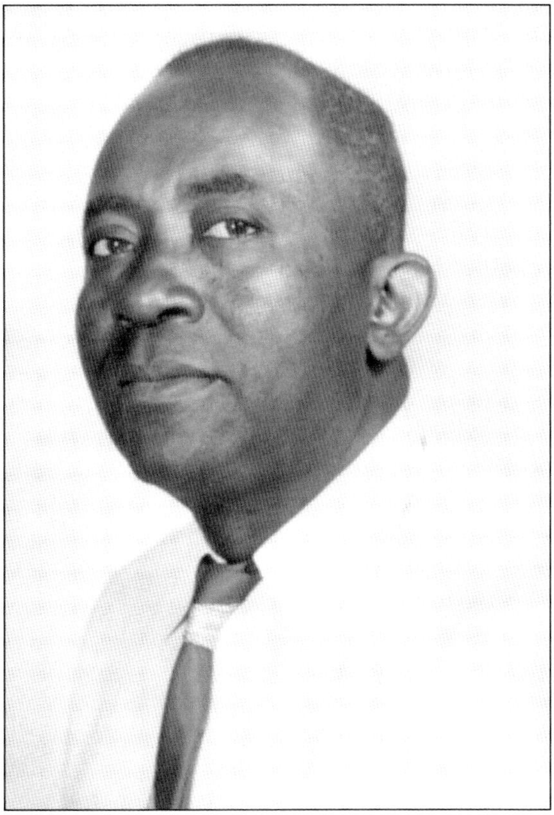

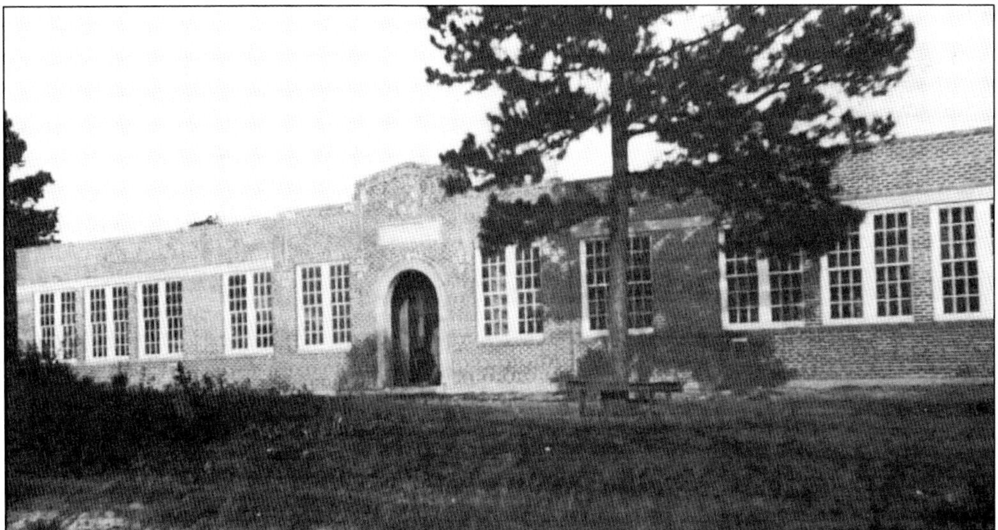

In 1926 or 1927, a six-teacher Timpson Colored School was built. The Rosenwald Fund, established in 1917 by Julius Rosenwald (chairman of the board of Sears Roebuck, and Co.) used matching funds to stimulate construction. Funding sources included Rosenwald's $1,500 and $23,700 from the general public. The school was built on a 10-acre site on the Old Tennessee Road. The school was closed in 1969. (Courtesy of Fisk University.)

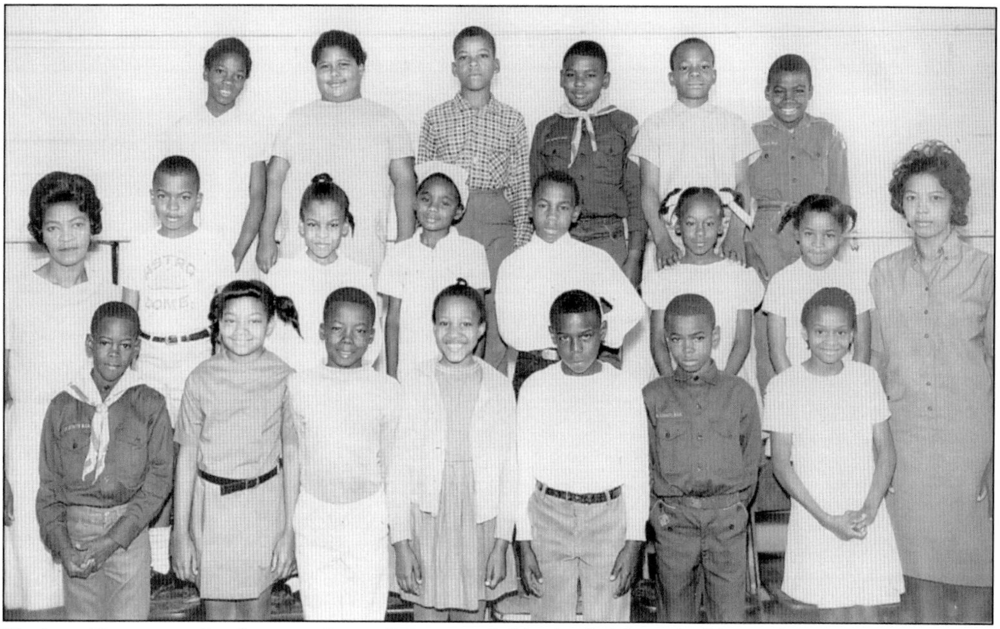

Nathan King was the first teacher of Timpson's black children, holding class in a one-teacher log house. The second school was a two-story plank structure that was torn down in 1926 when a two-story red brick school was built. After a fire, the school was rebuilt in 1929. Teachers Ruth Bussey (left) and Mary Driver are shown above with a group of their 1967–1968 students. (Courtesy of Ruth Bussey.)

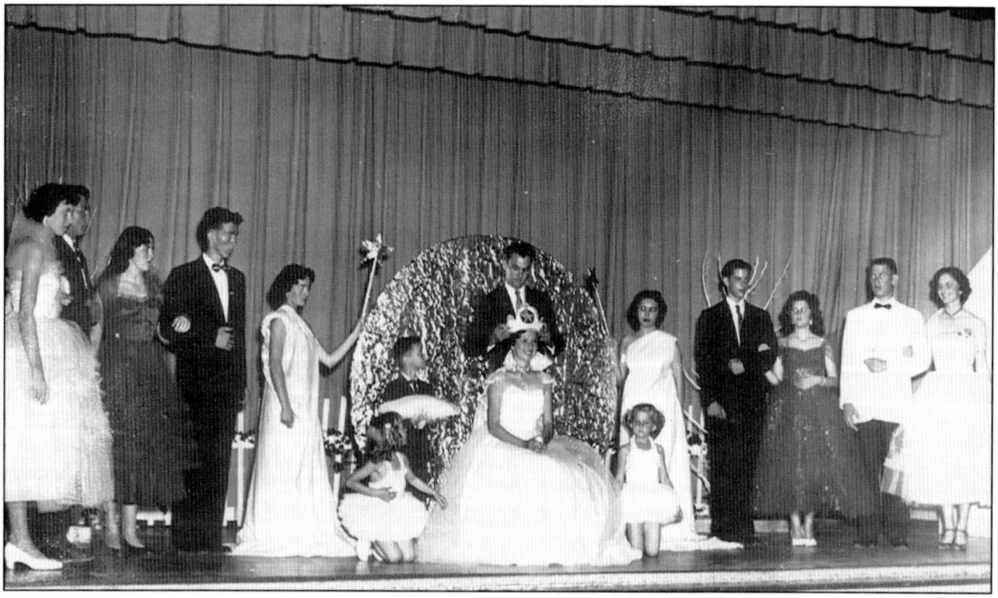

The 1955 Parent Teacher Association Halloween Coronation and festival were held on October 27 at Timpson High School. Miss Ina Dora Baker (queen) was crowned by King Barkley Bowlin. Shown here are, from left to right, Phabreece Bryce, Loy Dean McGowan, Mary Alice Hooper, Willie Herndon, Nina Ruth Billingsley, Janis Mora, Stephen Towns, Barkley Bowlin, Ina Dora Baker, Caroline Milford, Orine Pate, Everett Crawford, Rosaline Moore, Franklin Hairgrove, and Tempie Ann Green. (Courtesy of TAGHS.)

Everyone in Timpson looked forward to football season, especially the cheerleaders. This was the time for them to get the crowd excited about the game and root for the Bears, their beaus, and their friends. Shown here are, from left to right, (first row) Sue Stilley, Jan Wigley, and Diane Bowlin; (second row) Freeda Eberlan and Becky Eakin. This 1958–1959 group wore the traditional black and gold colors of Timpson High School. (Courtesy of Diane Bowlin Tolmachoff.)

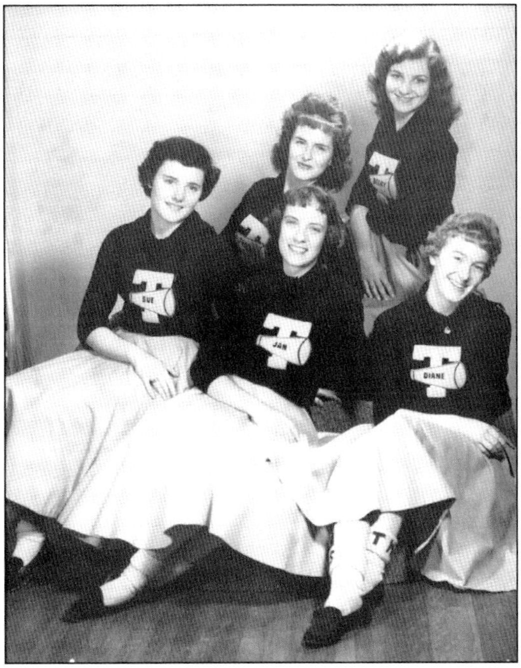

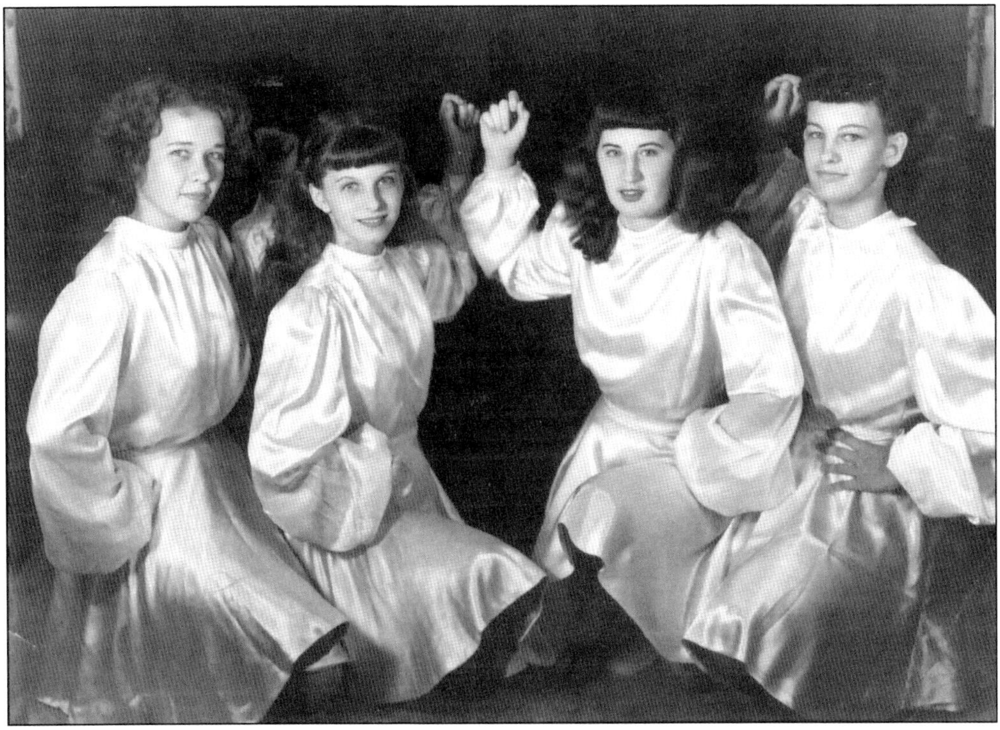

The excitement of a fall night, bright lights, and pretty girls encouraging the crowd to cheer on the team was palpable during a Timpson Bears football game. These 1948 cheerleaders knew their crowd and how to get the best from them. Shown here are, from left to right, Billie Joy Fitts, Jane Smith, Jeanette Hayes, and Elaine Billingsley. They wore solid white taffeta uniforms lined with gold, and gold tights. (Courtesy of Billie Joy Allen.)

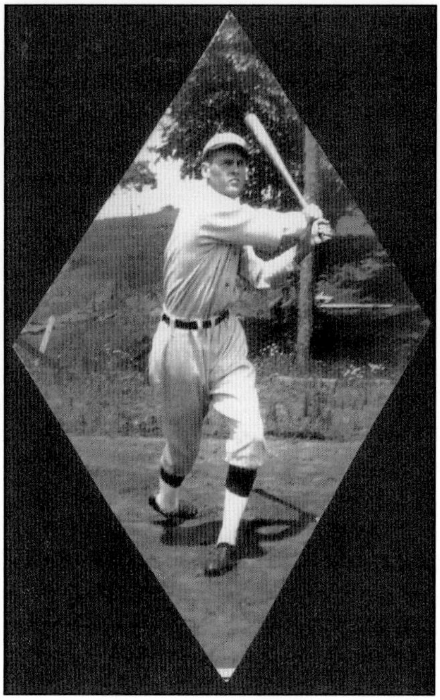

Clinton McClellan played professional baseball for several teams in East Texas and Arkansas from 1929 to 1933, including the celebrated Longview Cannibals. In the spring of 1930, he was with the Houston Buffs, a St. Louis Cardinals farm club. In the springs of 1931 and 1932 he was at a Detroit Tigers rookie camp in Beaumont. His teammates included future hall of famers Dizzy Dean (Buffs) and Hank Greenberg (Tigers). (Courtesy of Tom McClellan.)

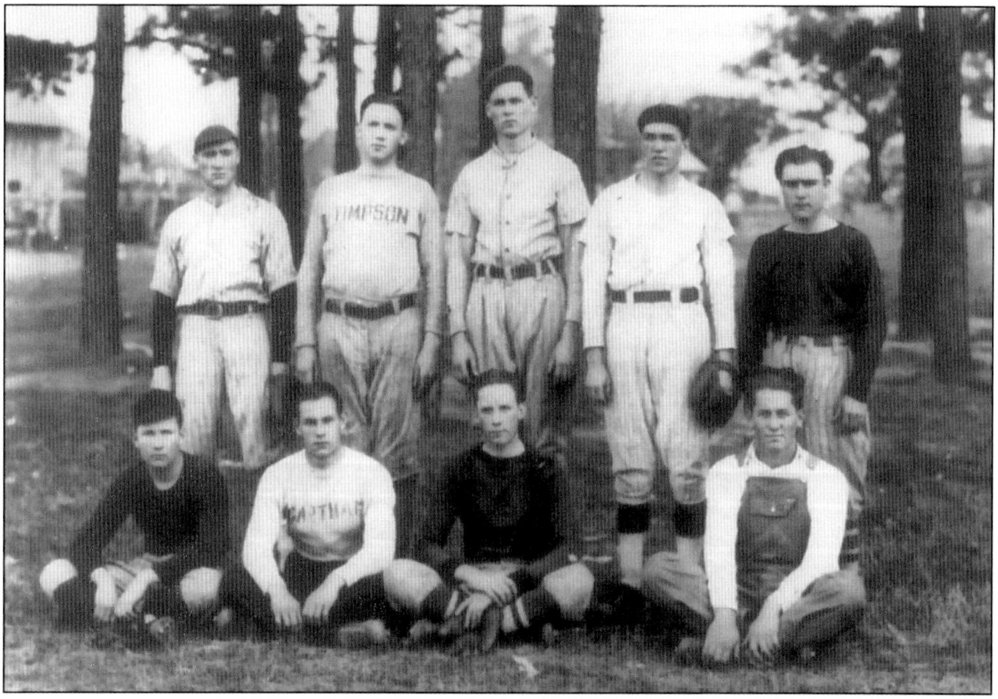

This 1927 photograph shows members of the city of Timpson baseball team. Identified for certain are Clinton McClellan (first baseman), back row center, and brother Lindsay McClellan (catcher, infielder), on his left. All others are unidentified but could include J.B. Adams and Vic Frazier. *Timpson Weekly Times*, April 23, 1927, newspaper accounts show a 19-inning Timpson win over Tenaha, 2-0, and an 8-3 Timpson win over Center on April 22, 1927. (Courtesy of Tom McClellan.)

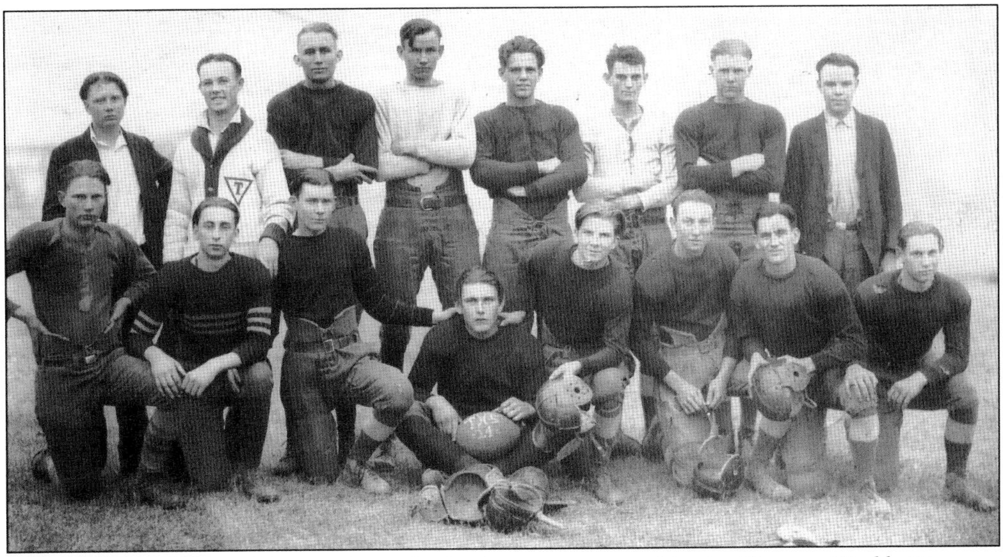

Calvin Hammer, second from right in the back row, was quoted in the *Timpson Weekly Times* on October 14, 1960: "Our 1924 team had no reserves for substitutions; we played both offense and defense. Our field was Dr. Dan Bussey's cow pasture. We did not have bands, cheerleaders, or pep squads. We were coached by Wallace Kristensen on his own time, and we were proud to play for him and Timpson High." (Courtesy of Tom McClellan.)

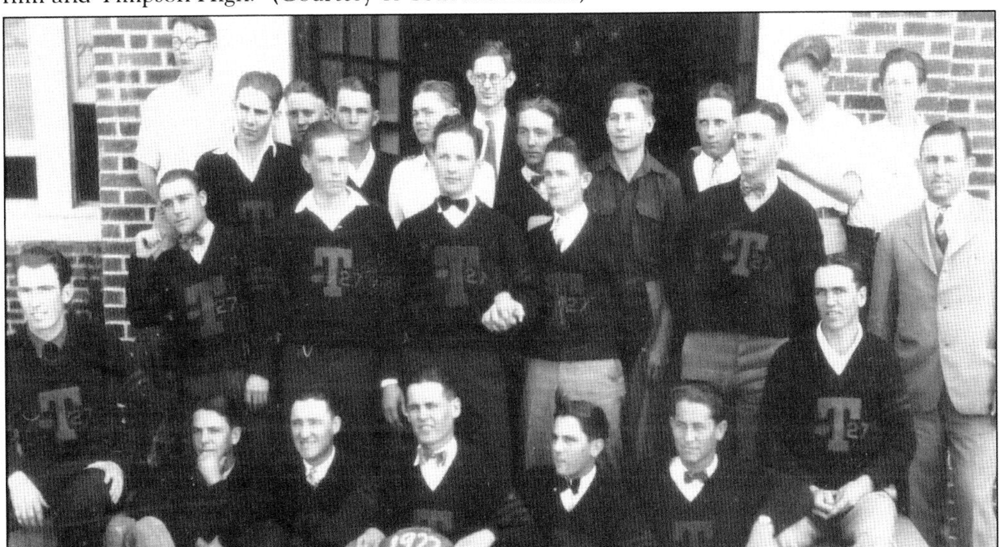

This 1927 football team is shown in front of Timpson High School. Team captain Clinton McClellan is holding the ball. Kavanagh Francis (back row, first person on the left, in white shirt) played right tackle for all four high school years, and was team captain his junior and senior year. He was the center for the Alabama's Rose Bowl team in 1935, which won the national football championship title. (Courtesy of TAGHS.)

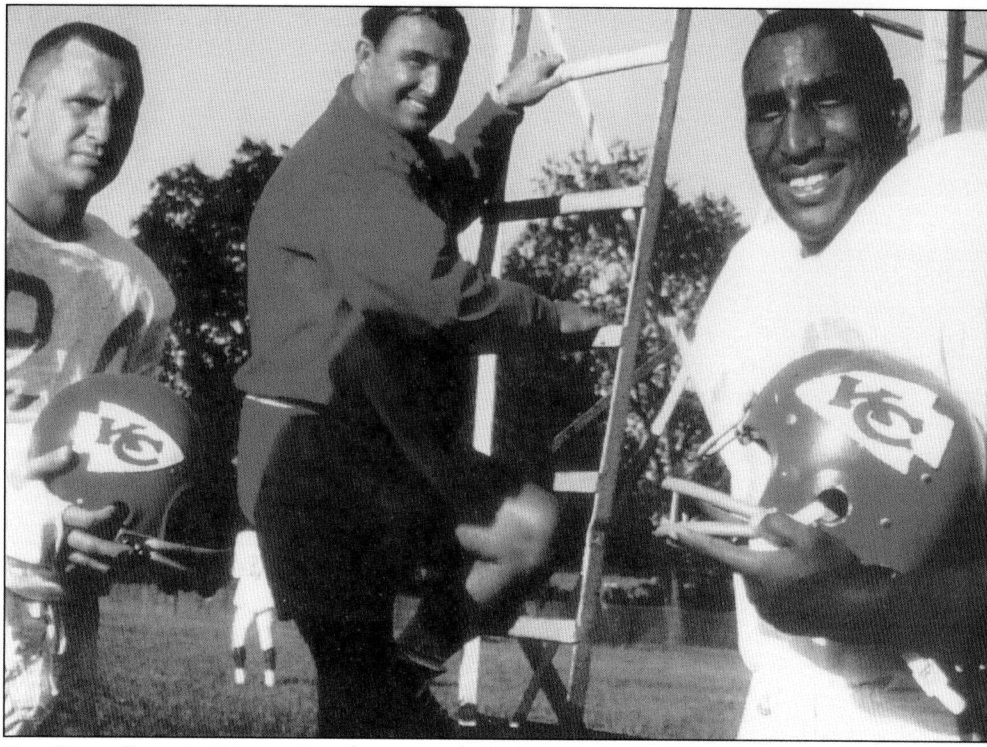

Bert Coan (born in Timpson) is shown on the left with Kansas City Chiefs coach Hank Stram and fellow halfback Curtis McClinton. Coan, an All-American High School football player at Pasadena, Texas, began his professional career with the San Diego Chargers. As a halfback for the Kansas City Chiefs (No. 23), he played in both Super Bowl I and Super Bowl IV. After retirement, he returned to Timpson. (Courtesy of Bert Coan.)

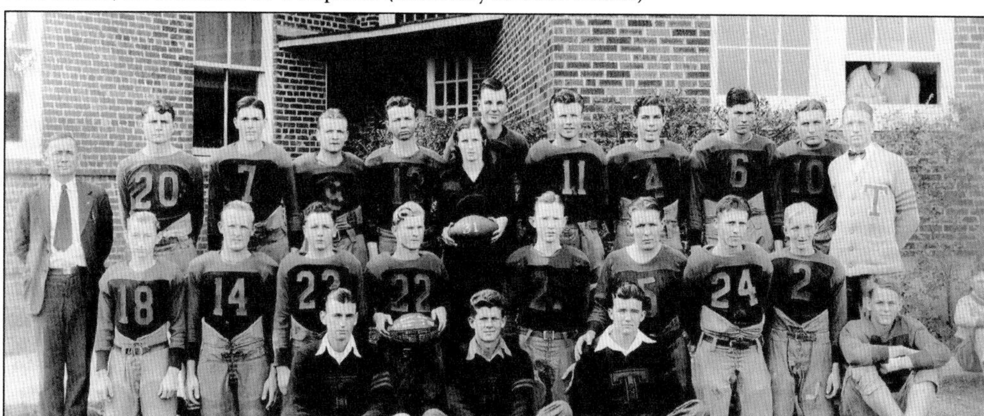

Two Timpson football teams from the early 1930s were district champions—the 1931 and 1934 teams. Bo Griffin was the 1931 fullback (back row, sixth from left, number 11). He later attended the University of Alabama. His freshman year, football teammate Kavanagh Francis was a senior, along with Paul "Bear" Bryant. Griffin also excelled at low hurdles and the 100-yard dash. (Courtesy of TAGHS.)

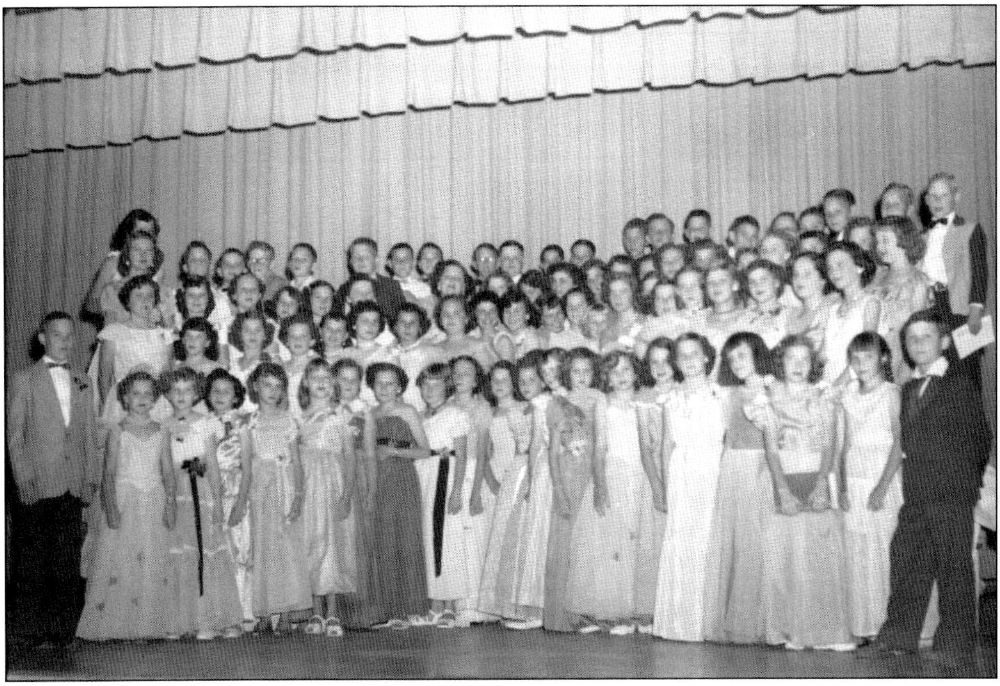

Four rows of young students in formal dress are presented on the Timpson School Auditorium stage. This is probably an elementary choir group comprising at least three class levels (sixth, seventh, and eighth grades) in the 1952–1953 school year. Irene Horton would have been the piano accompanist. (Courtesy of Pat Crawford.)

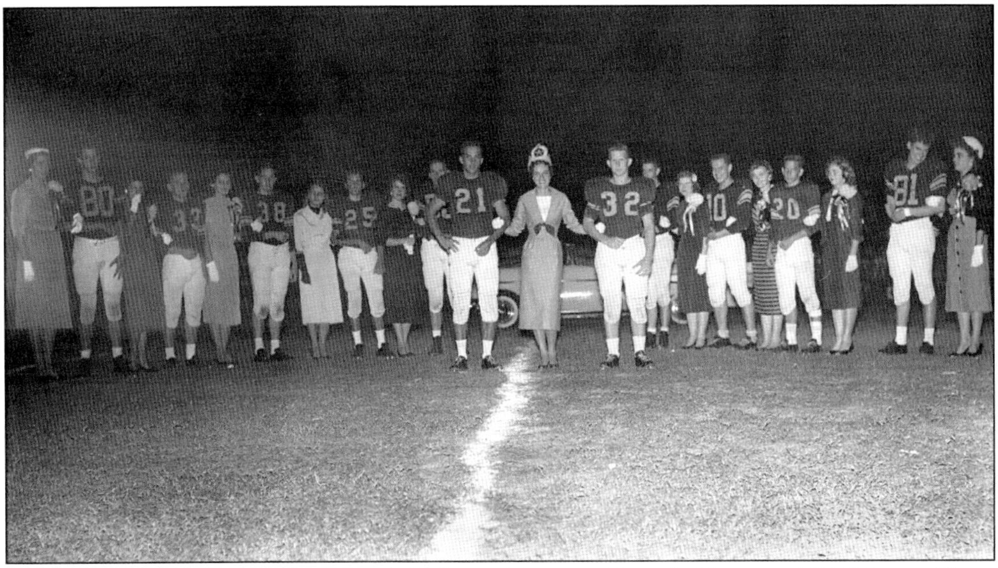

The homecoming court took center field during Timpson Bears halftime in 1957. Honored here are, from left to right, Patricia Ann Powers, Everett Crawford, Betty Lou Crump, H. M. Fletcher, Lou Ann Strickland, Johnny Earl Robinson, Diane Bowlin, Gilbert Rhodes, Joyce Webb, Johnny Yarbrough, Ray Powers, Queen Jan Wigley, Billy Ray Brunson, Harry Herndon, Cynthia Galbreath, Robert Pate, Helen Woodfin, Jerry Lynn Fitts, Martha Mathis, Vanard McDaniel, and Elaine Phelps. (Courtesy of Jan Wigley McGowan.)

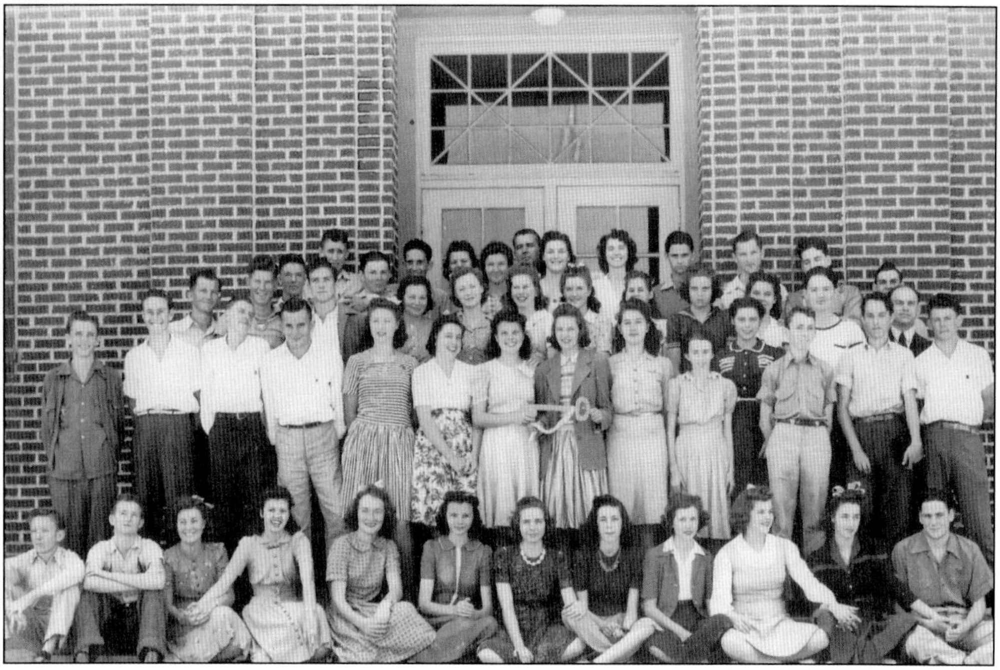

This 1942 class included many pretty girls. But Nellywn Gasway (center, in solid white, holding key) had a most unusual way of meeting her man. While working at a tomato packing shed, a World War II troop train stopped on the siding to let another train pass. The soldier she met there, Gerald Kent Bickford, became her husband in 1945. (Courtesy of Paul Wendell Amos.)

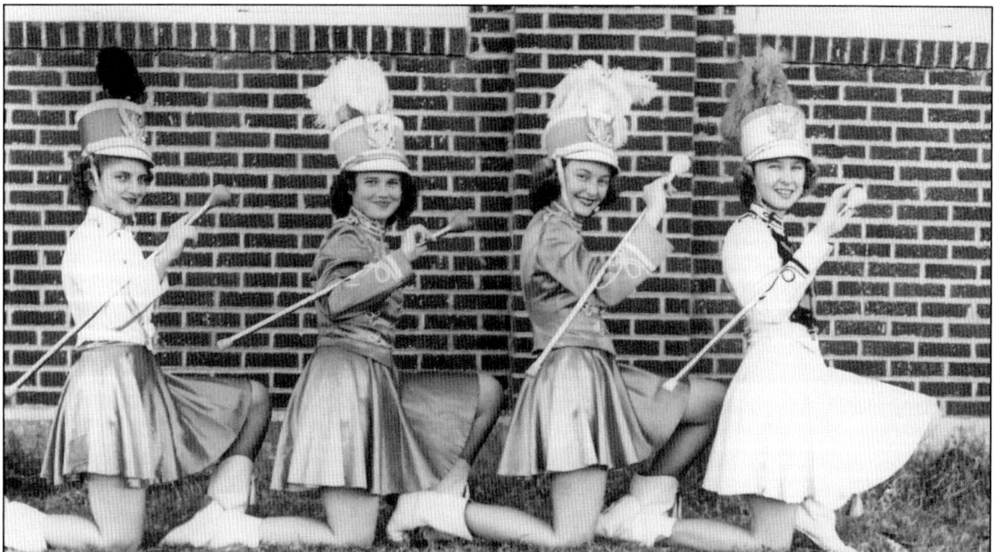

When the Timpson High School band reorganized after World War II, this was the first group of young ladies selected to serve as majorettes. Shown in front of a portion of the high school building are, from left to right, Jo Ann Lindsley, Wanda Eakin, Sadie Rae Shepherd, and drum major Barbara Young. (Courtesy of Barbara Young Bogue.)

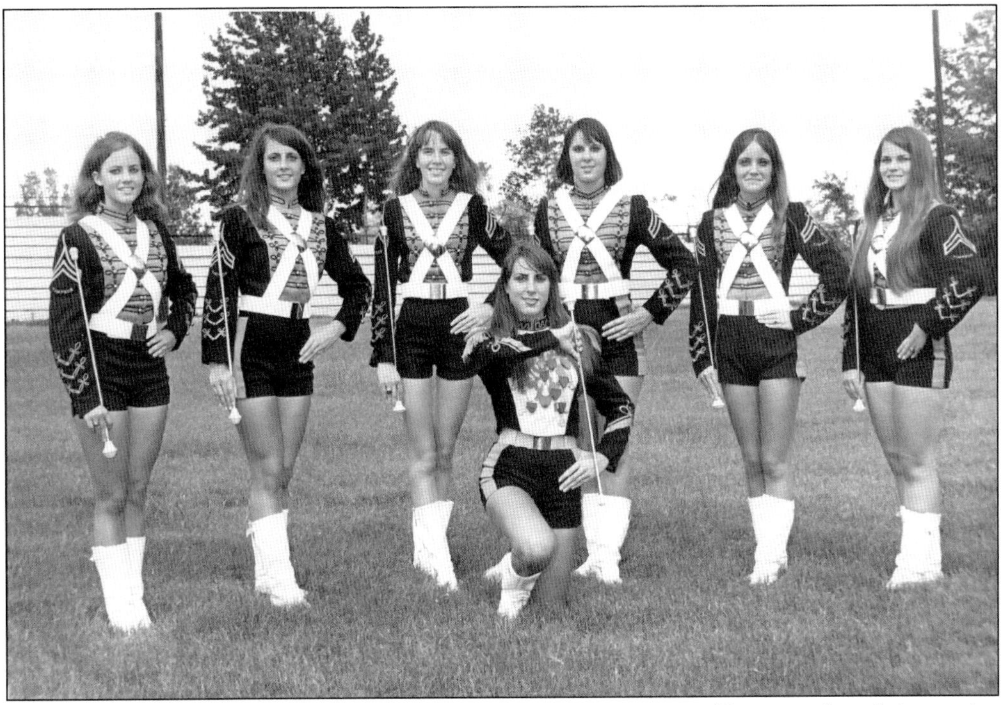

Shown in their military uniforms, the 1970–1971 majorettes pictured here are, from left to right, JoAnn Kaluza, Drew Ann Smith, Linda Windham, Diane Bogue, Lila Rogers, and Jean Collins. Drum major Becky Bogue is in front. Competition medals adorn the uniform of the drum major. (Courtesy of Barbara Young Bogue.)

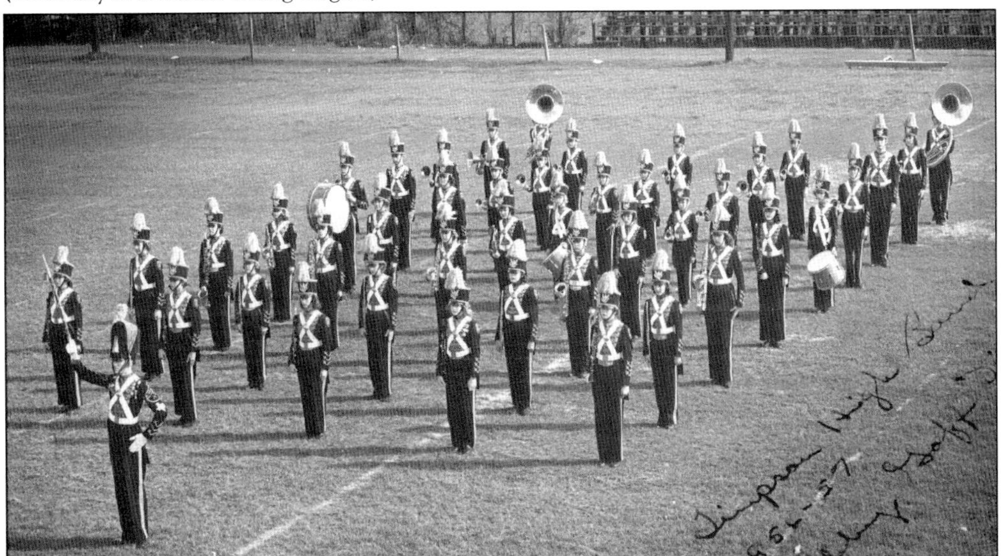

Under band director Bobby Goff, the 1956–1957 Timpson High School Band won acclaim for both musicianship and marching. Goff, who played an important part in establishing the continuing tradition of excellence for the Timpson band, was posthumously named to the Texas Bandmasters Hall of Fame in 2005. (Courtesy of The East Texas Research Center, R.W. Steen Library, Stephen F. Austin State University, Nacogdoches, Texas.)

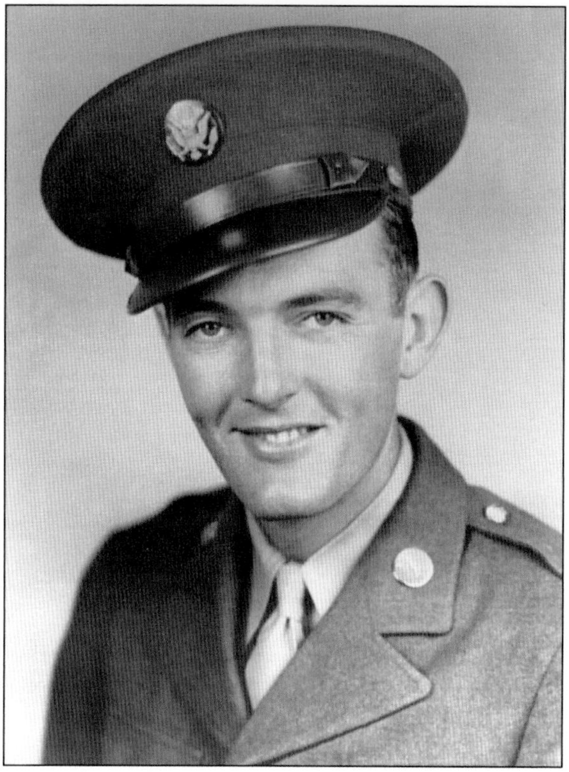

William Earl "Billy" Baker, a Timpson native, recognized the importance of education and used his life savings to improve opportunities for young graduates. After World War II, Baker was employed by Texaco in Port Arthur, Texas, retiring in the early 1980s. In 1988, his estate set aside $423,000 in scholarship funds to be used at Stephen F. Austin University in Nacogdoches, Texas, by Timpson graduates. This contribution from Baker is the largest individual donation that had ever, to that date, been given for scholarships in the history of the university. He also gave $150,000 for the administration building (below) carrying his name, located across the street from the present Timpson school plant. All funding was done in memory of his older brother, Bruce C. Baker Jr., who was killed during World War II. (Courtesy of Timpson Independent School District.)

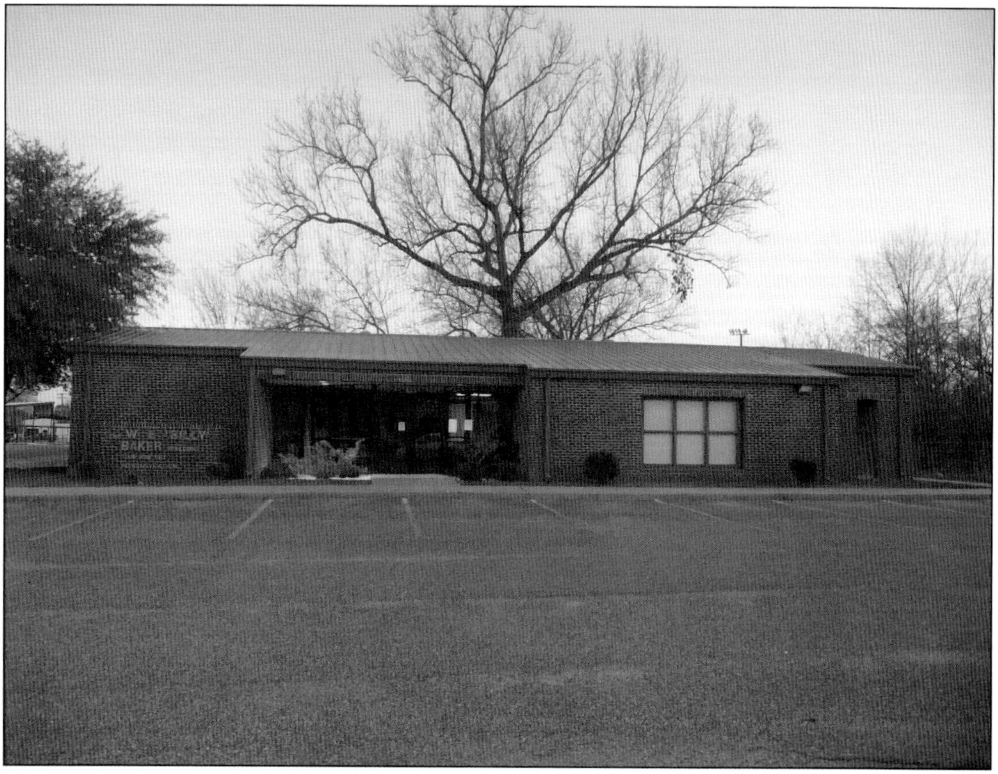

Four

COMMUNITY LIFE

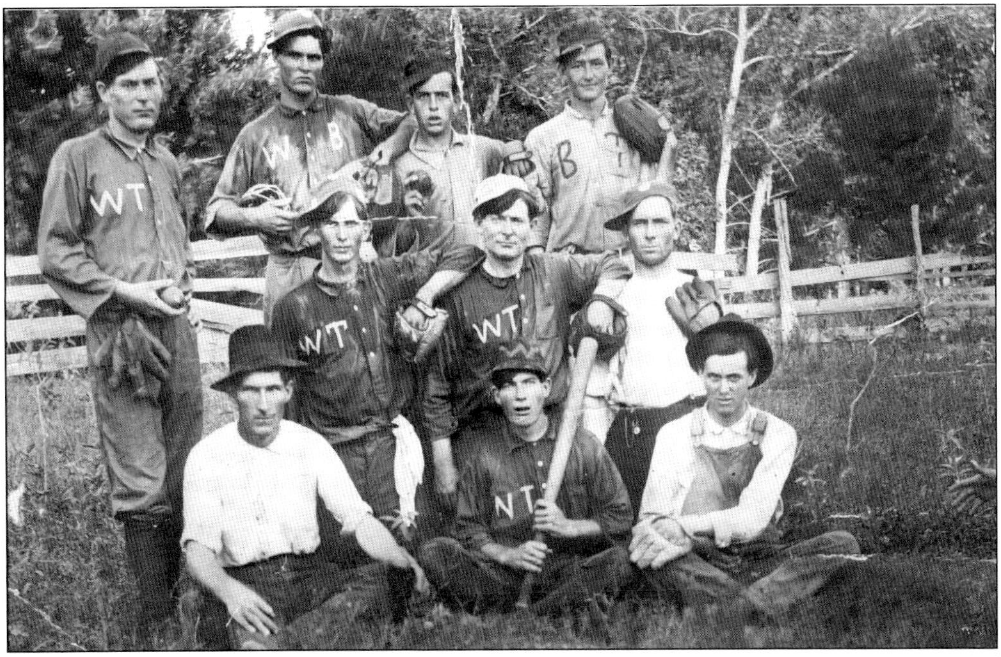

The Wedgeworth Baseball Team, shown here in the mid-1930s, had all the equipment they needed to enjoy America's national pastime—a ball, a bat, some gloves, and eager players. Tramping through high grass didn't hinder them. After a hot game, what better way to cool off than an ice-cream supper? The *Timpson Daily Times* wrote of Clem Eakin treating the "Wild Nine" to just such a treat on July 8, 1933. (Courtesy of the Herbert Eakin family.)

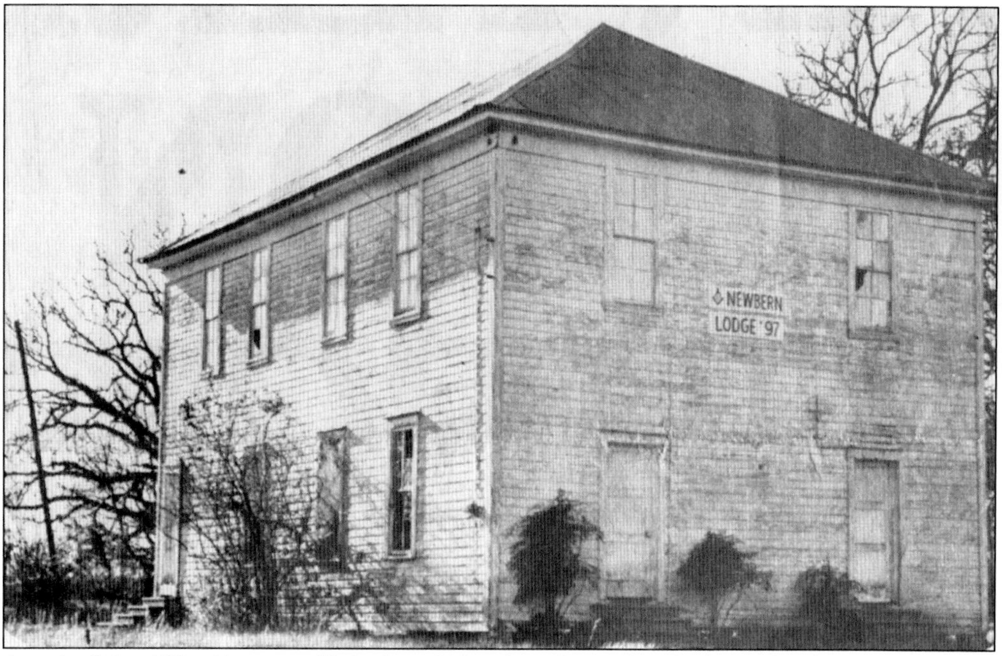

Arcadia School No. 60 was established in 1895 and was housed in the lowest level of the Woodmen of the World building, near the intersection of FM 138 and FM 1645. Later, this building housed Newbern Masonic Lodge No. 97. There are three accounts of its closing—when it became Myrtle Springs No. 60 in 1921; consolidation with Cooper School in 1924; and/or consolidation with Huber School in 1934 or 1935. (Courtesy of Fannie Watson.)

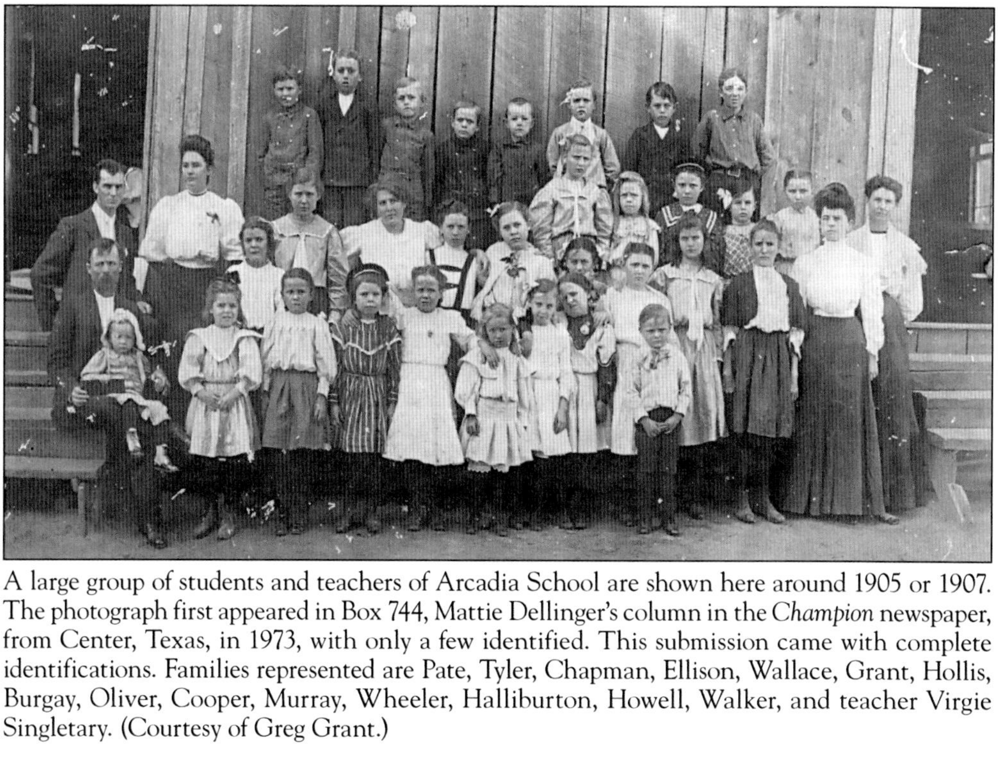

A large group of students and teachers of Arcadia School are shown here around 1905 or 1907. The photograph first appeared in Box 744, Mattie Dellinger's column in the *Champion* newspaper, from Center, Texas, in 1973, with only a few identified. This submission came with complete identifications. Families represented are Pate, Tyler, Chapman, Ellison, Wallace, Grant, Hollis, Burgay, Oliver, Cooper, Murray, Wheeler, Halliburton, Howell, Walker, and teacher Virgie Singletary. (Courtesy of Greg Grant.)

Once owned by Ransom Beauregard Neal, this dogtrot home was bought by Jake and Dee Smith around 1915. The house was equipped with electricity and droplights in 1949. The droplights are still in use. Ruby Dee Smith, daughter of Jake and Dee, owned the house and closed in the dogtrot around 1969. Now owned by Neil and Jackie Grant, the house was restored in 2005 by Jake and Dee Smith's grandson Greg Grant. (Courtesy of Greg Grant.)

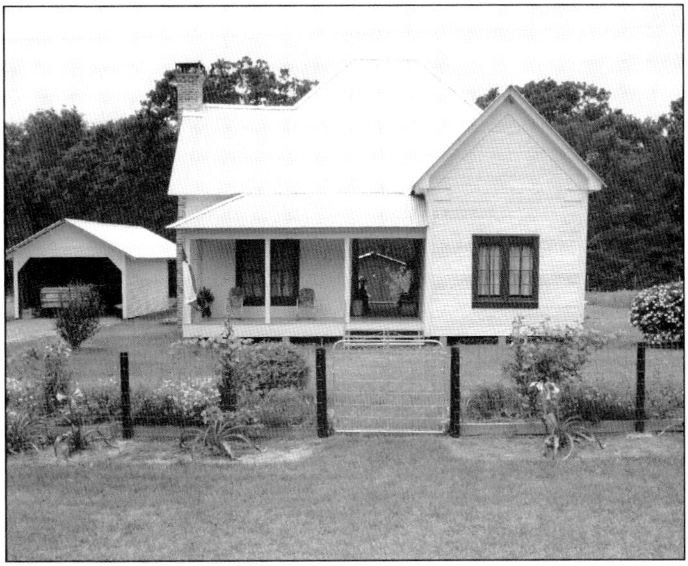

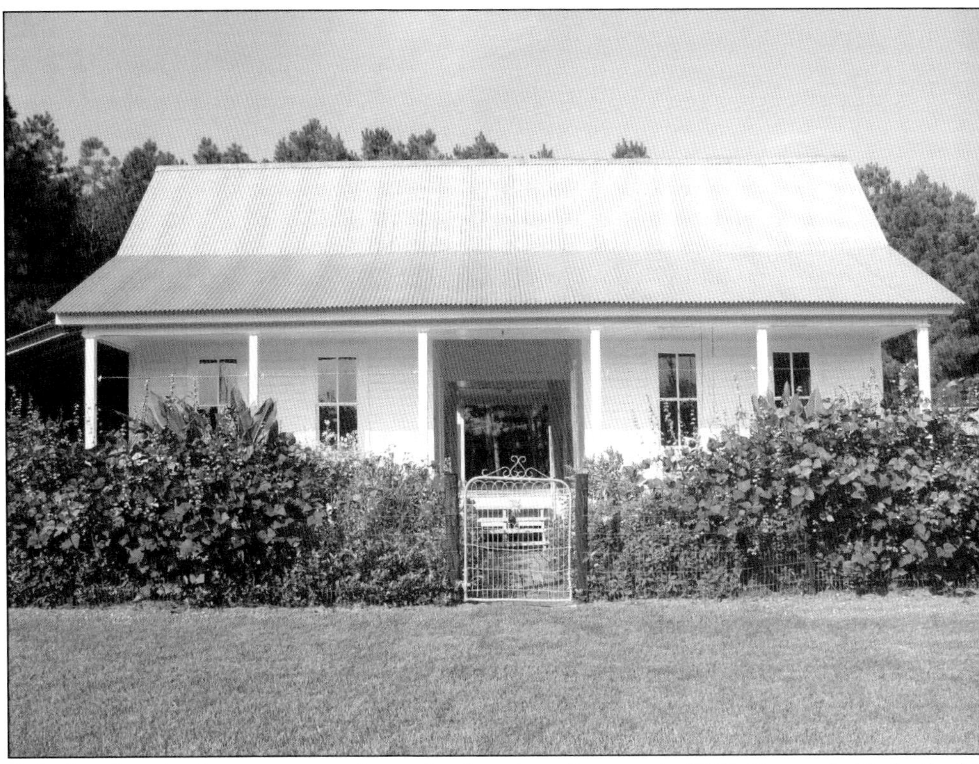

O.S. Cox bought the property and ran the first Arcadia store in 1887. Cox probably built this dogtrot house. It was the first home in Arcadia to have carbide lights. Voyd and Nara (Emanis) Hughes modernized the house, enclosing the dogtrot. Eventually, the house was bought by Eloy and Marquette Emanis. Greg Grant reversed the modernization, restoring the house to its original appearance. (Courtesy of Greg Grant.)

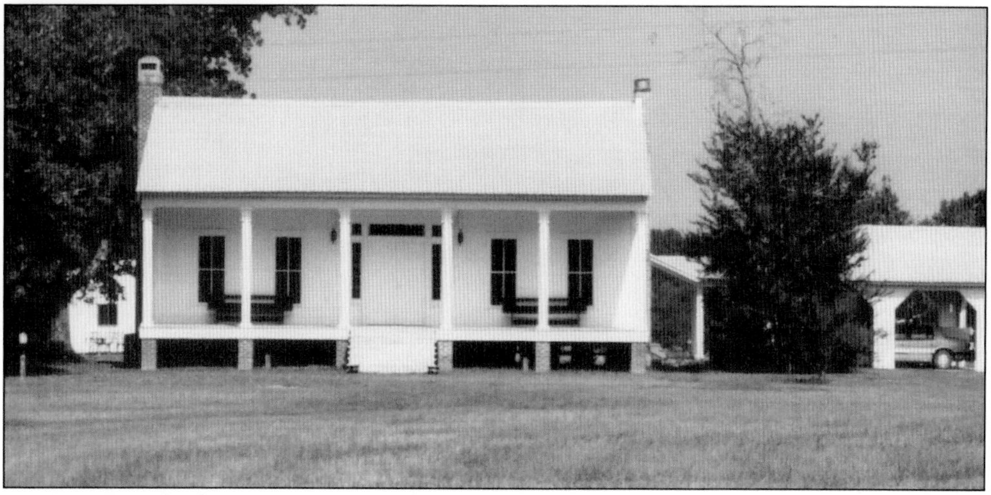

In 1904, David Alvis Hairgrove purchased a 220-acre farm and a 50-year-old home from Sarah A. Bryan. Hairgrove paid $3,500 for the Buena Vista property, paying it off over a 10-year period through his horse-breeding business. He died in 1915, after only 10 years of marriage to Martha (Cammack) Hairgrove. The home was restored in 1993–1994 by their grandson, David Leon Hairgrove. (Courtesy of Kenneth Hairgrove.)

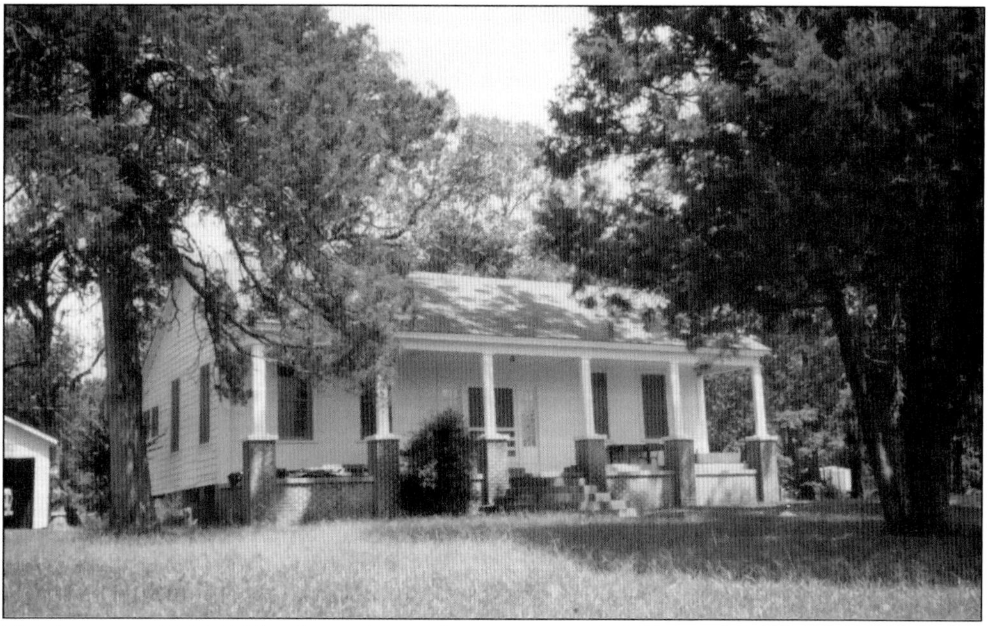

This home, on FM 1645, has housed several generations of Morrisons. John C. Morrison opened the first store in Buena Vista in 1847. Later, his son Eli built and operated a gristmill and a cotton gin. Eli Morrison was one of three men who went into a quarantined Shreveport, Louisiana, during the 1873 yellow fever epidemic to get supplies for the community. The other two men later died of the disease. (Courtesy of TAGHS.)

The Buena Vista Baptist Church was organized by Isaac Reed in 1839 and occupied three different buildings before this one was built in 1867. Eighty-seven years later, on July 4, 1954, it was torn down. The church bell was placed under the trees to wait for its new church home. Instead, it was stolen and never recovered. The new building was dedicated on Thanksgiving Day in 1954. (Courtesy of Martha Peters Brothers.)

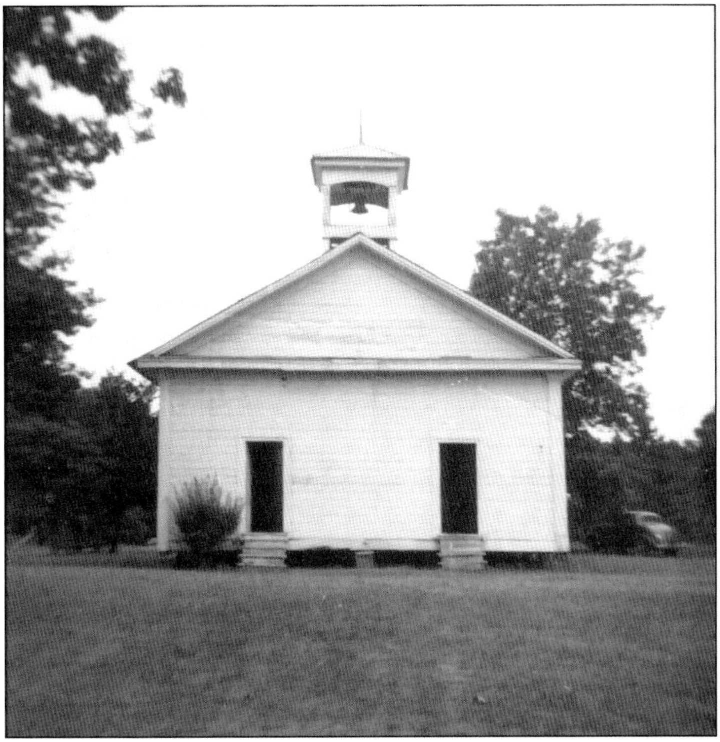

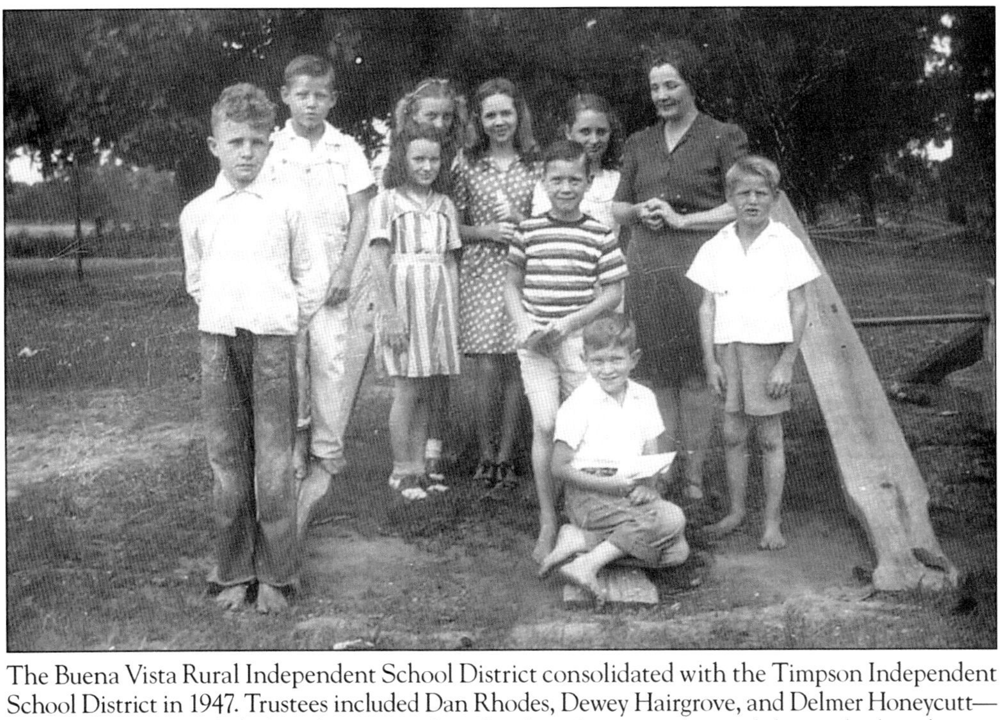

The Buena Vista Rural Independent School District consolidated with the Timpson Independent School District in 1947. Trustees included Dan Rhodes, Dewey Hairgrove, and Delmer Honeycutt—until his move shortly before this time. The school, at the time of consolidation, had grades one through six. Teacher Rachel Askins and some of the students were photographed in May 1947 on the last day of school in Buena Vista. (Courtesy of Kenneth Hairgrove.)

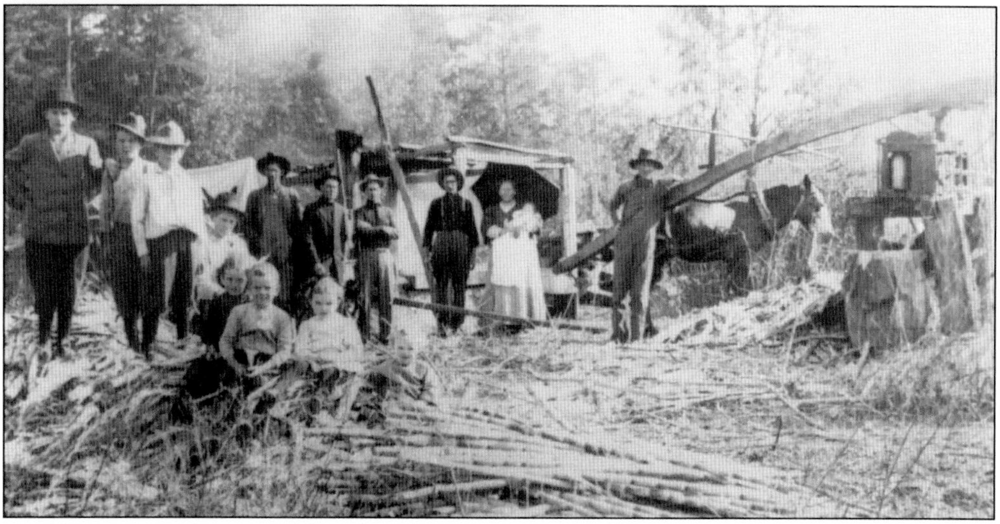

In 1909, an acre of cane could produce from 200 to 500 gallons of syrup and bring 50¢ a gallon. Shown here in 1912, the Hairgrove Mill was located in Buena Vista Community. Pictured from left to right are (first row, seated) Ima, Willie, Bernie, and Maurine Hairgrove; (second row, standing) unidentified, Otto Hairgrove, Wilburn Hairgrove, four unidentified, A.C. and wife, Jodie (Duke) Hairgrove, holding Mamie Lou Hairgrove, and unidentified. (Courtesy of Frances McIntyre.)

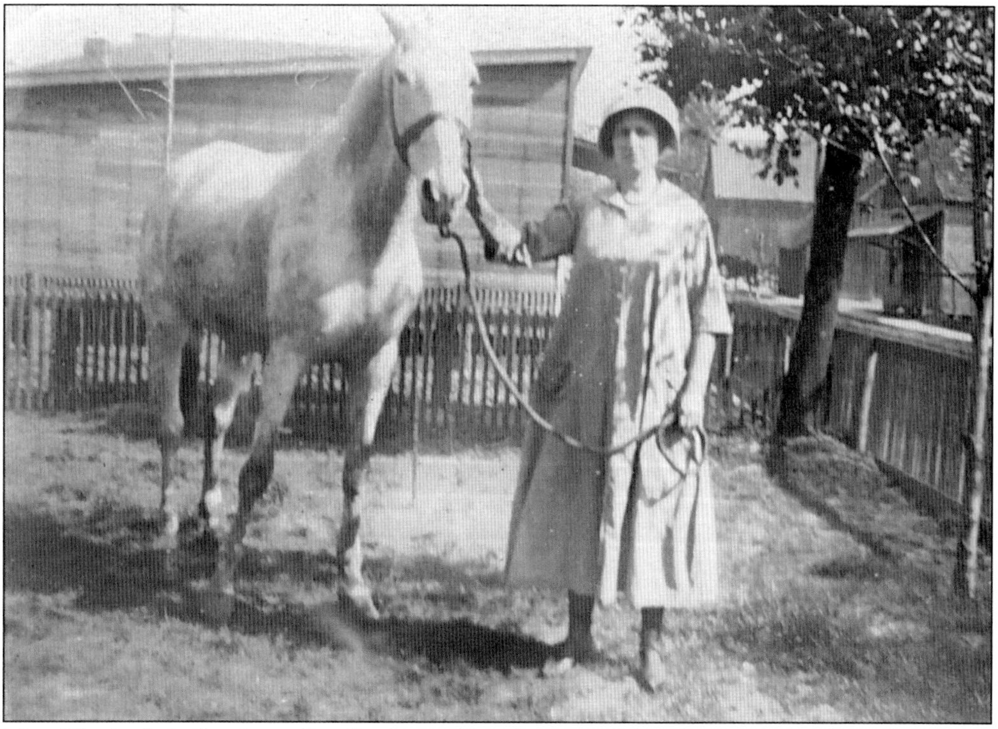

Mary Elizabeth Stilley, born October 28, 1887, is shown with her favorite buggy horse before she died on February 21, 1906. She caught her long skirt on fire while helping burn brush at the home of her sister Lucy Witherspoon. Lucy's husband, James, suffered severe burns to his hands and arms trying to extinguish the flames. Mary died as a result of the burns. (Courtesy of Margaret Witherspoon Oliver.)

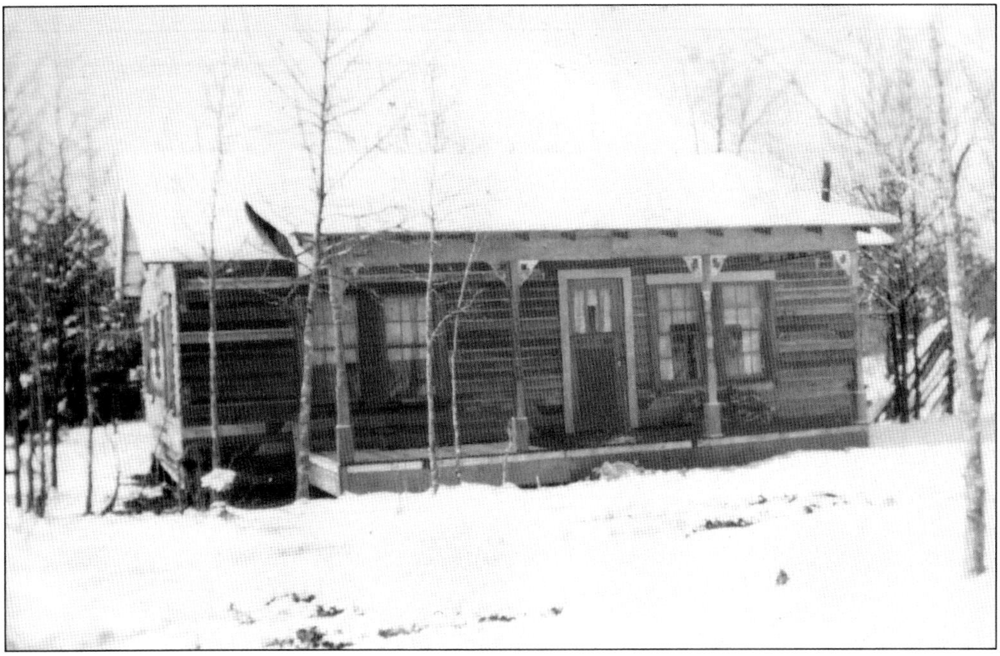

In the early 1940s, almost 100 years after Corinth Missionary Baptist Church began, the congregation built their first parsonage. Edd Rhodes, who had grown up in this church, surrendered to the ministry, married his sweetheart, I.T. Fisher, and was called to be their next pastor. Hugh Milford, who had raised Rhodes, spearheaded the building project on land obtained through a 100-year lease from the Booth family. (Courtesy of Annie Ruth Tate.)

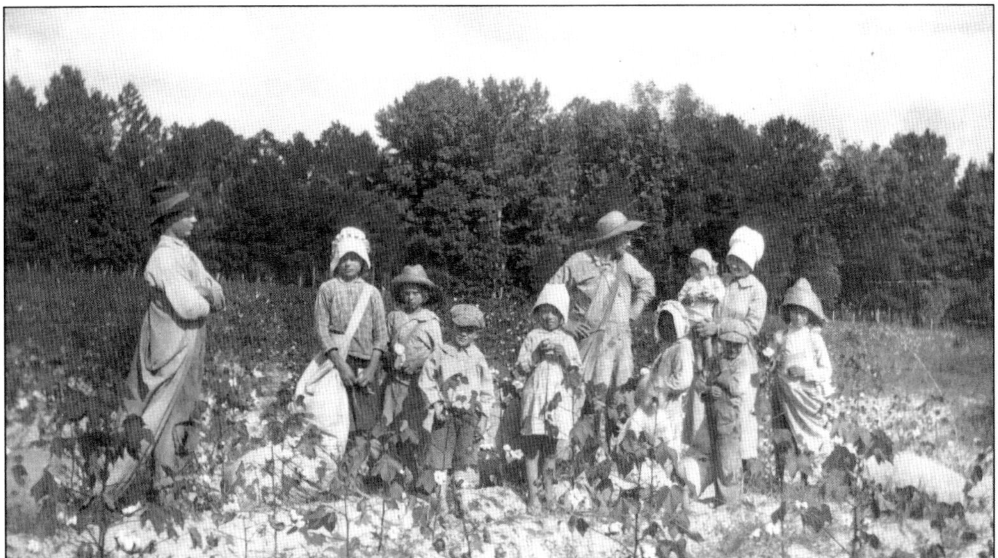

Picking cotton was hard work. Even the children were enlisted when the cotton was ready, and picking began around 5:00 a.m. Each picker had a sack with a long shoulder strap into which the cotton was placed. The sack became heavier and heavier as the day wore on, and temperatures in the area can rise to near 100 degrees. Haley Bush (left) is the only person identified in this photograph. (Courtesy of John Herbert Eakin family.)

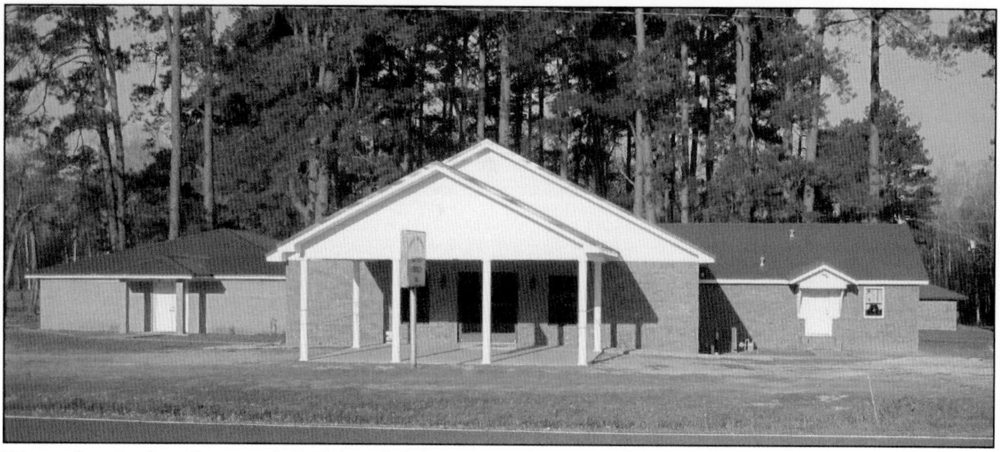

This rebricked and expanded Corinth Missionary Baptist Church is located on FM 1970 in the Corinth Community. It was established in 1852 when three families (Francis Wedgeworth, Thomas Milford, and Caswell Eakin) arrived by wagon train from Alabama. They chose a spot beside an Indian burial ground and spring for the log building that would serve as the church, school, and meeting place. This building was constructed about 1942. (Courtesy of TAGHS.)

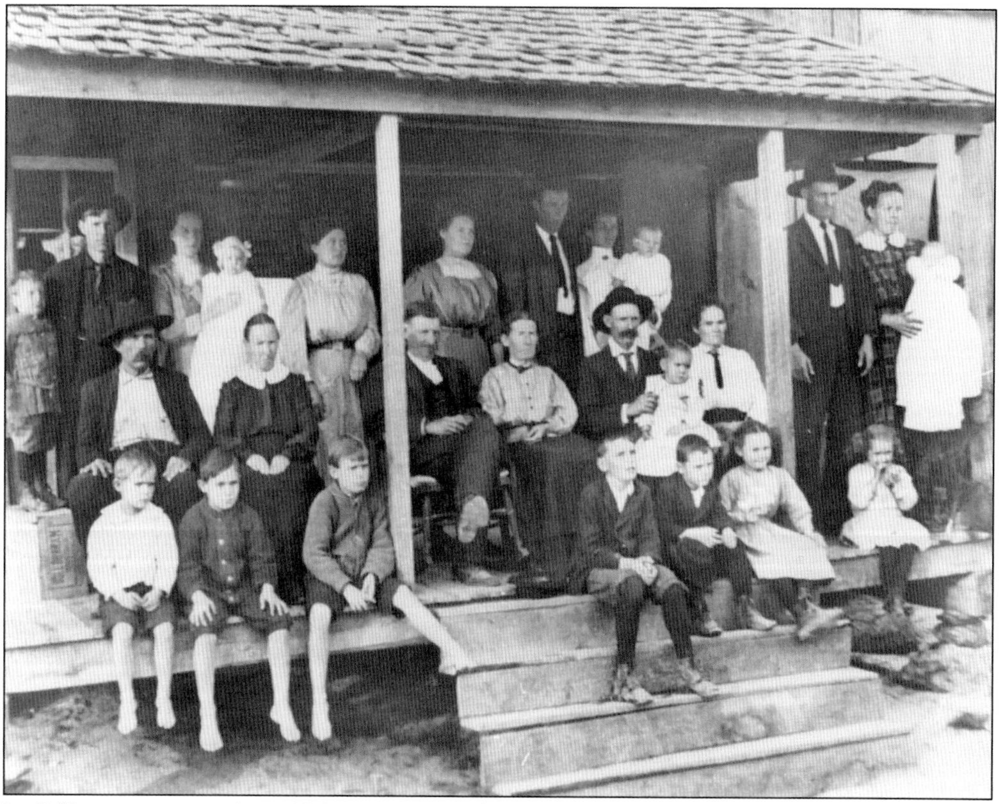

In 1852, a wagon train from Alabama was traveling through the pass at Shreveport when brothers John and Steve Stilley came riding up. They were chasing a disgruntled employee who shot their father, Mose Stilley. After the shooter was hanged, near present-day Timpson, Steve returned to Illinois. John stayed to marry Easter Ann Wedgeworth, from the wagon train. The John Stilley family is shown in 1911 in the Corinth community. (Courtesy of Sandra Brownlow.)

The Milford Store had to be moved from the roadway when FM 1970 was constructed through the Corinth community. They sold coal oil and gasoline, as well as everything from school supplies to groceries. Shown here in the early 1940s are, from left to right, Ruth Witherspoon, Hazel Milford, Emma Lee Milford (who ran the store for years), and Ethel Milford, Emma and Hazel's mother. (Courtesy of Annie Ruth Tate.)

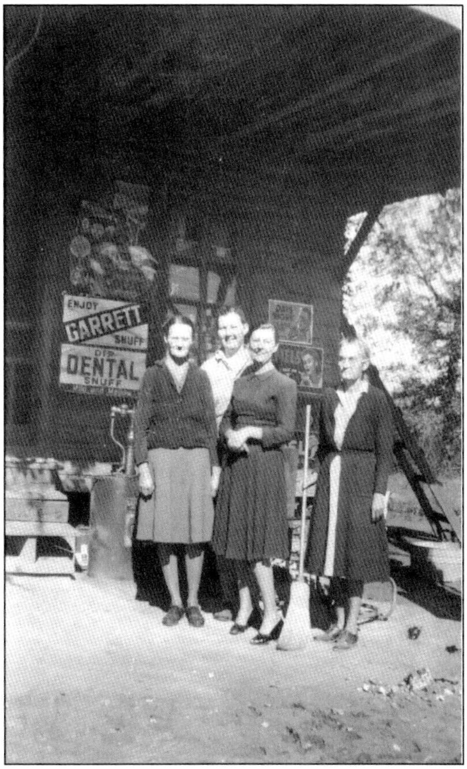

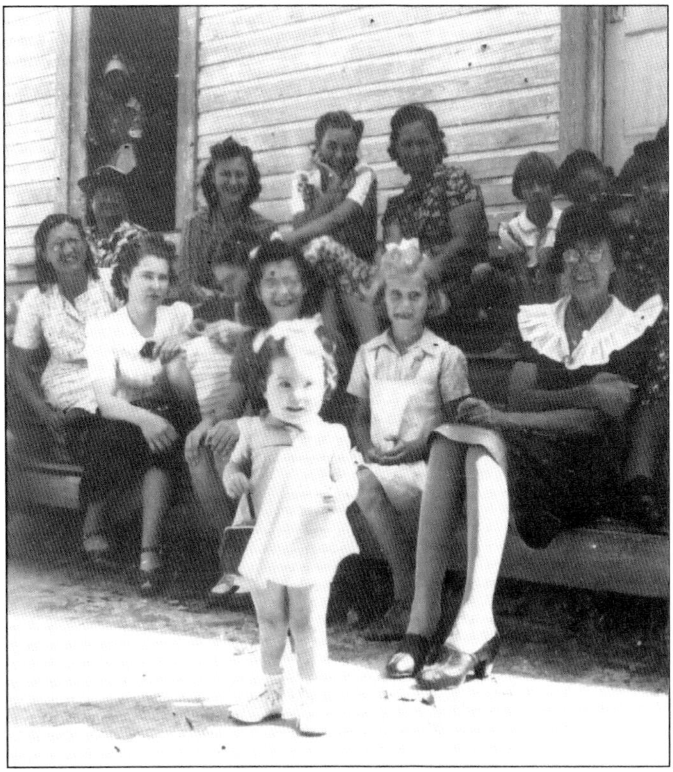

During World War II, it was not uncommon for a crowd to gather and watch as troops passed by. This group of women is seated in front of the old wooden Corinth Church, located on the south side of Farm Road 1970, for that purpose. On this occasion, troops wanted their picture taken with two-year-old Patricia Ritter, the young redheaded girl in front. (Courtesy of Annie Ruth Tate.)

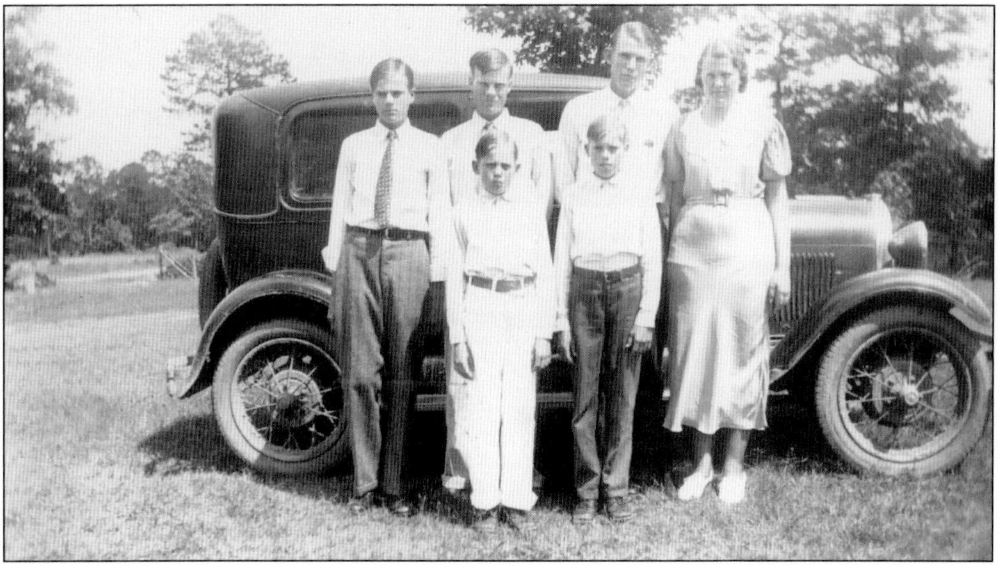

The children of Jones and Sallie (Anderson) Harvey stand beside the family car at their parents' home in 1935. The home was located west of the Wedgeworth School, near the Rusk and Panola County line. Shown here are, from left to right, (first row) Veston and Elton Harvey; (second row) Burtis, Donnie, Ralph, and Bonnie Harvey. Four Harvey brothers (Burtis, Donnie, Ralph, and Elton) served in World War II. (Courtesy of Esther Marie Harvey.)

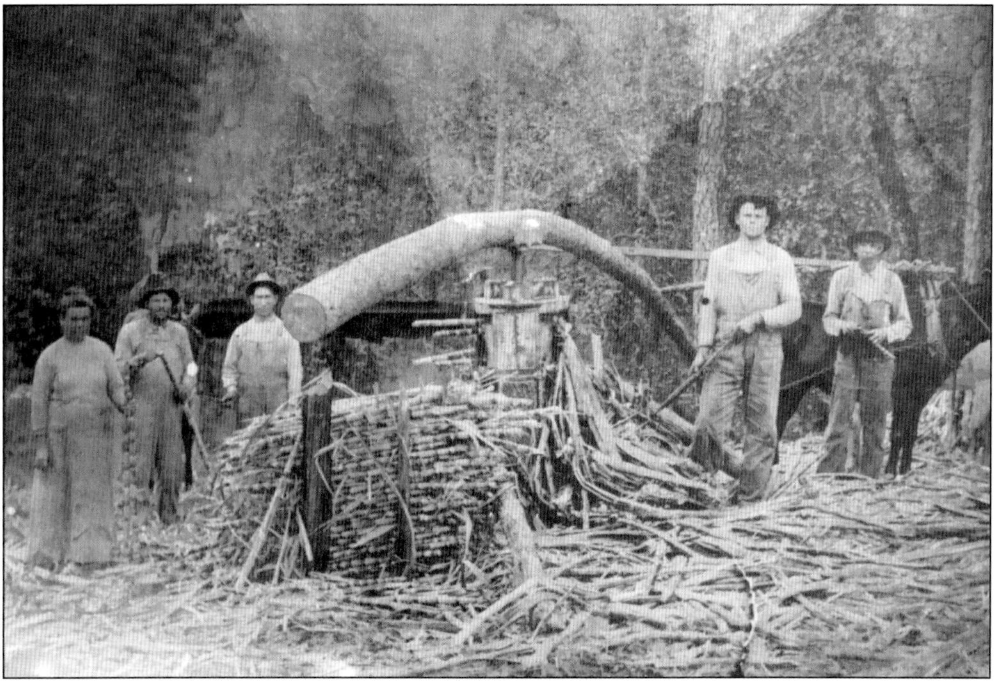

Syrup mills were not uncommon during the early 20th century in rural East Texas. Ribbon cane molasses (sugarcane syrup) could be a source of income or just a family affair. The Downing Mill, located in Wedgeworth Community, is shown in 1912. Those identified are, from left to right, Nancy (Gary) Downing, Nute Downing, Jim Humphries, Lonnie Downing, and William Downing. (Courtesy of Jan Magness Barrett.)

The Wedgeworth Basketball Team is pictured here on the steps of the Wedgeworth School in the 1930s. The players are, from left to right, (first row) Lovis Eakin, Burtis Harvey, coach Herbert Eakin, Tom Humphries, and Bob Bates; (second row) Ralph Harvey, Jack Hudson, Lem Hudson, and John Eakin. These same players also made up any other school sports team. (Courtesy of Marilyn Corder and John Herbert Eakin family.)

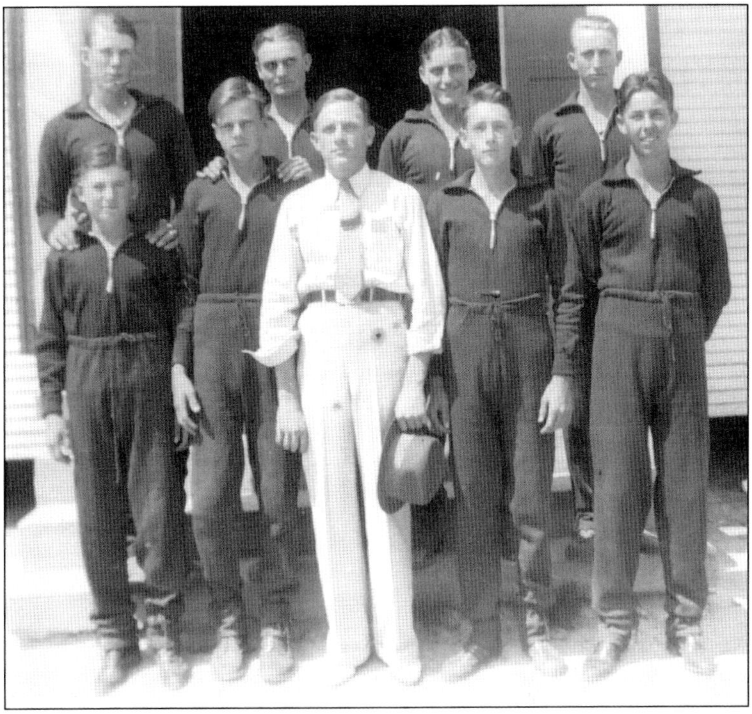

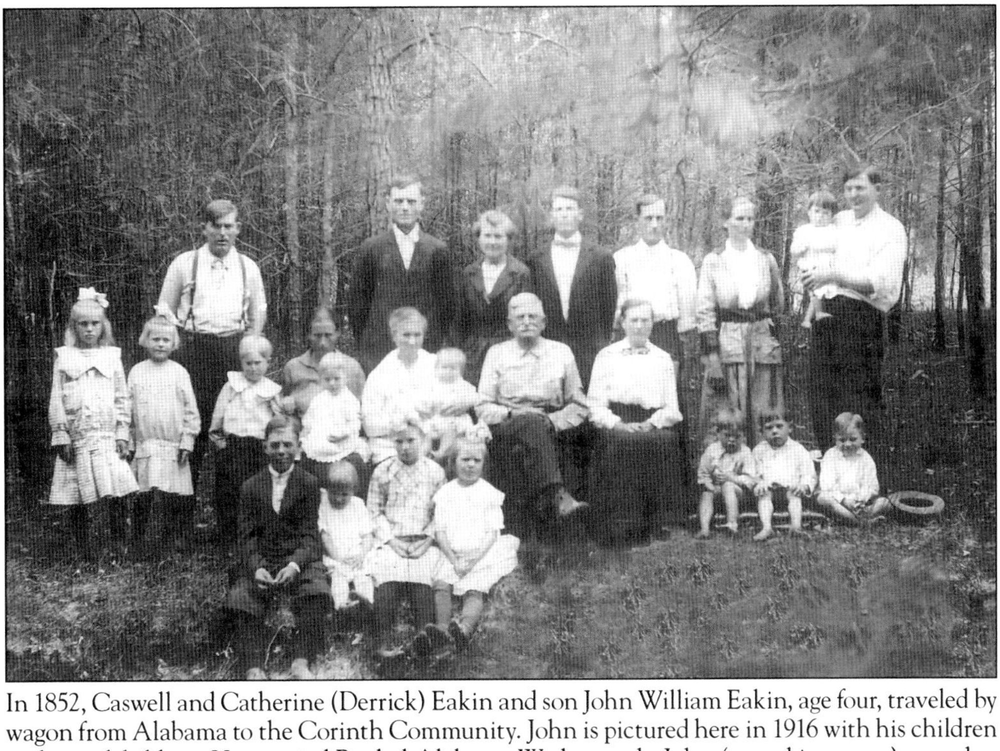

In 1852, Caswell and Catherine (Derrick) Eakin and son John William Eakin, age four, traveled by wagon from Alabama to the Corinth Community. John is pictured here in 1916 with his children and grandchildren. He married Rachel Alabama Wedgeworth. John (seated in center) served as constable in Timpson one year, but he mostly farmed. Their grandchildren became educators, elected officials, and successful car dealers. (Courtesy of John Herbert Eakin family.)

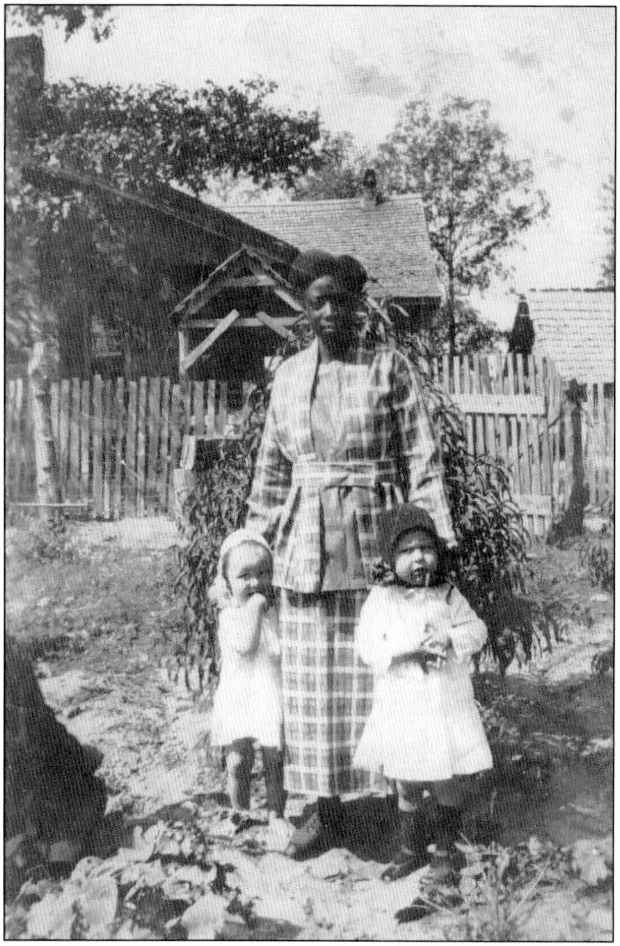

Hugh Henry Milford and Sallie Ethel Bush were married on February 23, 1916. Returning from Clayton, Texas, with several children left homeless by a house fire, they found homes for them with local Corinth families. Ida Pellum, the adult in this photograph, remained with the Milford family and was loved as one of the family. She is shown with two of the Milford children, Hazel Marion (left) and Emma Lee. (Courtesy of Annie Ruth Tate.)

In the early 1900s, many of the local farmers raised cotton as a cash crop. Cotton was picked and weighed in the field, then brought to one of the gins operating in Timpson and many other rural communities. L.D. McWilliams Sr., T.P. Todd, and Sam Smith were some of the first cotton gin operators. In 1953, the *Timpson Weekly Times* reported over 2,000 bales ginned in Timpson. (Courtesy of TAGHS.)

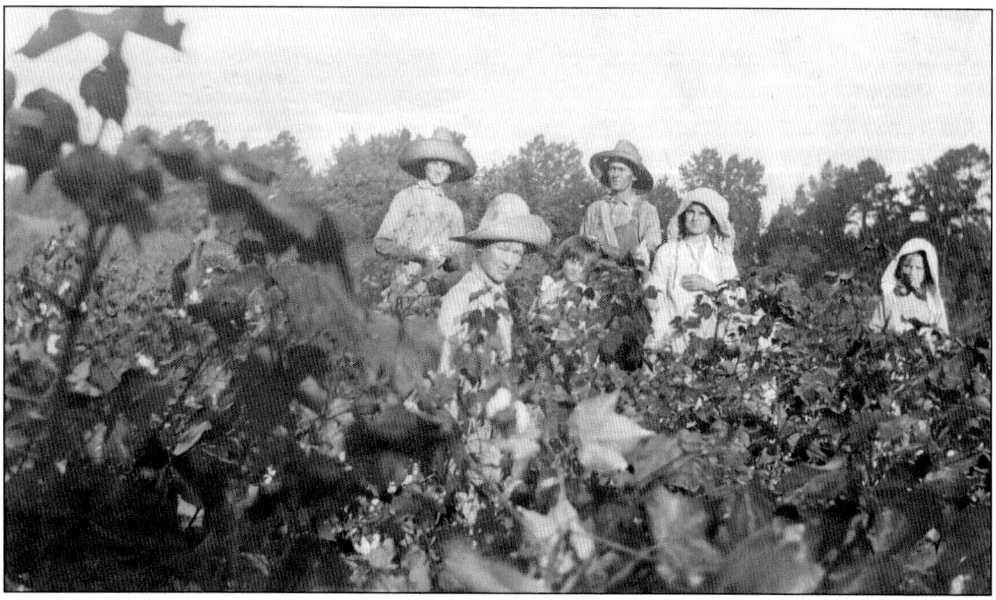

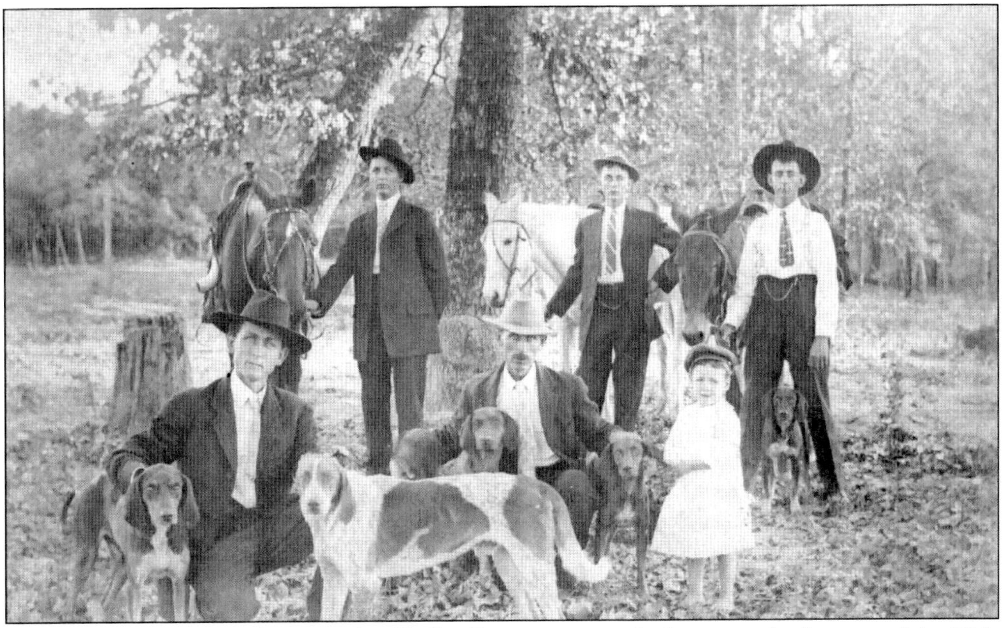

The Sparks family is set for a popular Shelby County sport—fox hunting. At the turn of the 20th century, hunters established the National Hall of Fame of Foxhounds Cemetery at Boles Field in the Sabine National Forest. These Timpson hunters are shown in 1907 and identified as, from left to right, (first row) Walter, Jim, and Hollis Sparks; (second row) Charlie, Tom and Julian Sparks. (Courtesy of Dru Sparks Dickey.)

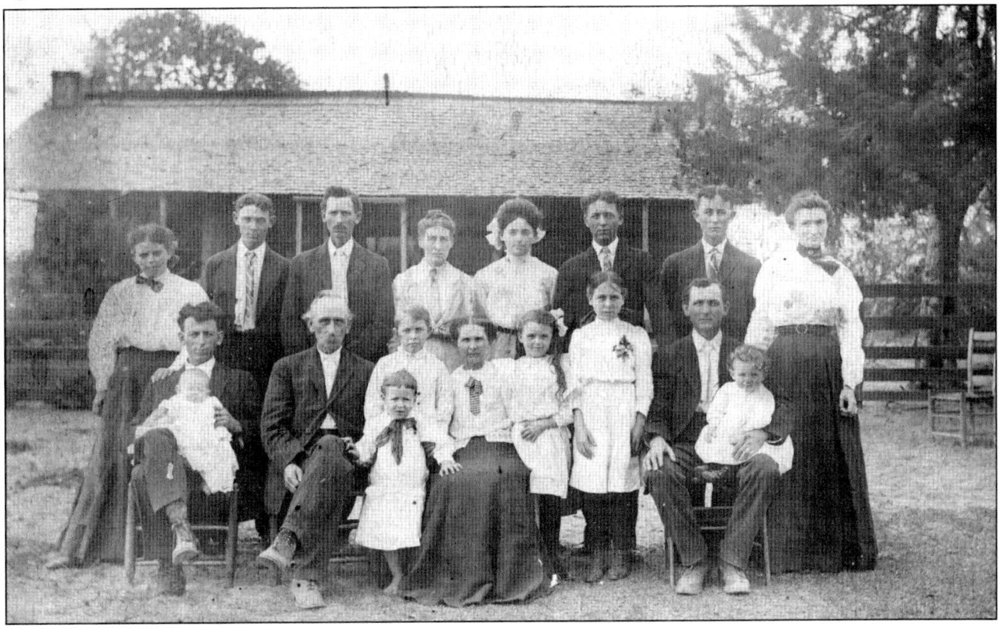

The family of Edmund Neeley and Mary Emma Martin Sparks are shown here around 1908, near their home off of FM 1971. They are, from left to right, (first row) Julian, Clifford, Edmund, Hollis, Ed, Emma, Vera, Winnie, Walter, and Velma Sparks; (second row) Lena (Amos) Sparks, Elbert, Jim, Fannie (Gregory) Sparks, Helen, Charles "Buddy" Sparks, Tommy, and Minnie Ola (Moore) Sparks. (Courtesy of Dru Sparks Dickey.)

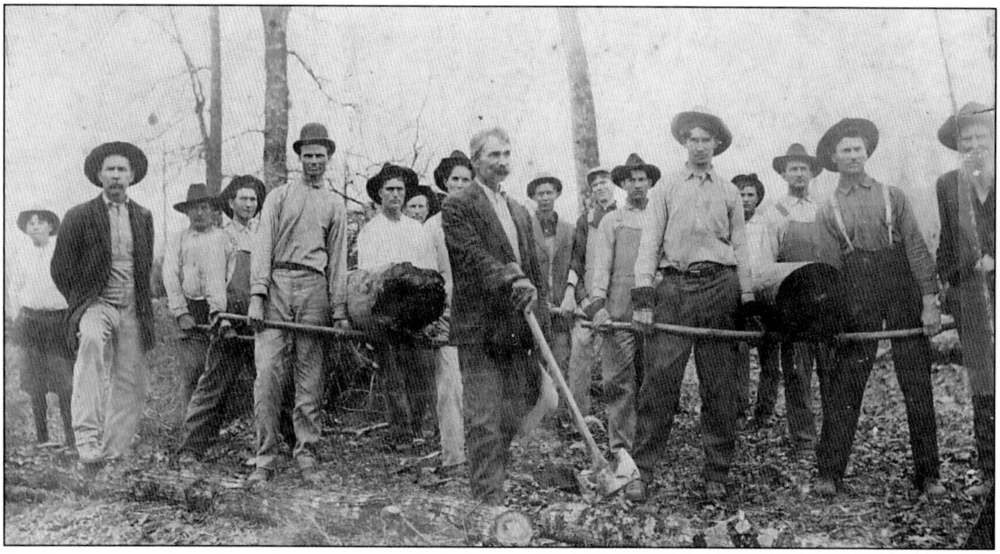

Settlers coming into East Texas in the early 1800s encountered vast forests of pines and hardwoods. The logging business became the primary focus of activity in the region. In addition to cutting tasks, forest workers transported logs, worked on roads, and set miles of ties for railroad tracks. Lawrence A. Risinger, second from right, is the only one identified in this work party. (Courtesy of Margaret Oliver and Barbara Bogue.)

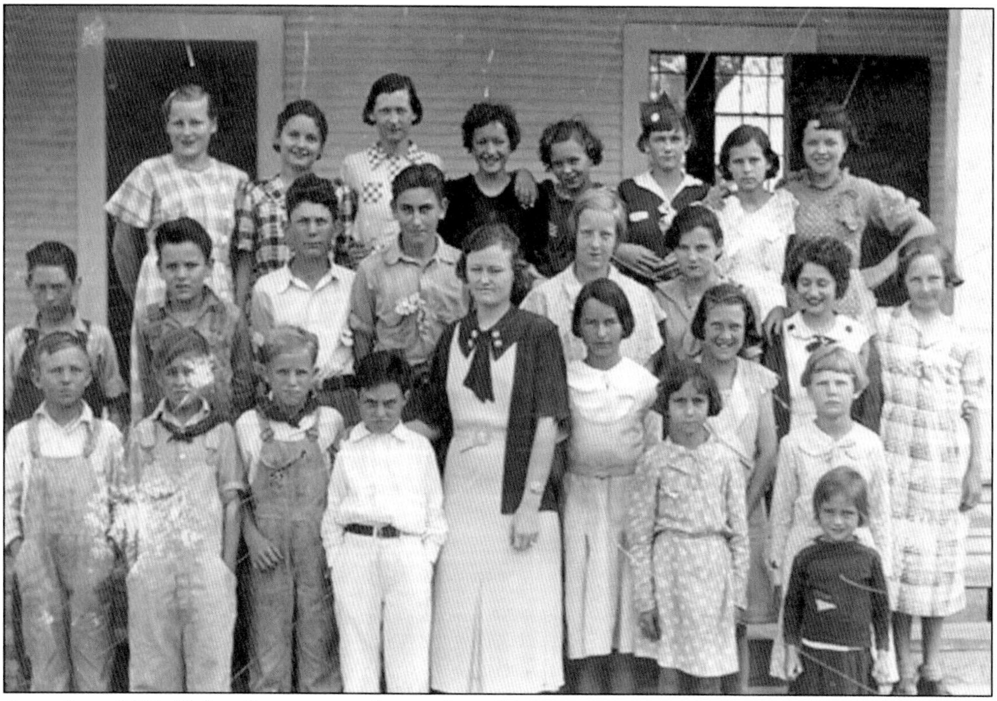

As early as 1893, Huber Community, located south of Timpson on State Highway 87, had a school. The district also encompassed Mt. Gillian School (a colored school). Teacher Vallie (Hughes) Clark is shown with her students on the steps of the Huber School in 1934 or 1935. At one time, as many as 132 students attended the schools in this district. Huber consolidated with Timpson in the fall of 1945. (Courtesy of Pat Crawford.)

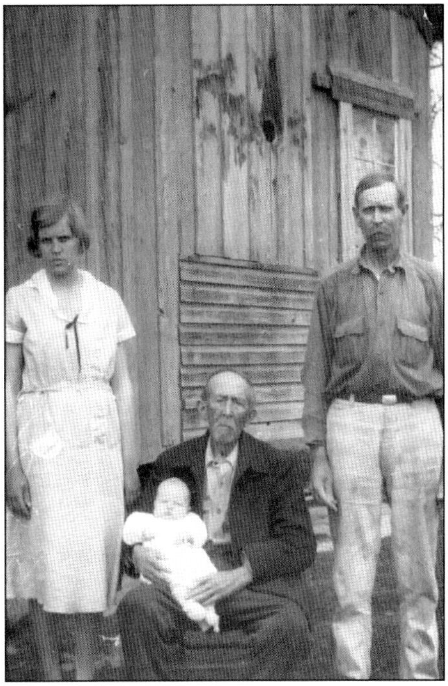

Four generations of Driggers are shown at A.M. and Ina Mae Darnell's home in the Shady Grove Community in 1931. Pictured here are, from left to right, Ina Mae (Driggers) Darnell, Emmett Eugene Darnell (baby), James L. Driggers, and Thomas Jefferson Driggers. Great-grandfather James served in the Confederacy from 1862 to 1865, coming from Alabama to Texas in 1894. Emmett Eugene was in the Korean War from 1952 to 1954. (Courtesy of Esther Marie Darnell Harvey.)

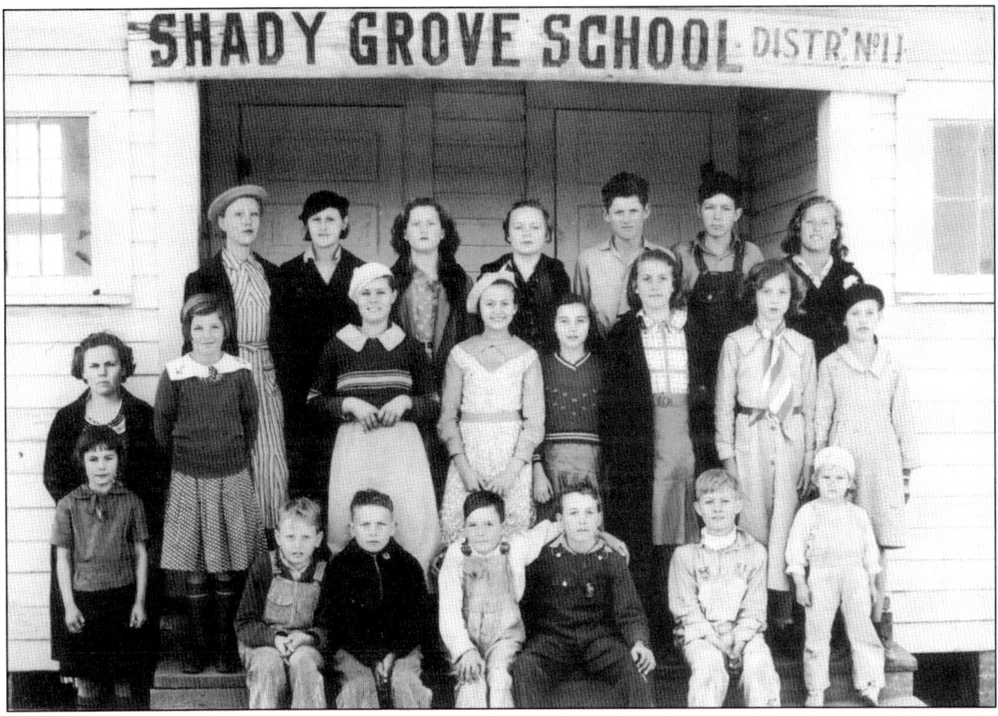

Standing in front of the school on "picture day" are students in the upper grades at the Shady Grove Elementary School around the 1930s. Identified in this photograph are, from left to right, (second row) teacher Joella Crawford, two unidentified, Agnes Childs, and Ernesteen Ramsey. All others are unidentified. Shady Grove School was established in 1893 and continued until it consolidated with Timpson in 1943. (Courtesy of Pat Crawford.)

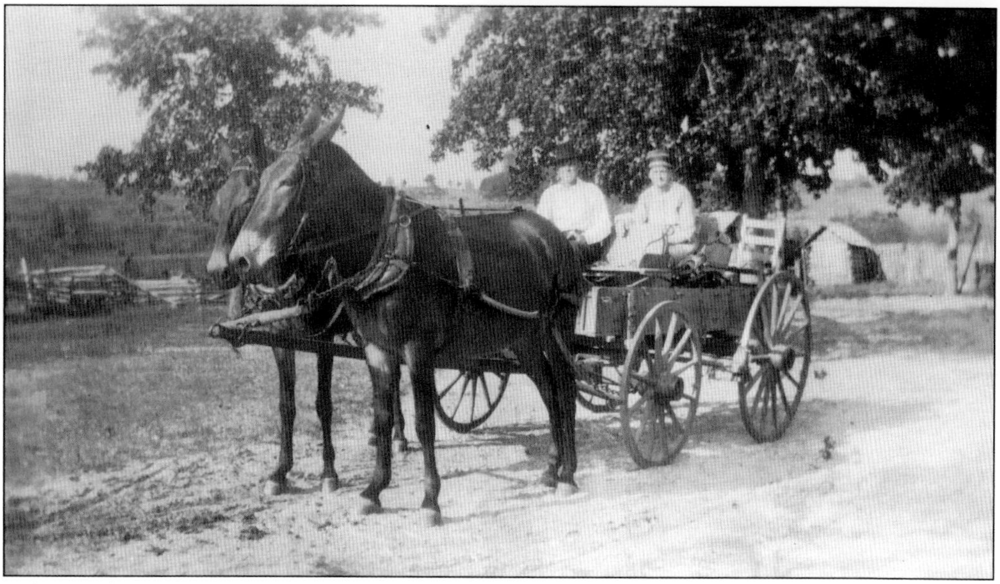

Robert and Jennie Darnell Rhodes raised five children on their farm in the Shady Grove Community. They grew vegetables and cotton and raised pigs, cows, and plow mules. Their only purchases were salt, coffee, fabric to sew, and a few other items. They made mattresses from their own cotton or chicken feathers, built fences from their own timber, and more. Farm life in the 1920s was simple and safe. (Courtesy of Esther Marie Harvey.)

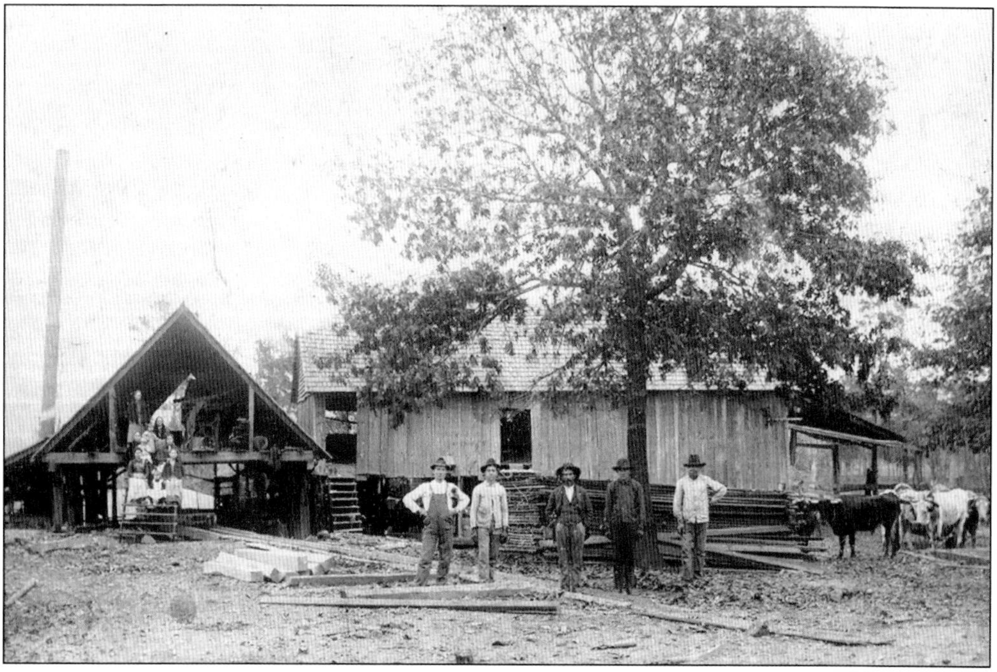

The community of Silas was settled before 1865 and got a post office in 1896. The community had a rural agricultural economy, with crops including cotton, corn, hay, sugar cane, peanuts, and truck crops. Timber was mostly yellow pine, and some was milled at Jess Parker's sawmill, located between Silas and Stockman. Shown in 1907, the mill used the Waterman Lumber Company tram to send lumber to Timpson and beyond. (Courtesy of TAGHS.)

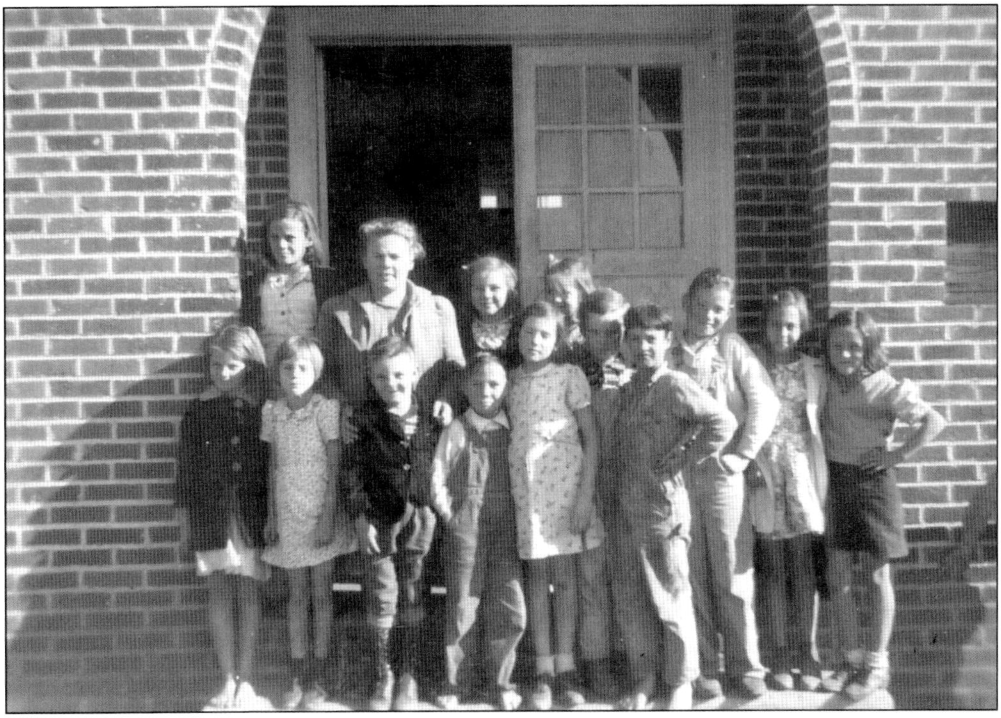

Stockman School was formed in time for the 1910–1911 school year, and school was held in a church building for several years until a school was constructed in 1920. In 1932, a new brick structure replaced the original building. In 1936, high school students were bused to Timpson. This photograph was taken between 1938 and 1944, when Joella Crawford taught these elementary school students. (Courtesy of Pat Crawford.)

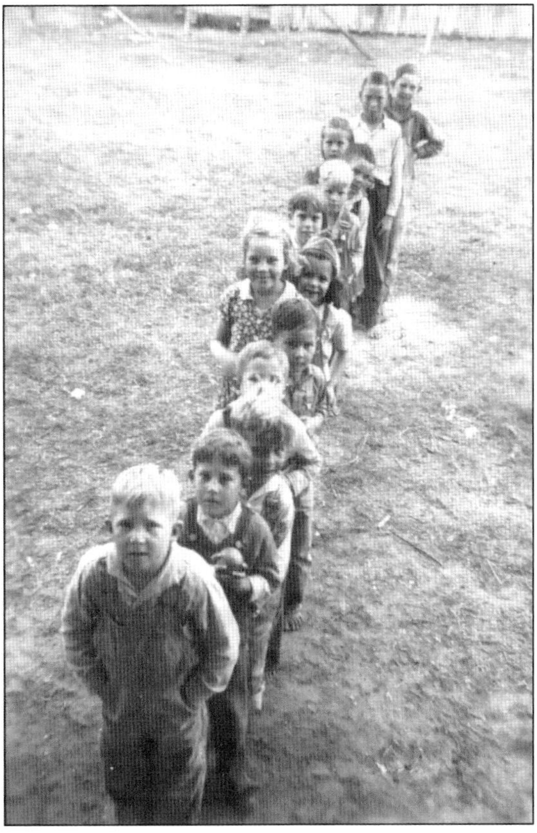

In 1910, Stockman was a small village situated on the branch railroad line out of Timpson. It was located on what is now FM 415, near the Attoyac River. Before the school was formed in 1910, students walked long distances to attend school at Silas. These young schoolchildren seem happy to form a line for the next activity at Stockman School. (Courtesy of Pat Crawford.)

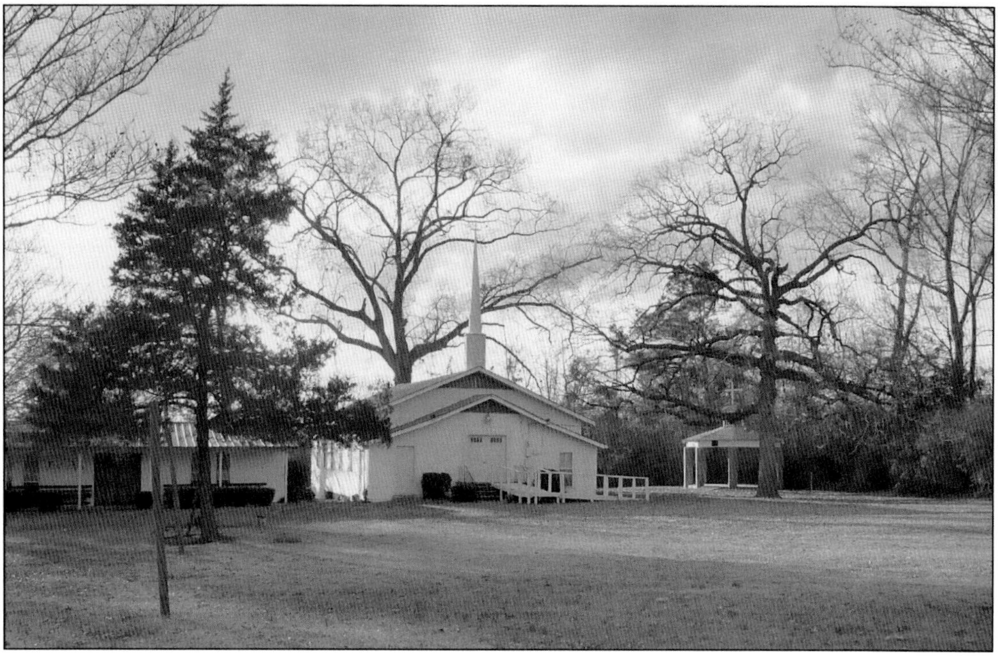

This Stockman Community Church building was constructed in 1928 or 1929. The original two-story church, which had served various denominations (Church of Christ, Christian, Pentecostal, Missionary Baptist, and both Congregational and United Methodist) was damaged by a storm, so it was dismantled and the materials were used in the new building. It is currently used for worship services by a small congregation of United Methodists whose ancestors chartered the church in 1930. (Courtesy of TAGHS.)

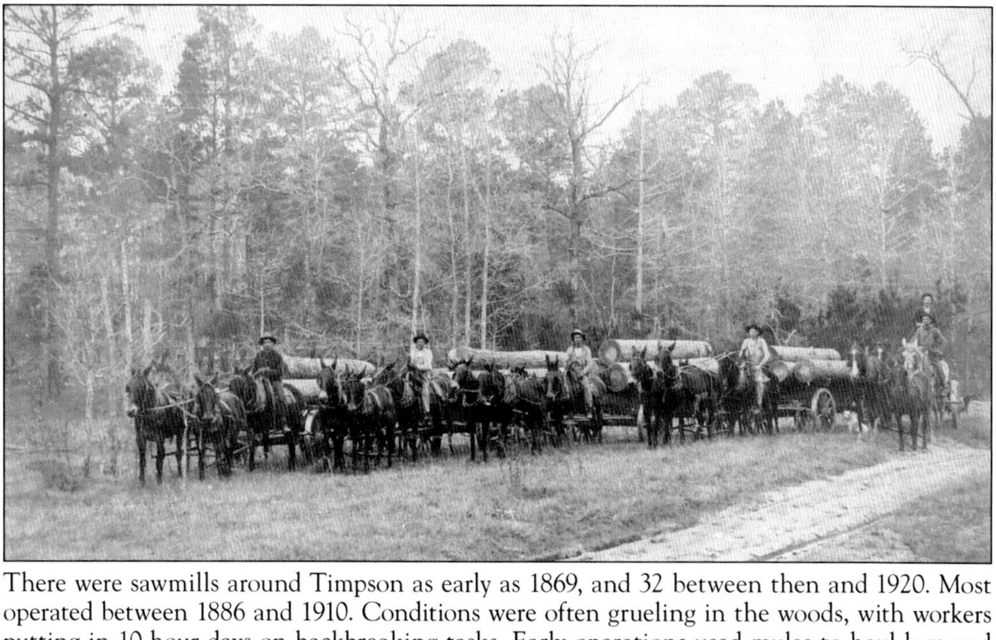

There were sawmills around Timpson as early as 1869, and 32 between then and 1920. Most operated between 1886 and 1910. Conditions were often grueling in the woods, with workers putting in 10-hour days on backbreaking tasks. Early operations used mules to haul logs and cross-load the logs onto flatcars. In this 1905 photograph, Columbus A. Stockman could be the first man on the left. (Courtesy of Shirley and Kenneth Bates.)

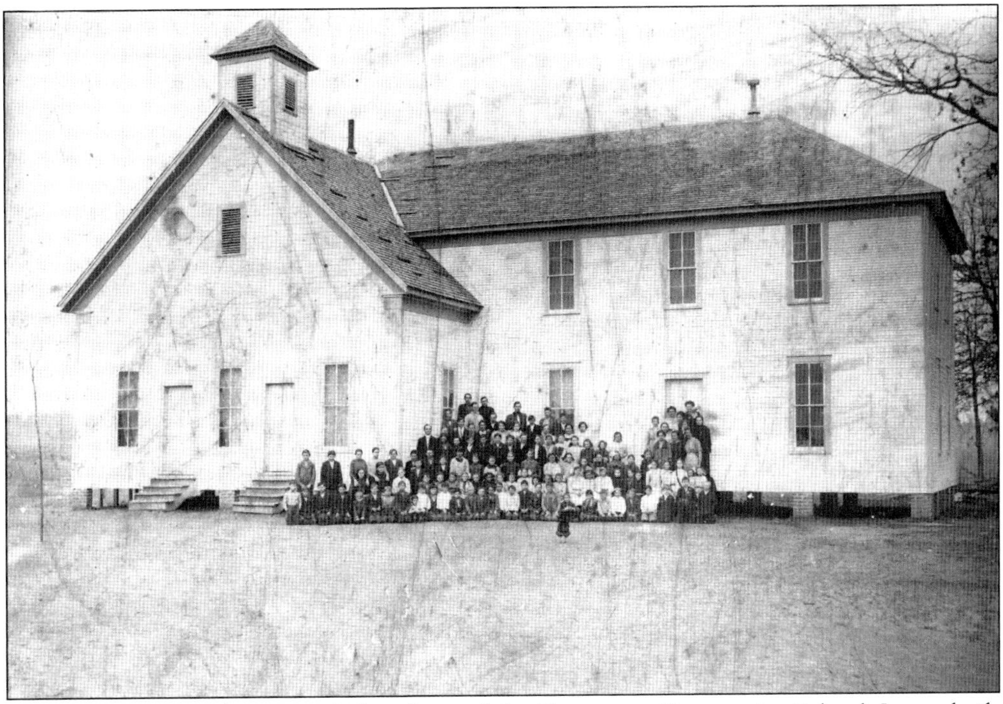

Many students are shown in 1915 in front of the Tennessee Community School. It was built around 1913 and was located seven miles east of Timpson on what is now FM 947. In 1910 or 1911, there were 86 students. When the school burned in 1933, it was replaced with a brick building. After 1937, high school students were transferred to Timpson and Tenaha. Consolidation was completed in 1954. (Courtesy of Billie Green.)

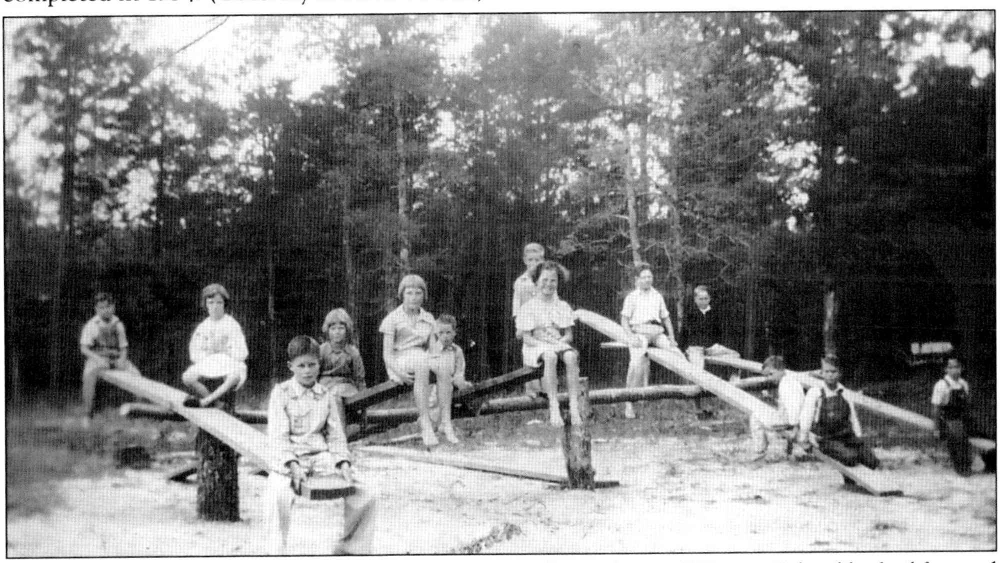

Even though the playground equipment was homemade, students of Weaver School looked forward to recess. There were seesaws and a device for swinging that consisted of an iron pole with a high ring of metal from which a number of "swings" dangled. A child grasped the swing and ran around in a circle, moving fast. Students also played ring-around-the-rosy, may I, red rover, and dodgeball. (Courtesy of Ralph Corry.)

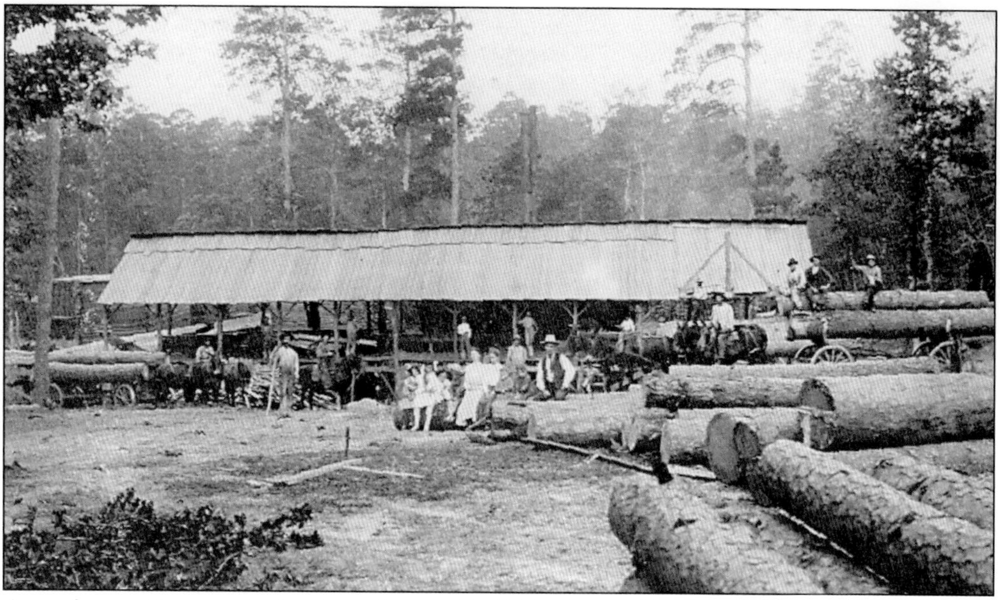

According to *Garrison in the News*, August 29, 2002, "Sawmilling ranged from large operations that cut up to 100,000 feet per day and more to small operators that cut a few hundred feet per day, often referred to as 'peckerwood' mills and 'jake leg' mills. The community of Waterman . . . near Stockman . . . was the site of two mills, one pine and one hardwood, that could each cut 100,000 feet of timber a day." (Courtesy of TAGHS.)

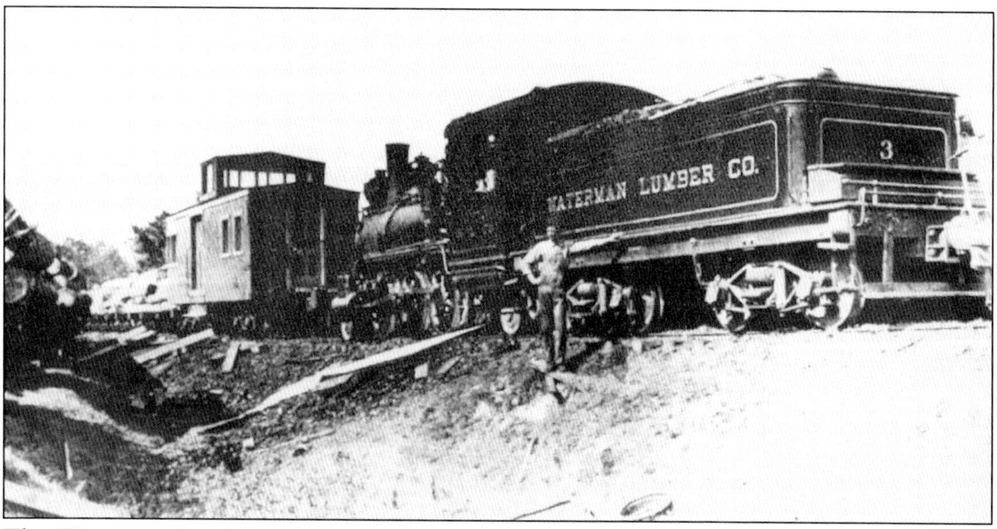

The Waterman Lumber Company operated from 1902 to 1909 along the Attoyac River in Waterman. The train (tram) transported both logs and timber workers from the forests to the mill town, and to Timpson. The lumber plant consisted of the sawmill, the planning mill, a boilerhouse, powerhouse, a machine shop, waterworks, an electric light plant, houses, buildings, structures, and steam machinery. After the longleaf pines were gone, Waterman took his mill and left. (Courtesy of TAGHS.)

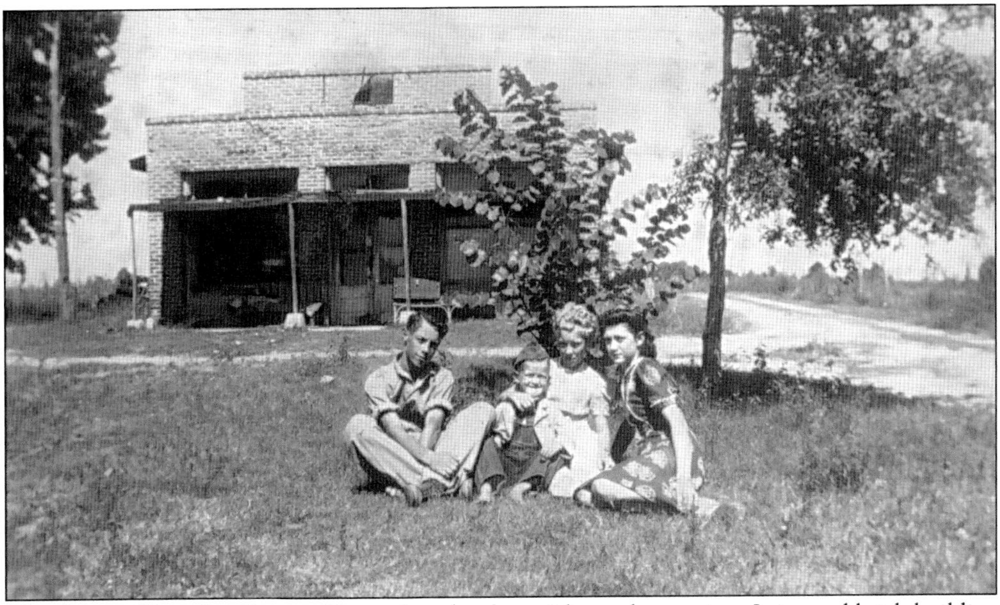

The George Herndon Store still stands today, but without the awning. It is a red brick building and, although some changes have been made with time, it is still recognizable. The store is located in what was called Georgetown, named for George Herndon, who built the store. Shown here around 1942 or 1943 are, from left to right, Charles Jackson, Willie Herndon, Lou Nell Jackson, and Jane Herndon. (Courtesy of Ralph Corry.)

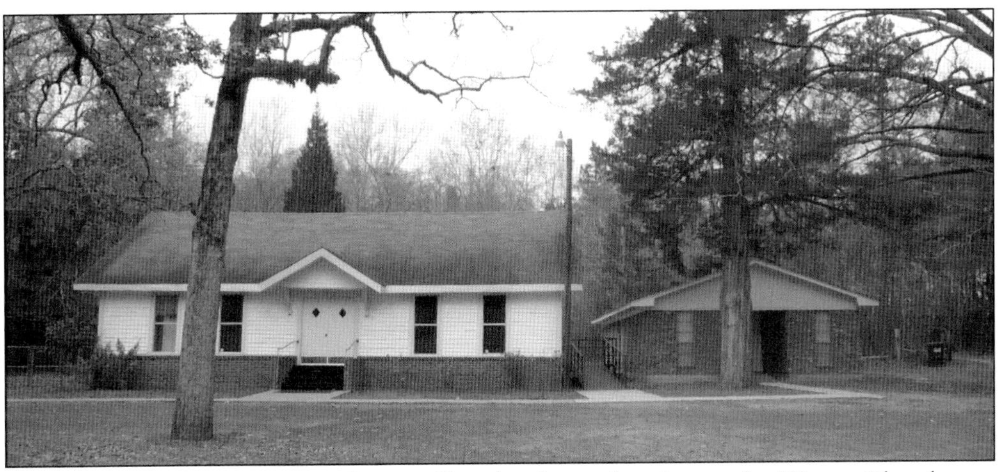

The New Columbia Missionary Baptist Church, often referred to as the Weaver Church, was originally called the Sulfur Springs Baptist Church. The first church in Weaver was a Christian church. Later, it disbanded and became a Baptist church. In the early days, the church building also served as the school building. This is the second building for the Baptist church. Today, services are still held each Sunday. (Photograph by Tempie Green Pike.)

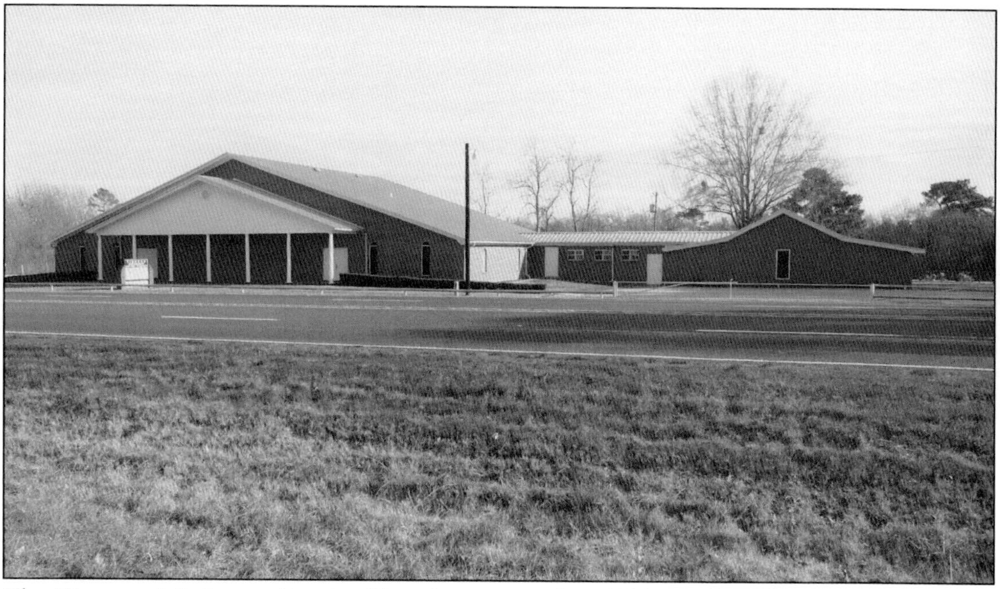

The Timpson Missionary Baptist Church, organized in 1950, purchased one acre of land on US 59 from F.R. Bussey and began a building project. The first service held in the new building was in March 1951. Two long-serving pastors were Ottie Reed (14 years) and Sammy Eldridge (28 years). Today, a greatly expanded church building and cemetery sit on four acres just north of Timpson. (Courtesy of TAGHS.)

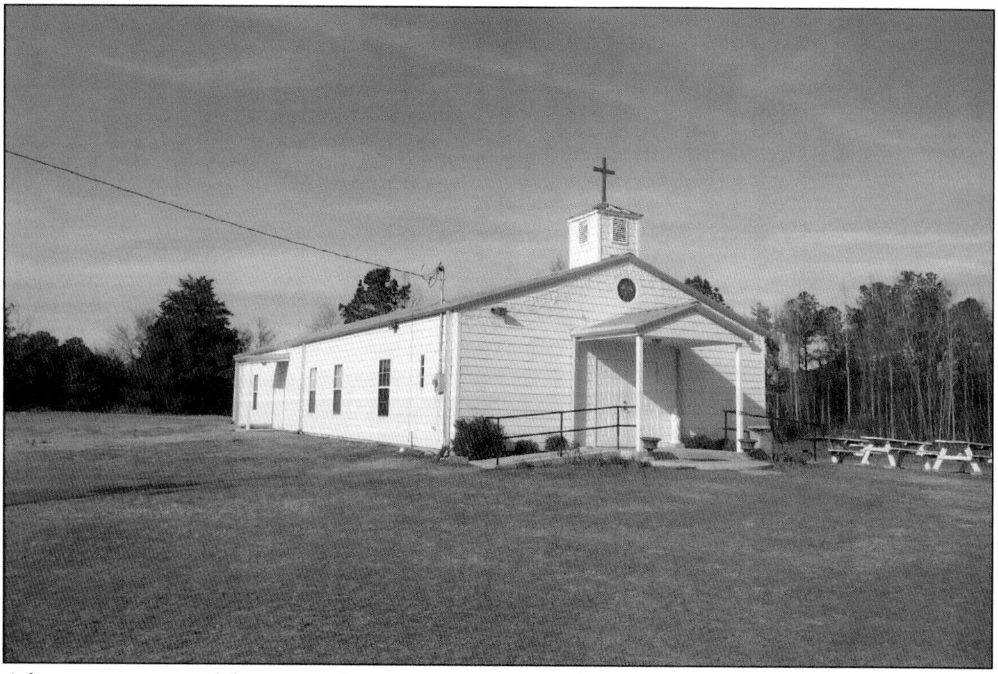

After many years of driving to larger towns to attend Mass, Janeice Eakin Carrington, her mother, Margaret Eakin, Margery Massey, and others established a Catholic Mission in Timpson. In January 1996, the Epiphany Catholic Mission celebrated the first mass in Timpson. In 1998, they purchased a home on Highway 59 south of Timpson. A new church building and fellowship building were dedicated on September 13, 2006. (Courtesy of TAGHS.)

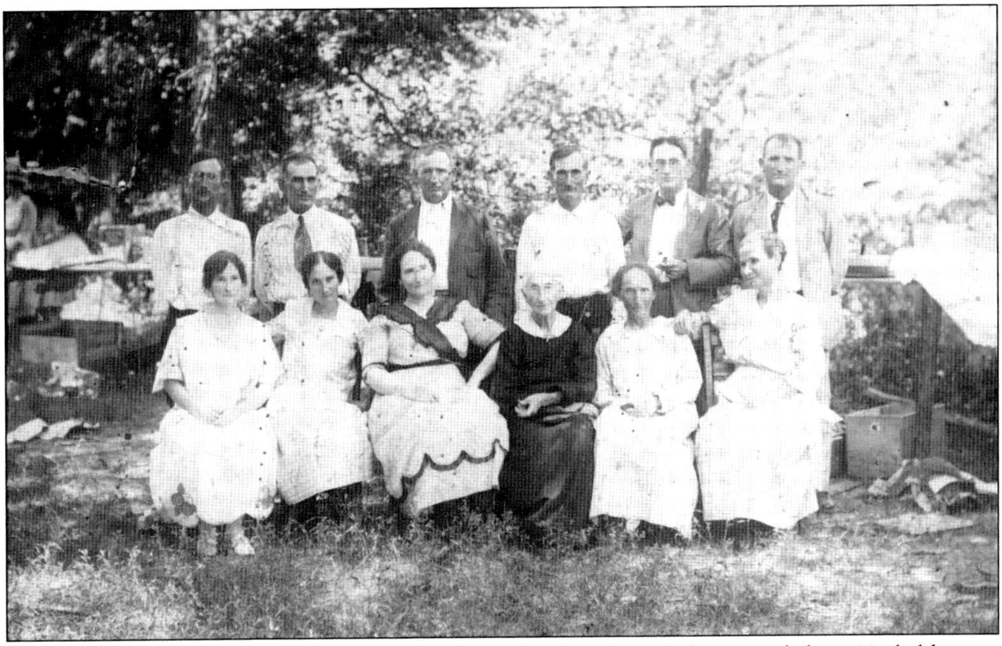

Martha Foster and William J. Hartt were both born in Alabama but raised their 11 children in neighboring Garrison. Shown here around 1920 are, from left to right, (first row) Alice, Ollie, Luella, Martha (mother), Virginia, and Betty Hartt; (second row) Jimmy, Berry Foster, Tommy, Gilford, William, and Hubbard Hartt. Son William G. practiced medicine in Timpson for a time. Daughter Alice married Hugh Shepherd of Timpson. (Courtesy of Shirley and Kenneth Bates.)

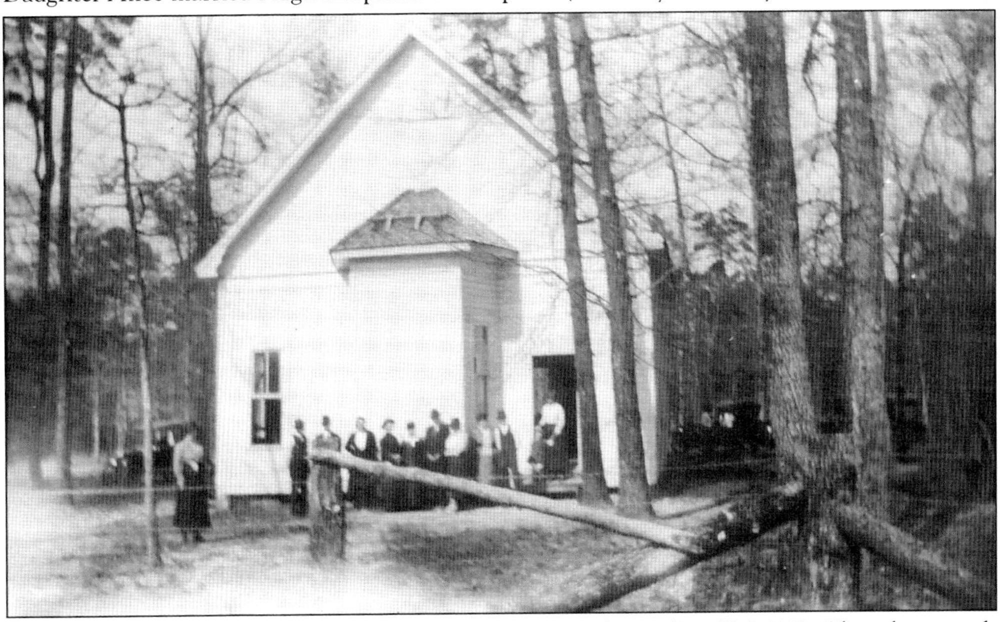

Mt. Zion Methodist Episcopal Church (1870–1970s) was located on FM 1490. This photograph was taken from the cemetery, looking toward the back of the church. John Mills was called to pastor the church in 1935 and stayed for the next 33 years. His sister played the piano there during their childhood. Mills is buried beside his wife, Kay (Kent) Mills, in the Mt. Zion Cemetery. (Courtesy of Greg Grant.)

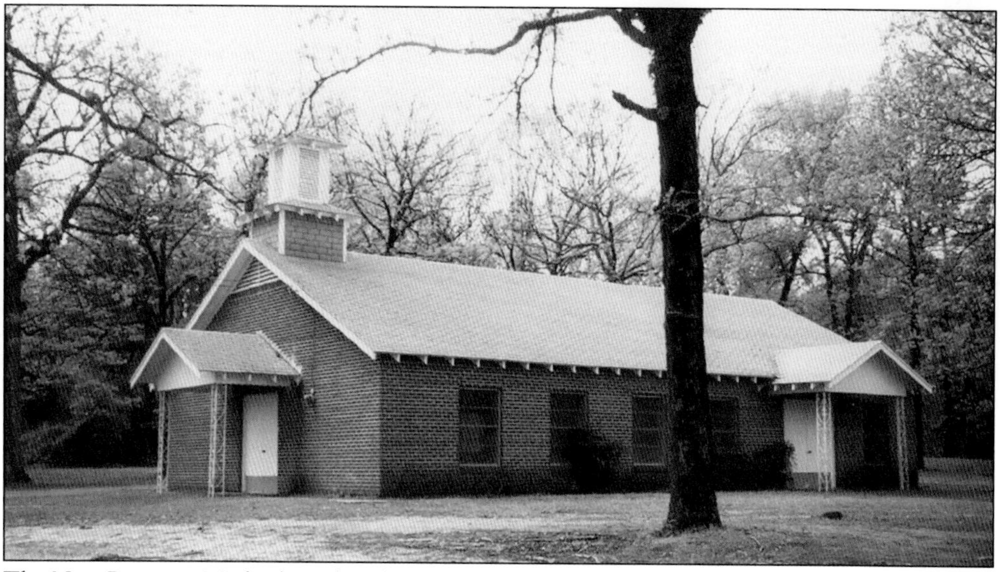

The New Prospect Methodist Church was organized in the early 1850s. Services were first held in a log building. A later wooden church, built in 1903, was destroyed by lightening in 1957 and replaced with a brick building. In 1968, the congregation had dwindled and they decided to join with the Timpson Methodist Church. The brick building is used only in June for homecoming. (Courtesy of Beth Shepherd.)

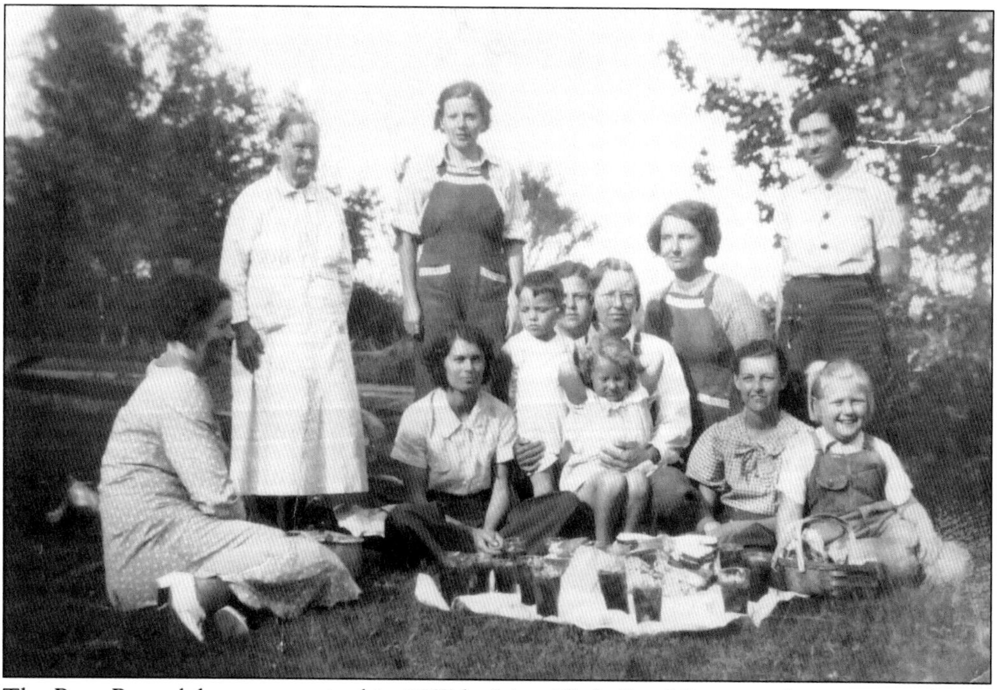

The Busy Bees club was organized in 1937 by Mrs. Clyde Reed Bussey, who was a teacher at Wedgeworth School. Enjoying a picnic are, from left to right, (seated) Mildred Witherspoon, Evie Lou Witherspoon, (child) David Wayne Crawford, Judie Crawford, Blanch Wedgeworth, (child) Peggy Stilley, Emma Lee Milford, and Annie Ruth Milford; (standing) Leecy Witherspoon, Onita Stilley, Esther Rider, and (kneeling) Irene Wedgeworth. (Courtesy of Annie Ruth Tate.)

Five

They Served Their Country

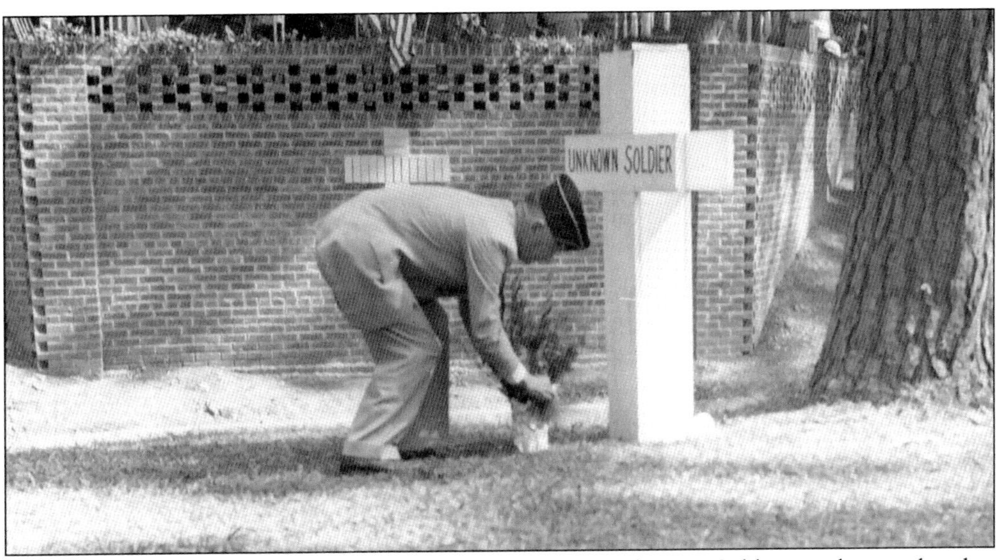

As part of the Memorial Day Services in SoSo Park, the Unknown Soldier was honored with a large white cross placed immediately in front of the bandstand/podium. Maj. Joseph J. Compton places flowers on the memorial spot sometime in the late 1940s as other attendees solemnly watch. (Courtesy of Lynn Hartt.)

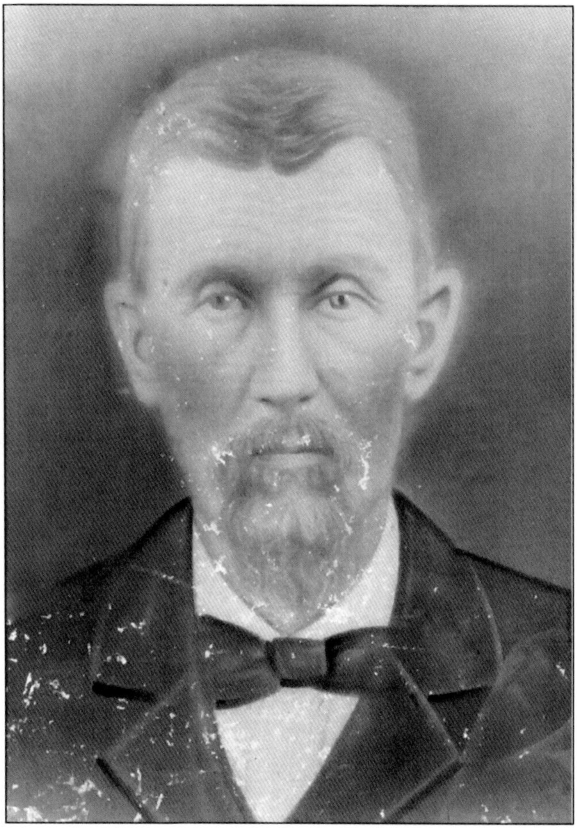

William Penn Burns (1842–1904) served in the Civil War with the 28th Regiment, Texas Cavalry, Randal's 1st Texas Lancers. His father, Joseph P. Burns (1809–1891), fought in the Mexican-American War as a lieutenant in Capt. E.M. Doggett's company in the famous Ranger regiment commanded by Col. Jack Hayes. Joseph Burns received a land grant for his service and settled in the Buena Vista Community. (Courtesy of Charlie Rhodes.)

In 1907, outfitted with guns, canteens, and sleeping rolls, a contingent of Company B 3rd Texas Infantry is ready to depart for Camp Mabry, near Austin, for training maneuvers. Standing front and center with his daughter, four-year-old Maurine, is 1st Lt. Buford M. Jennings, officer in charge. (Courtesy of TAGHS.)

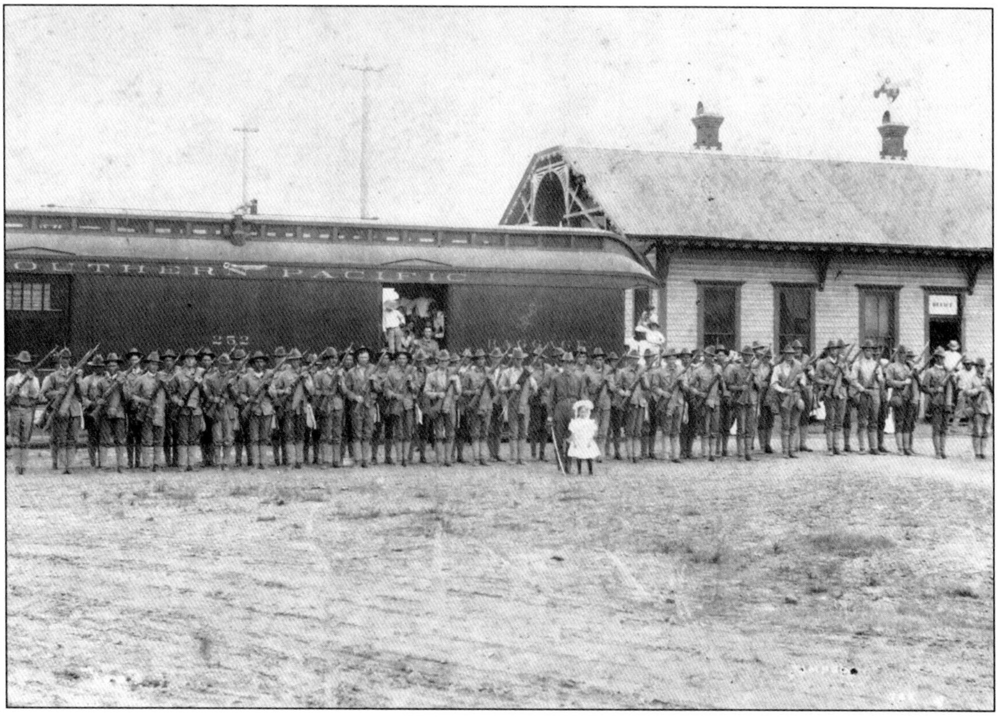

Pvt. William Bryant Francis, born December 3, 1896, in Timpson, registered for the Army on June 5, 1918. He was in the Demobilization Department at Camp Travis. Eugene A. and Nellie (Williams) Francis were his parents. William Bryant Francis was a retired oil field worker when he died on January 31, 1988, in Center, Texas. He was survived by his wife, Florence, and was buried in Dixon Cemetery. (Courtesy of Shirley Bates.)

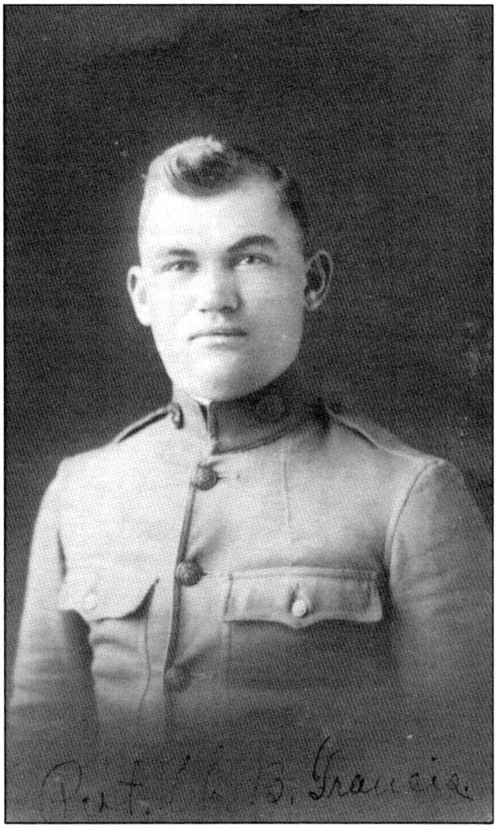

Company B, 3rd Texas Infantry was formed on February 25, 1902. It was nicknamed "Fory Fusileers" for Howard Russell Fory, who, in 1899, donated land behind the Christian church for militia use. The officers were Cpt. John D. Jennings, Lt. E.A. Booth, and Lt. J.P. Anderson of Center. Company B is shown here in 1908 on the steps of the First United Methodist Church, proudly displaying their marksmanship trophy. (Courtesy of First United Methodist Church.)

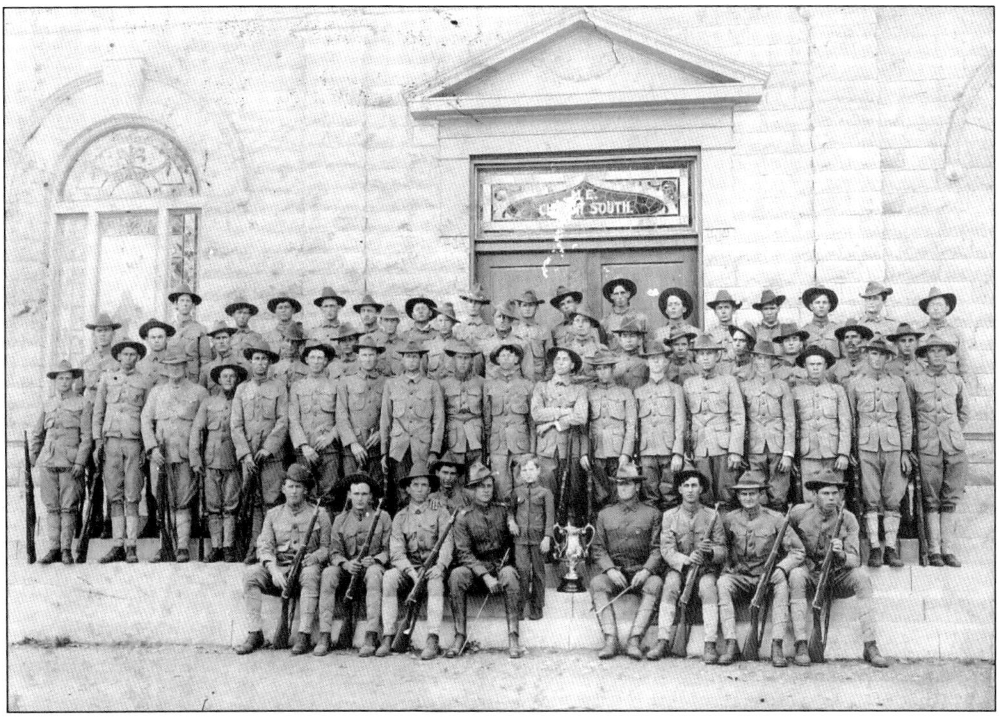

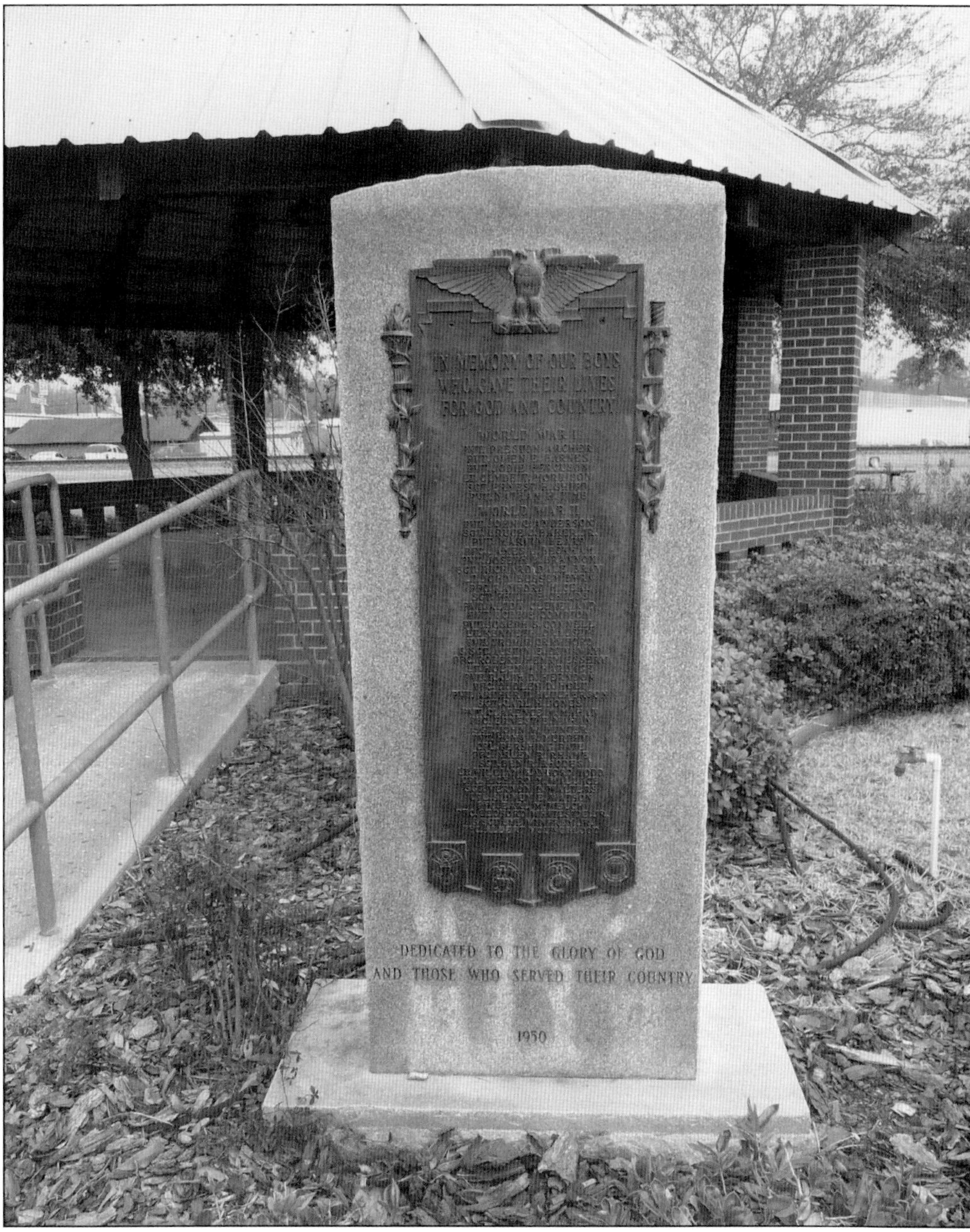

On November 5, 1950, the dedication of a memorial plaque honoring Timpson's fallen soldiers from both world wars was held in Memorial (SoSo) Park. The bronze plaque, erected immediately in front of the American Legion Building, listed six men from World War I and 36 from World War II. E.W. Crawford Jr., veteran of World War II, delivered the dedication address. In describing the memorial, Crawford drew attention to the placement of the eagle, the emblem of our great nation, with its strength and protective nature. On the left of the scroll of names was the torch of peace, and on the right, the sheathed sword. But honoring the sacrifice of those whose names were scribed on the tablet was the most important task of the day. The American Legion and the Legion Auxiliary sponsored local fundraising events to purchase the plaque and hosted the dedication event. (Courtesy of TAGHS.)

Joseph James Compton served over 30 years in the military, primarily associated with the Timpson Volunteer Guard, or Texas National Guard. He saw service in the Mexican Border War in 1916–1917 and in World Wars I and II. He was promoted to major in 1941, when he assumed command of the 1st Battalion, 144th Infantry. He became principal of Timpson High School in 1921 and superintendent in 1922. (Courtesy of Lynn Hartt.)

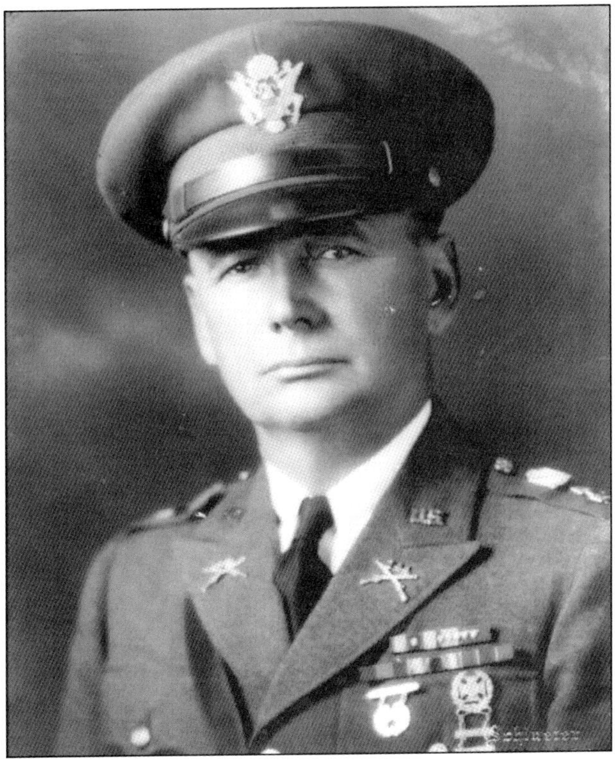

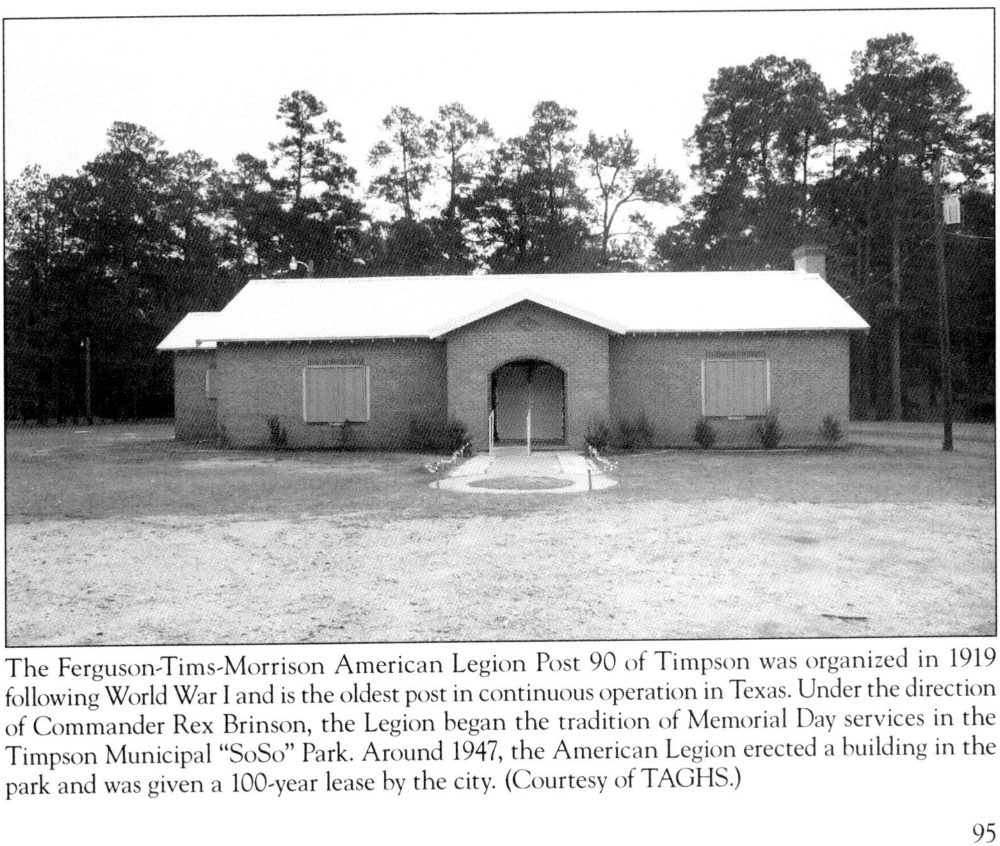

The Ferguson-Tims-Morrison American Legion Post 90 of Timpson was organized in 1919 following World War I and is the oldest post in continuous operation in Texas. Under the direction of Commander Rex Brinson, the Legion began the tradition of Memorial Day services in the Timpson Municipal "SoSo" Park. Around 1947, the American Legion erected a building in the park and was given a 100-year lease by the city. (Courtesy of TAGHS.)

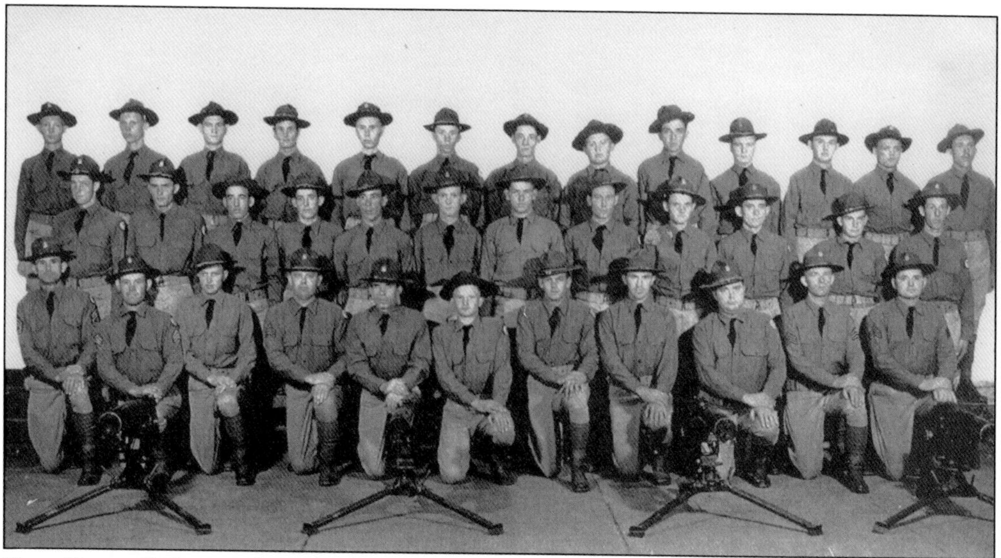

Gen. George P. Rains, of Marshall, visited Timpson in 1921 to establish a new military unit and gave the command to James S. Taylor, a World War I captain, with 1st Lt. Joseph J. Compton and 2nd Lt. Peter W. McKittrick as officers of the new unit. The first sergeant was Thomas C. Clements. General Rains designated the new unit Company D, 144th Infantry, a machine gun company. (Courtesy of TAGHS.)

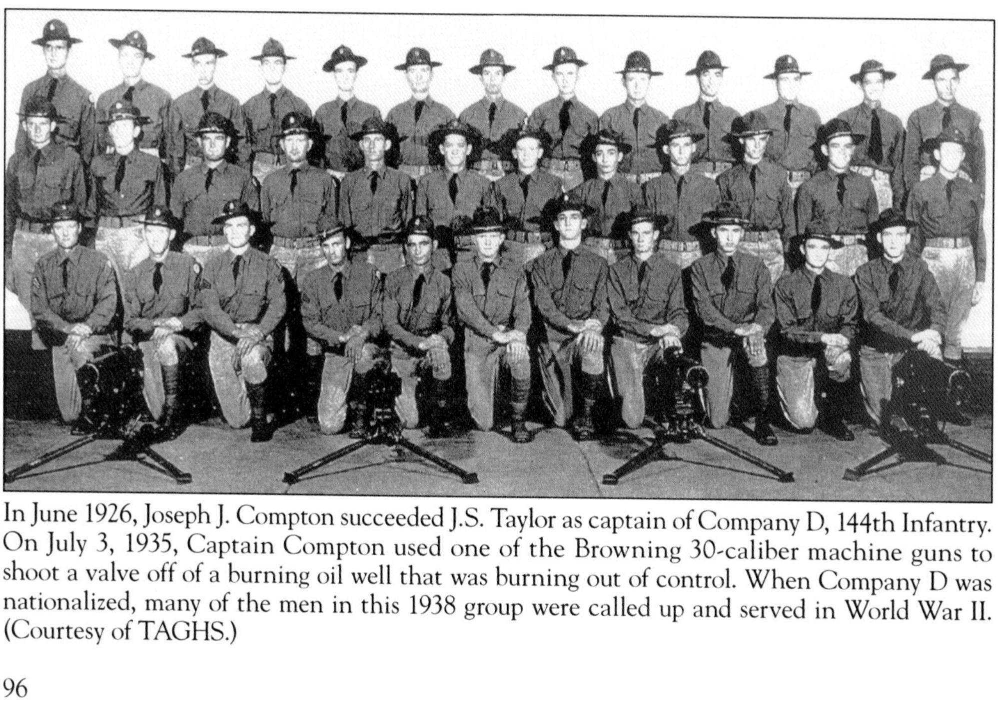

In June 1926, Joseph J. Compton succeeded J.S. Taylor as captain of Company D, 144th Infantry. On July 3, 1935, Captain Compton used one of the Browning 30-caliber machine guns to shoot a valve off of a burning oil well that was burning out of control. When Company D was nationalized, many of the men in this 1938 group were called up and served in World War II. (Courtesy of TAGHS.)

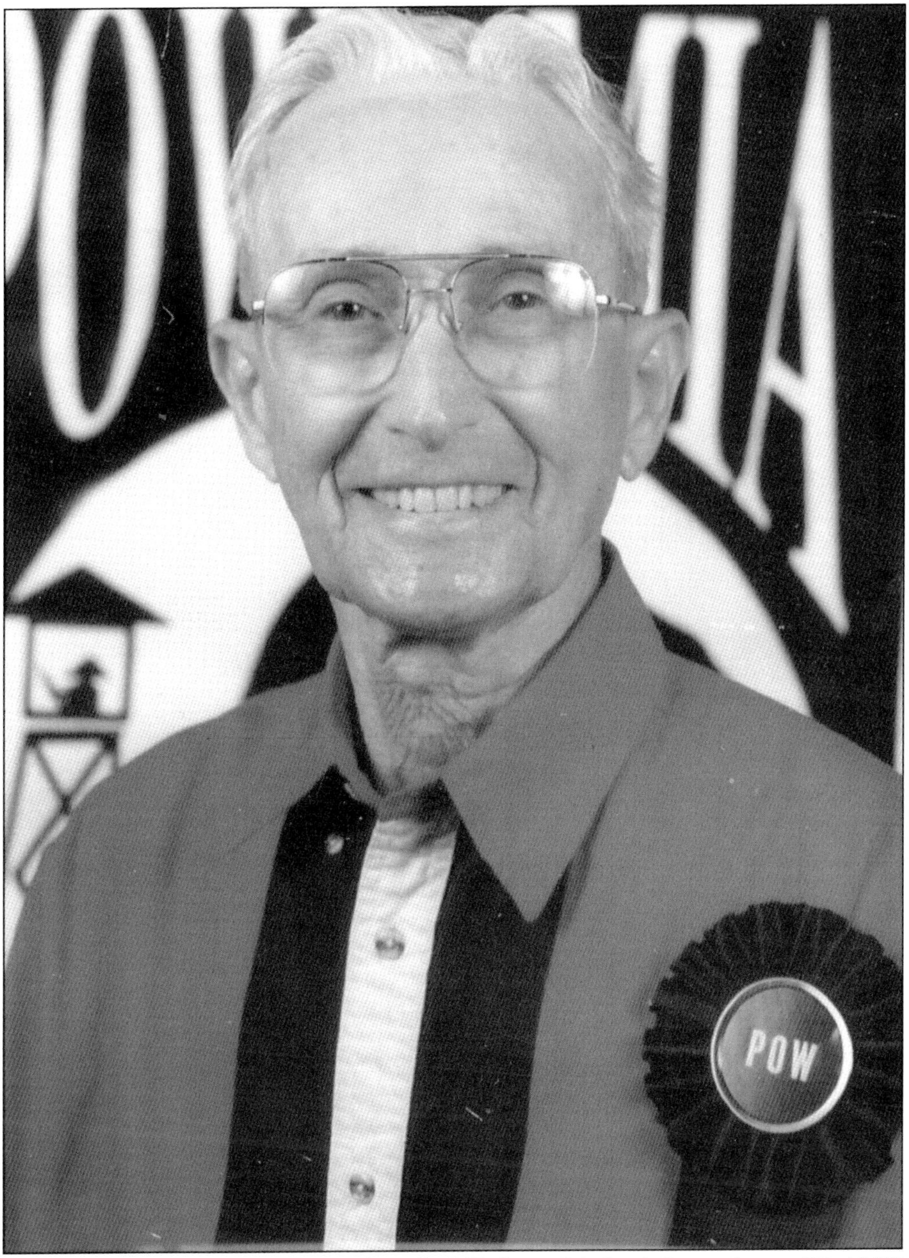

Charles Donald "Jimmy" Rogers served in the US Army Medical Corps during World War II. His unit set up a hospital in the Philippines at Bataan, and, while helping the wounded, he was hit in the leg by shrapnel. Rogers was in the hospital when the Philippines surrendered to the Japanese on April 9, 1942. He became a prisoner, and after caring for those who survived the death march and readying the injured Filipinos to return home, he began a long imprisonment of slave labor. He was finally sent to Japan in the hole of a coal ship with standing room only, arriving in late December 1944. Rogers was freed when the war was over, having been a prisoner of war for 42 months. He received two Purple Hearts and the POW medal. Upon returning home, Rogers transferred to Timpson with the US Postal Service, retiring after 31 years. (Courtesy of Mary Eva Rogers.)

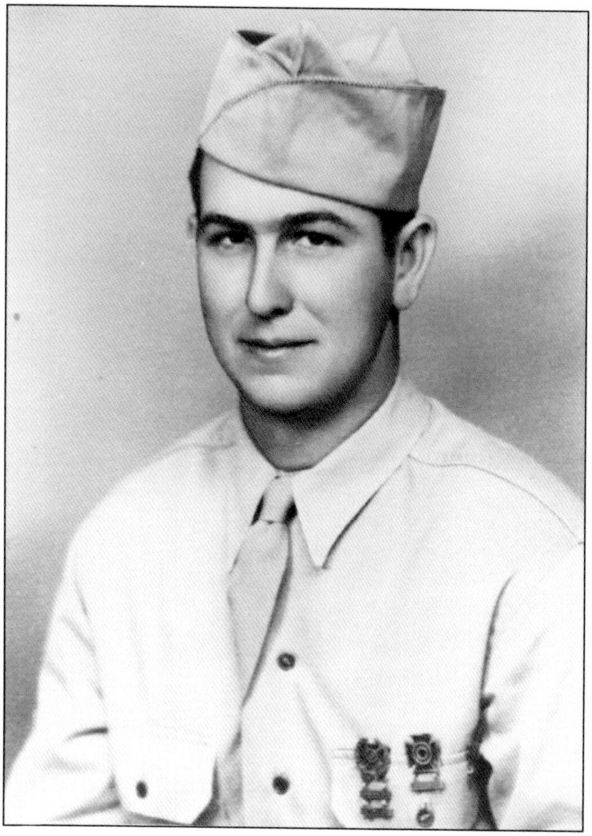

Joe Dillon was one of many Shelby County young men drafted for World War II. Trained to become a Sherman tank gunner, he served in Company D, 3rd Platoon, 740th Tank Battalion, seeing action in the Battle of the Bulge in Belgium, and in Germany. After the armistice, Corporal Dillon came home and was later severely injured in the 1947 Texas City Disaster, the worst industrial explosion disaster in American history. He now lives in Blair. (Courtesy of Joe Dillon.)

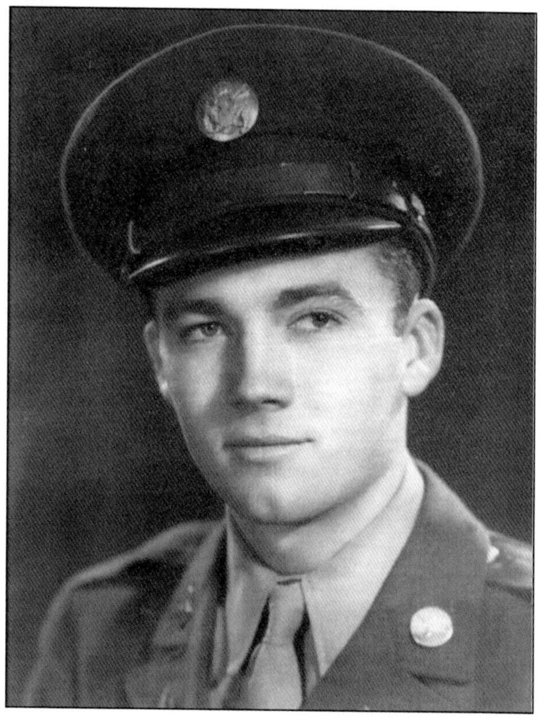

Bruce Cleveland Baker Jr. entered the Army Air Corps in 1942 and served more than 15 missions over enemy territory while in the 92nd Bomber Group, Thurleigh, England. He was awarded two Air Medals with an Oak Leaf Cluster. On July 15, 1944, Baker was fatally injured while on a training mission. He was reinterred in New Prospect Cemetery exactly four years after his death in England. (Courtesy of Timpson Independent School District.)

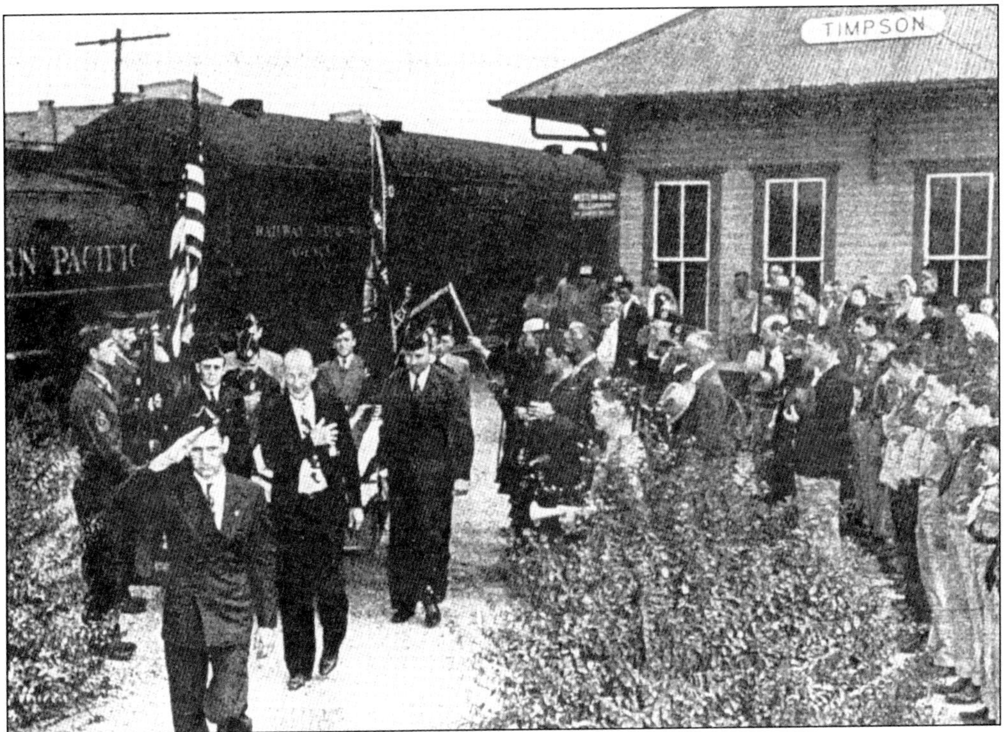

Servicemen were on hand at the Timpson rail depot in November 1948 when the body of Sgt. Vernon B. Walters was returned from a prisoner of war camp at Camp O'Donnell in the Philippines. Sergeant Walters was reported missing in action in 1944 and his body was recovered from a gravesite near the camp in 1948. This was an all-too-familiar sight. (Courtesy of TAGHS.)

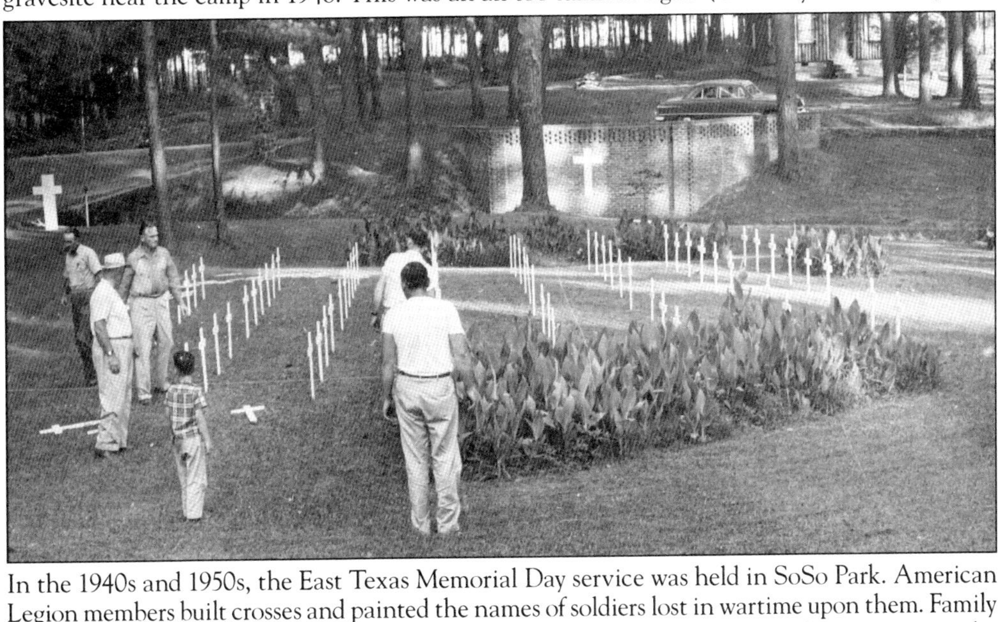

In the 1940s and 1950s, the East Texas Memorial Day service was held in SoSo Park. American Legion members built crosses and painted the names of soldiers lost in wartime upon them. Family and friends placed wreaths upon the crosses as part of the commemoration. Those setting up the crosses are, from left to right, unidentified, Rex Brinson, Douglas Galbreath, Jimmy Galbreath, Theo Galbreath, and Mark Smith. (Courtesy of Sarah Smith.)

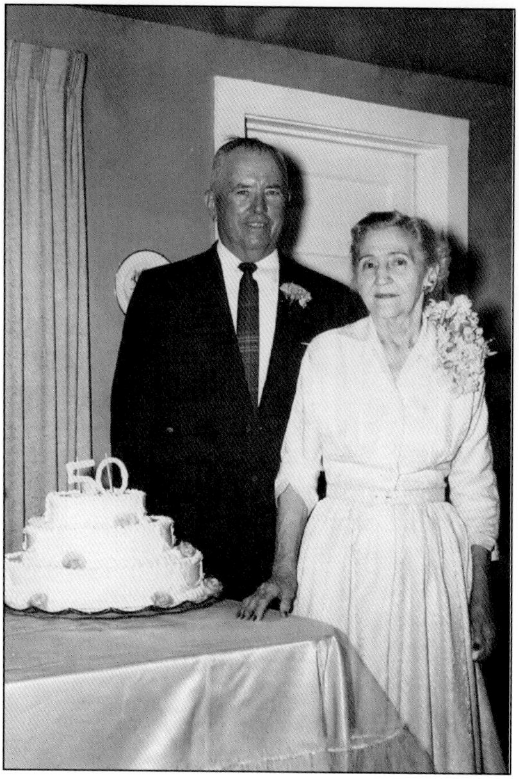

Richard Roberts "Dick" Morrison (left) was born in Timpson, Texas, in 1883, and married Henry Grady Hairston in 1907. They are shown celebrating their 50th anniversary in 1957. Morrison joined Company B, 3rd Texas Infantry in 1903, and was soon commissioned as a second lieutenant. He served on the Mexican border (1916–1917) and in both world wars. Morrison retired from the Army with the rank of colonel while serving as commander at POW Camp Clark, Missouri, in 1945. (Courtesy of TAGHS.)

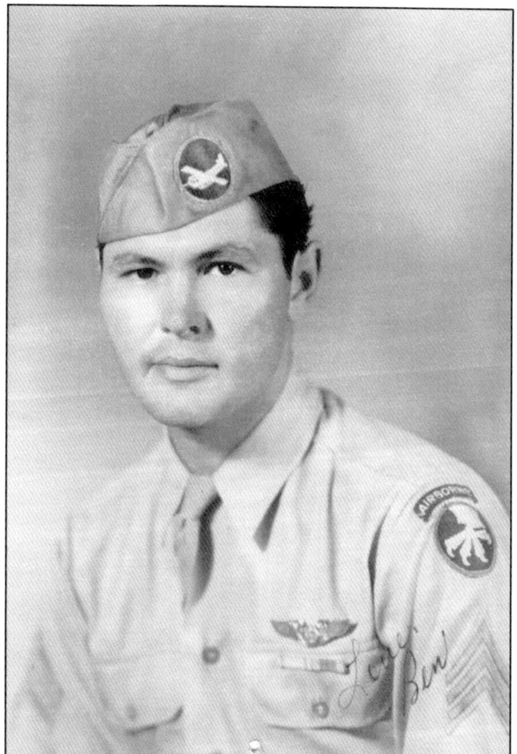

Benjamin Harrison "Ben" Burns, son of Hilliard Harrison and Fannie Burns, served in the US Army Air Corps during World War II from October 1939 to March 1945. He then joined the Merchant Marines, and had returned from a two-month trip to Japan and Korea when he fell into the water at dockside in Galveston on December 11, 1951, and apparently drowned. His body was never recovered. (Courtesy of Stanley Hairgrove.)

Pvt. Lonnie Benjamin Downing was one of the young men from the Wedgeworth/Corinth area who served their country in World War I. They faced poison mustard gas and other horrors of the German war machine. Lonnie married Maidie McClure and had two sons, Arthur Lee and Garland. Downing was born on March 23, 1893 and died on April 15, 1980; he is buried in the Mt. Bethel Cemetery. (Courtesy of Jan Magness Barrett.)

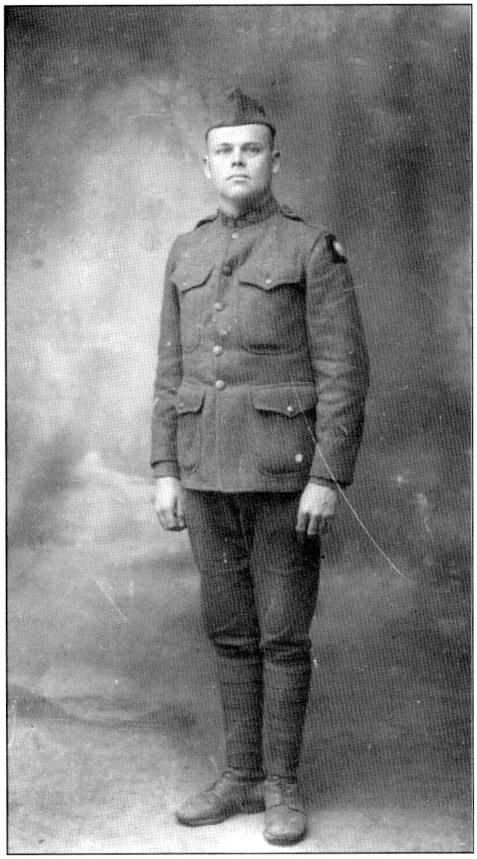

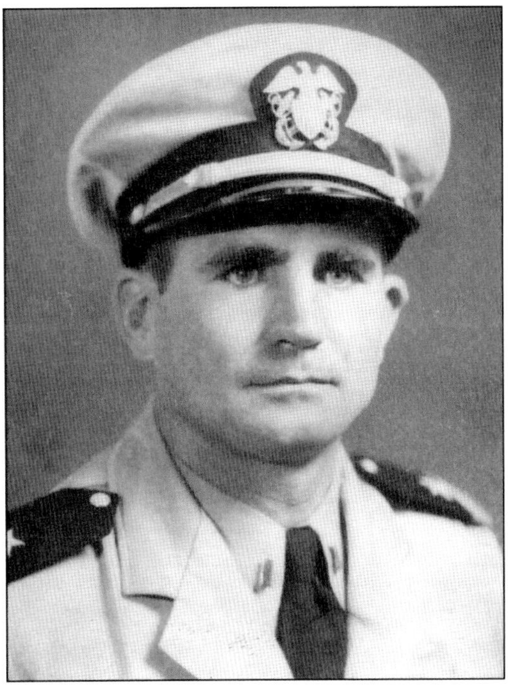

Herschel Randolph "Red" Ramsey, son of former Timpson residents William Elzie and Lettie Ross Ramsey, is shown here in his US Navy uniform. He is best known as a Texas Tech All-American and Philadelphia Eagles professional football player. Ramsey led Tech to its first-ever bowl game, the Sun Bowl, in El Paso in 1938. He played for the Eagles in 1938 through 1940 and in 1945. (Courtesy of Marion Shepherd.)

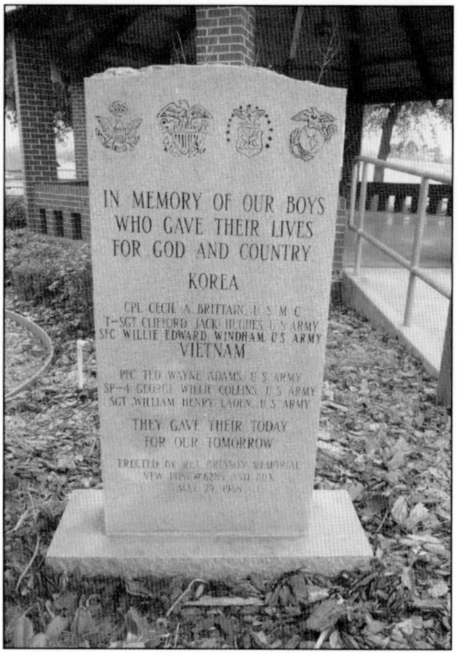

In 1988, Rex Brinson Memorial Veterans of Foreign Wars Post No. 6288 and the post auxiliary erected a memorial plaque to honor Timpson's servicemen that died in the Korean and Vietnam Wars. The plaque was placed in Park Plaza in downtown Timpson. Each year, local citizens gather on Memorial Day to honor these men and those lost in World Wars I and II and other conflicts. (Courtesy of TAGHS.)

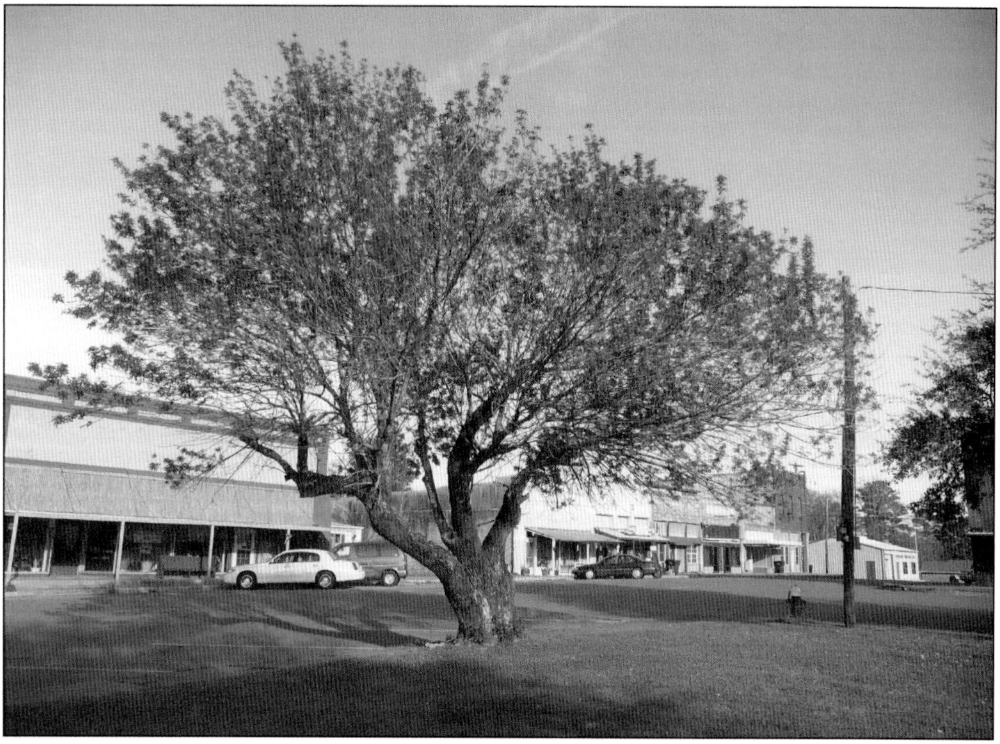

After 81 years, three Japanese elm trees planted in 1930 by the newly formed American Legion Auxiliary still stand in Park Plaza. They were planted in memory of three young men who gave their lives in World War I, and for whom the Ferguson-Tims-Morrison American Legion Post No. 90 was named. As the trees declined, Gilbert Rhodes, Eagle Scout and science teacher, assumed stewardship of them, extending their lives. (Courtesy of Tempie Green Pike.)

Six

Tenaha, Timpson, Bobo, and Blair

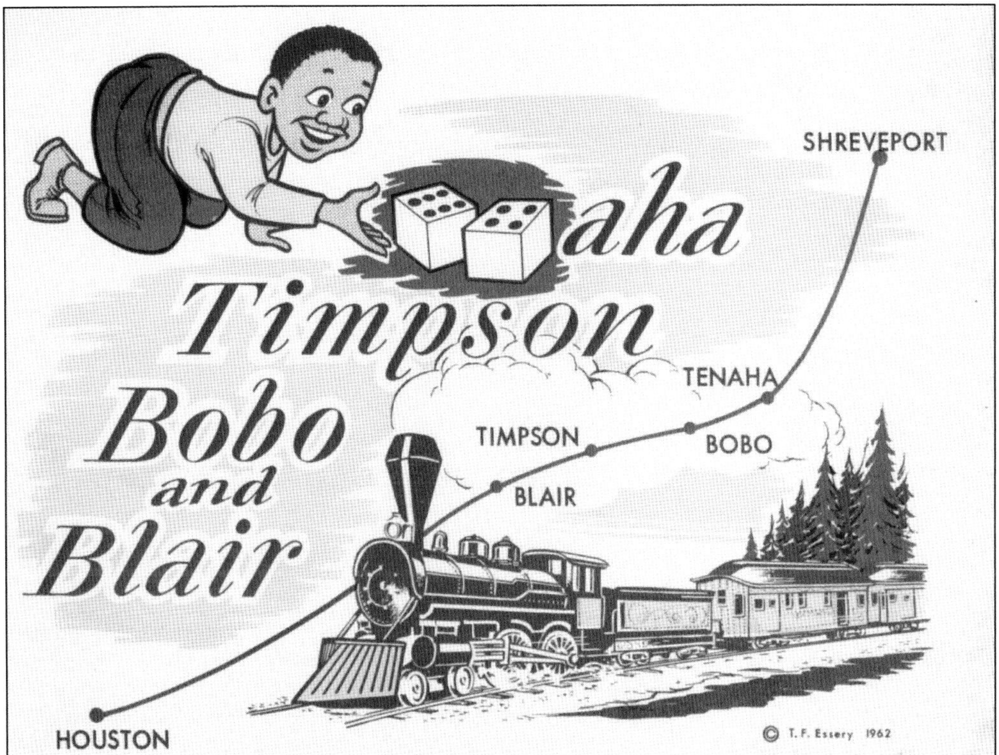

Tenaha, Timpson, Bobo, and Blair are towns and communities in East Texas along what was once the Houston East and West Texas (HE&WT) Railway. Crapshooters would chant "Tenaha, Timpson, Bobo, and Blair," hoping to roll a double five. Hobos on the trains were also said to chant the words. T.F. Essery, Timpson mayor, designed this jumbo postcard in 1962 as a souvenir card and to sell in his grocery store on North Second Street. (Courtesy of TAGHS.)

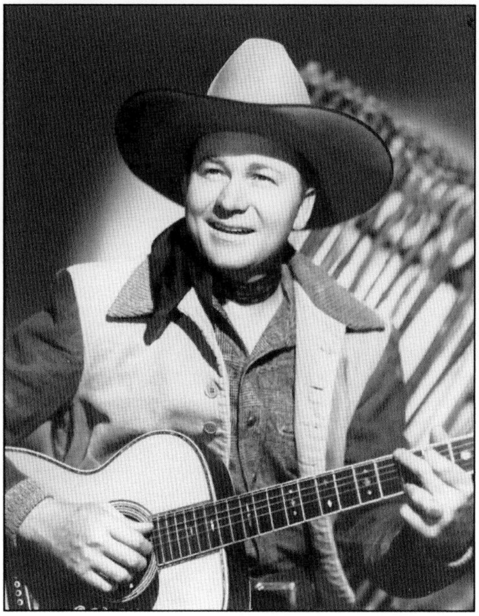

It is Tex Ritter's recording of "Tenaha, Timpson, Bobo, and Blair" that permanently binds Maurice Woodward "Tex" Ritter to Timpson. Born in 1905 in the nearby Panola County community of Murval, Ritter became American's Most Beloved Cowboy. He found success in radio, on the stage, and in the movies. He was honored as one of the first members of the Country Music Association Hall of Fame. (Courtesy of Bill O'Neal.)

The lyrics of "Tenaha, Timpson, Bobo, and Blair" speak longingly of the little towns and communities along the HE&WT. Tex Ritter immortalized them by recording the song in the 1940s. The lyrics were sung anywhere our local soldiers traveled during World War II, making this part of rural East Texas recognized even in faraway lands. (Courtesy of TAGHS.)

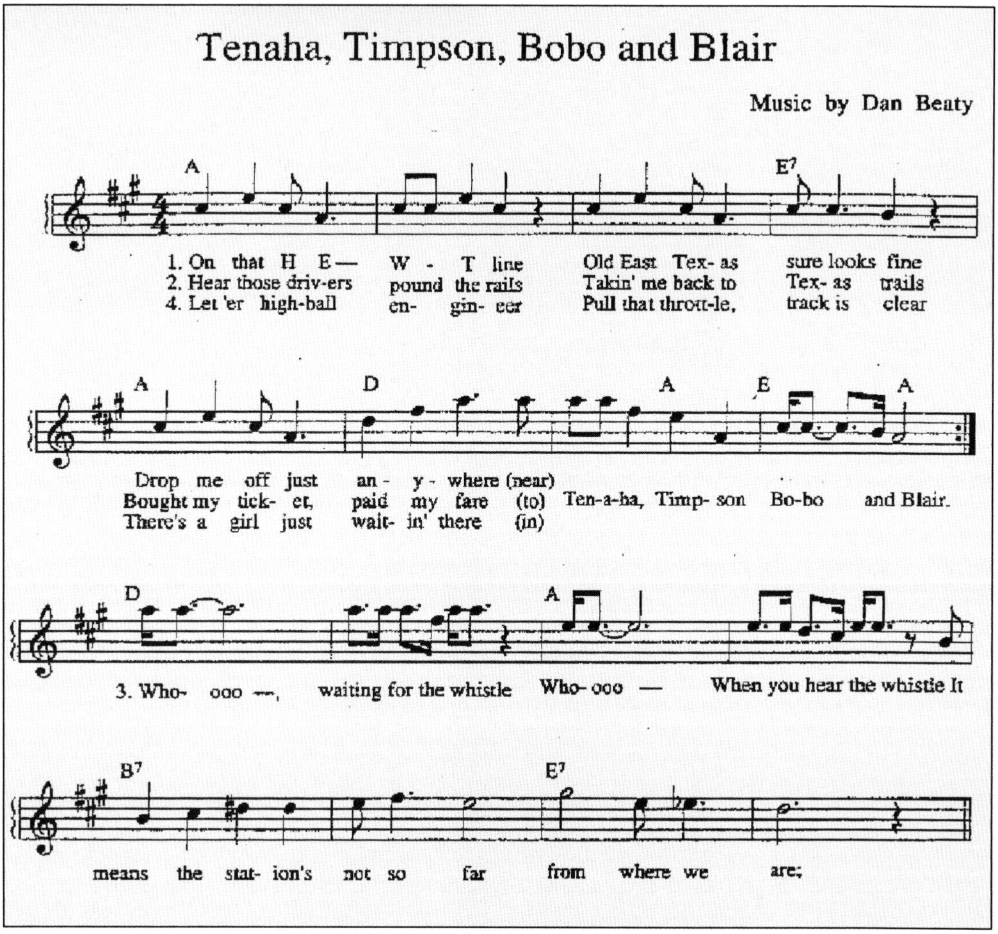

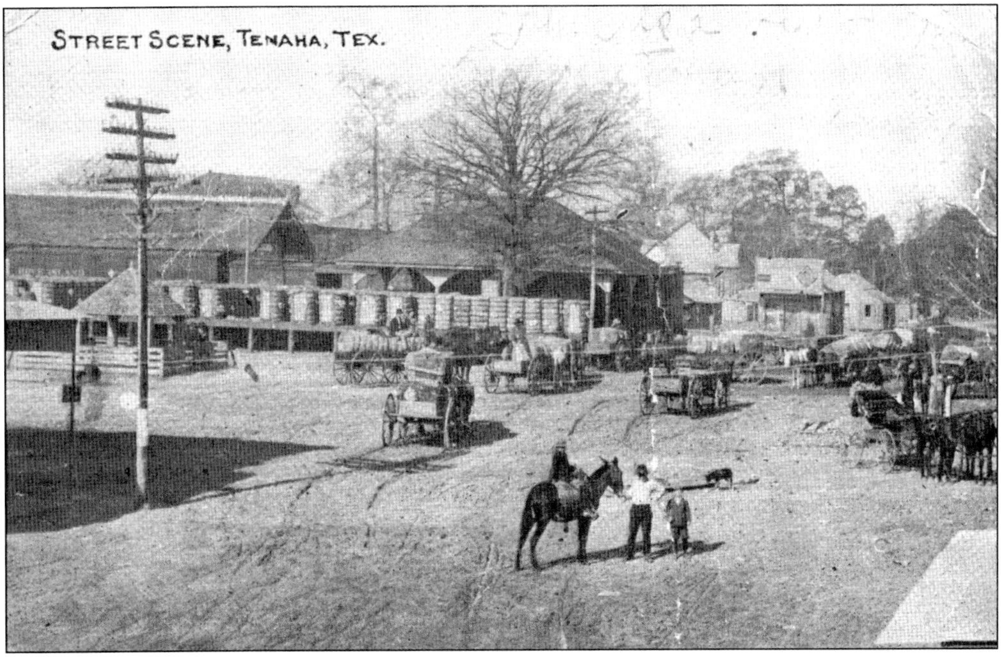

This Tenaha street scene is shown on a postcard mailed on January 12, 1912, at a cost of 1¢. At that time, the streets were unpaved, the buildings were made with wood siding, and transportation was by horse and carriage, or wagons pulled by horses or mules. In this scene, an abundance of cotton is baled and ready to be sent by rail to distant markets. (Courtesy of Lois Parker.)

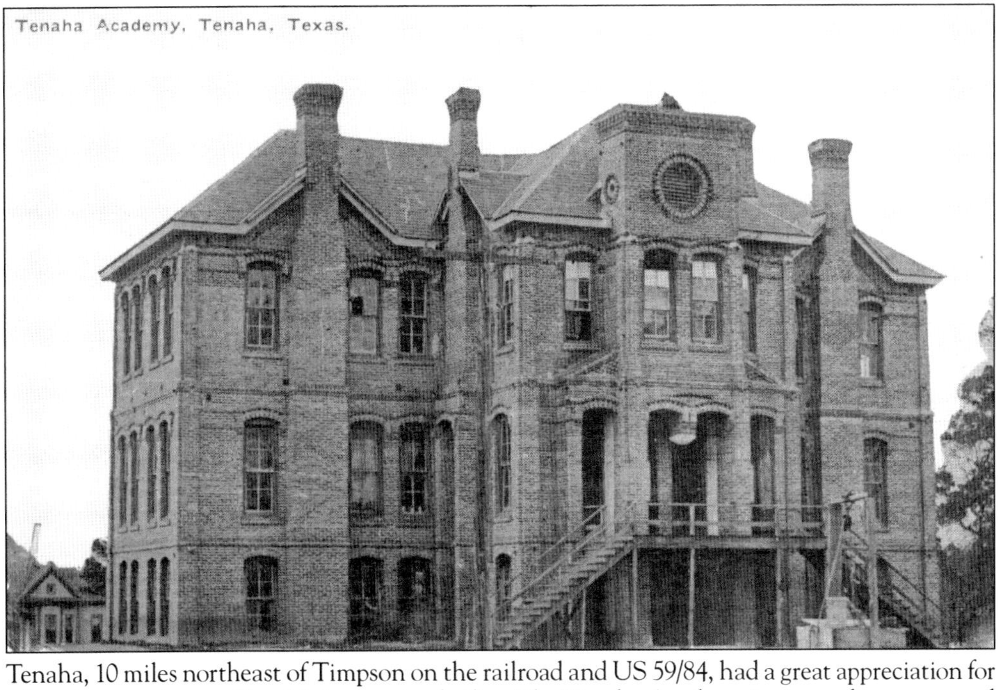

Tenaha, 10 miles northeast of Timpson on the railroad and US 59/84, had a great appreciation for education, as witnessed by this impressive facility. The Tenaha Academy is pictured on a postcard sent from Gary, Texas, to Ethel Rhodes, of Swansville, Texas, on November 11, 1911. Written on the front were the words, "Suppose you have seen the building?" (Courtesy of Lois Parker.)

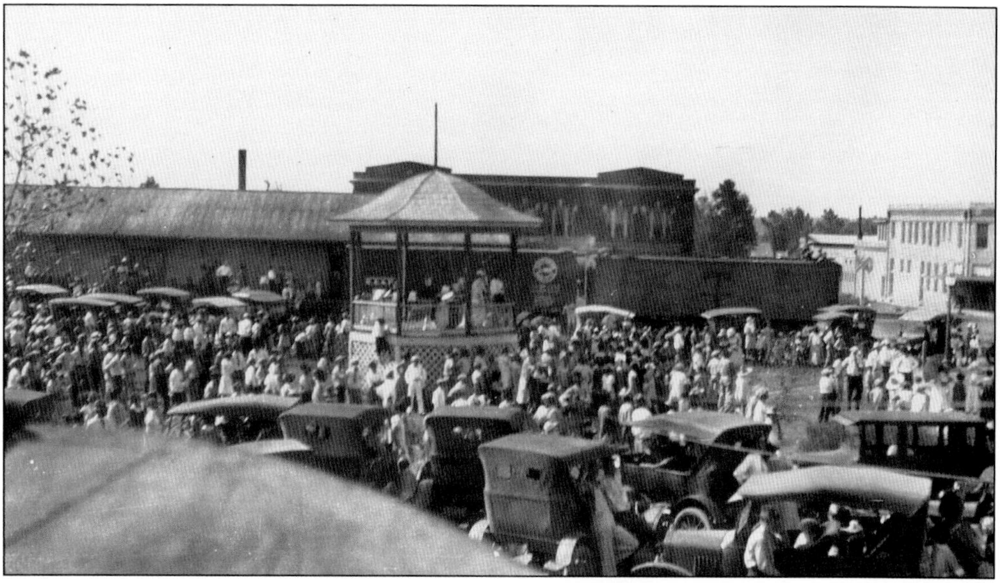

In the 1920s, scenes like this one were not uncommon in Timpson. Saturdays were full of people shopping and catching up on the news. Crowds often gathered on Park Plaza for the latest entertainment. In this scene, it appears a small band is in the gazebo with instruments. In the background are, from left to right, the train depot, Blankenship Hotel, boxcars, and Wallace Kristensen's Grocery and Market. (Courtesy of TAGHS.)

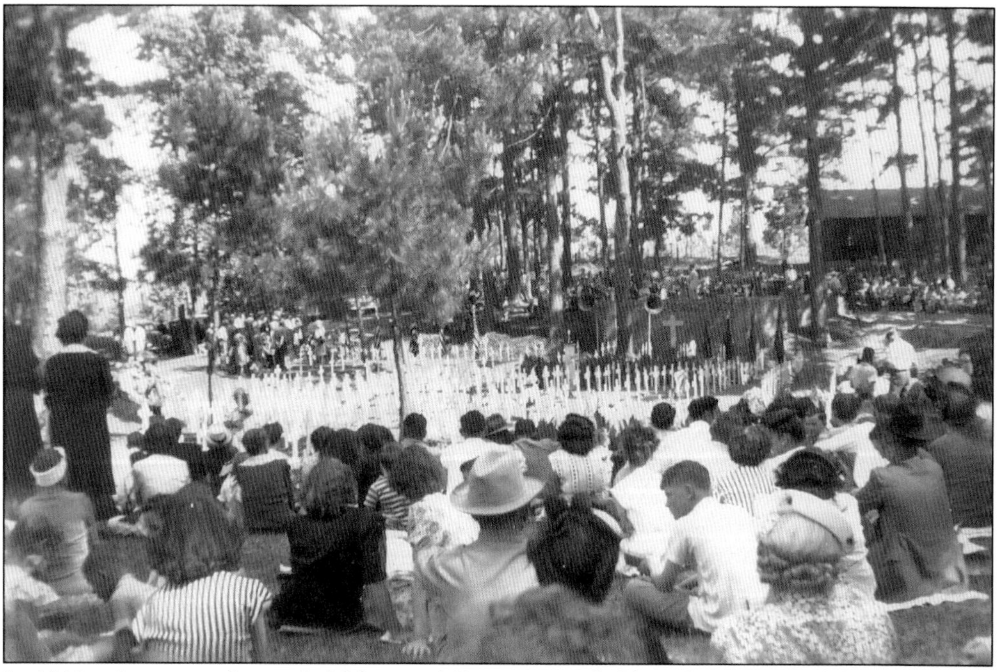

In 1946, a large crowd attended Memorial Day services held in the Municipal (SoSo) Park in Timpson. Just one year after World War II, the loss of so many young men was still fresh. The 11.5 acres used by the park was purchased in 1935 by the City of Timpson from the T.S. Garrison and C.E. Sanford estates. Easter Sunrise Services was another large gathering held in the park. (Courtesy of TAGHS.)

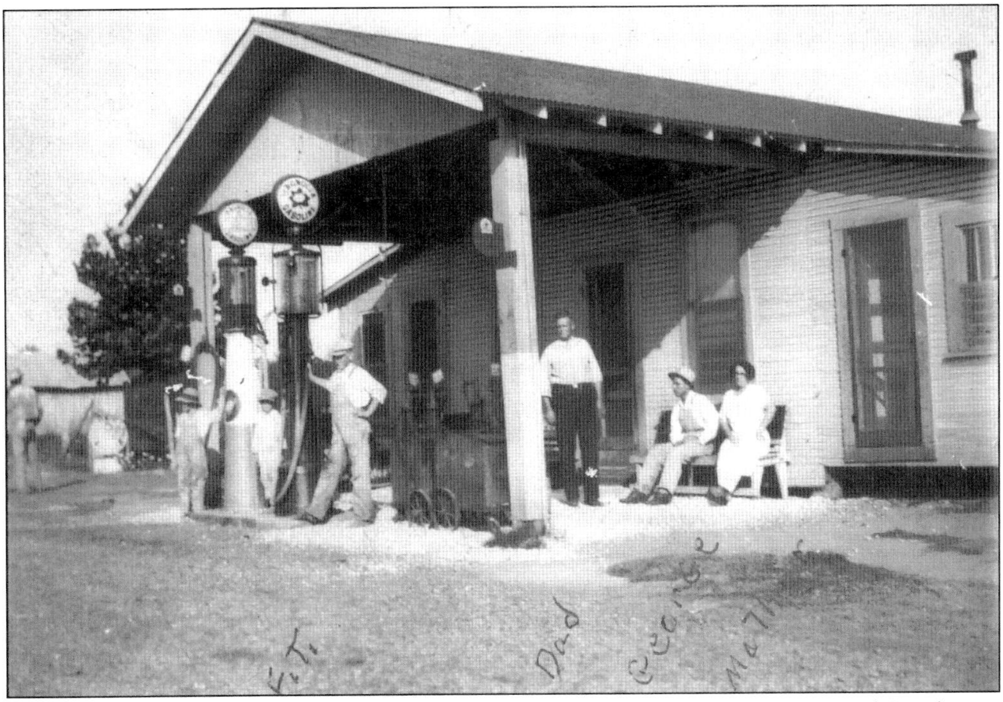

Green's general merchandise store and gas station was located between Timpson and Tenaha, on US 59, in the Bobo Community. The original store was built by George W. Green and operated by his son Luther Green from the early 1930s through the mid-1950s. Those in front of the store are, from left to right, unidentified man, two unidentified children, Fowler, Luther, George, and Victoria Green. (Courtesy of Victoria Green Clow.)

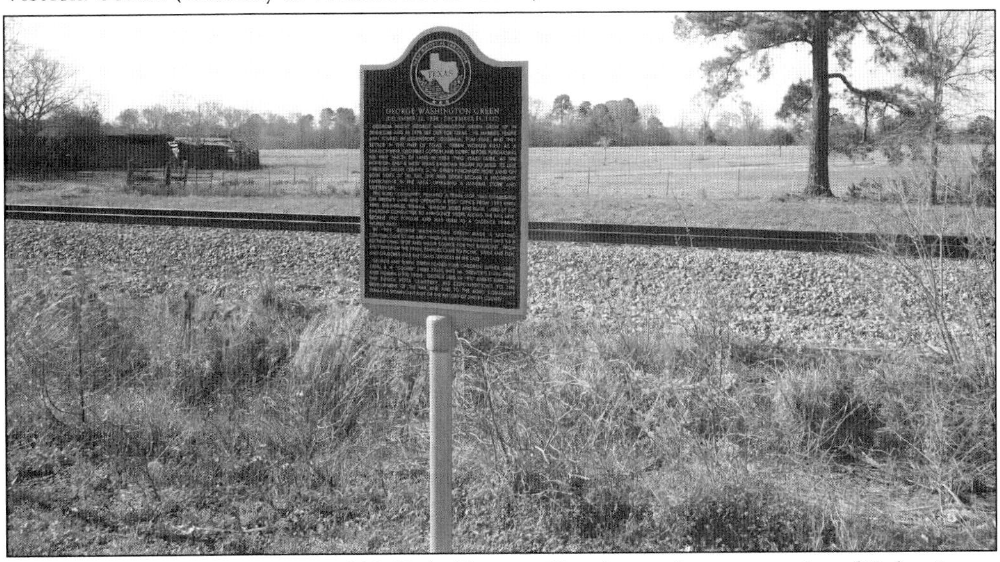

Heading east from Timpson on US 59, halfway to Tenaha, is the community of Bobo. It was named for John Henry Bobo, who operated a sawmill there. Bobo had a post office in the 1890s and was a flag stop for the train. Later, the steam locomotives stopped at Green's Lake to fill up with water. In 2001, a Texas Historical Marker was placed at Bobo to honor George Washington Green. (Courtesy of TAGHS.)

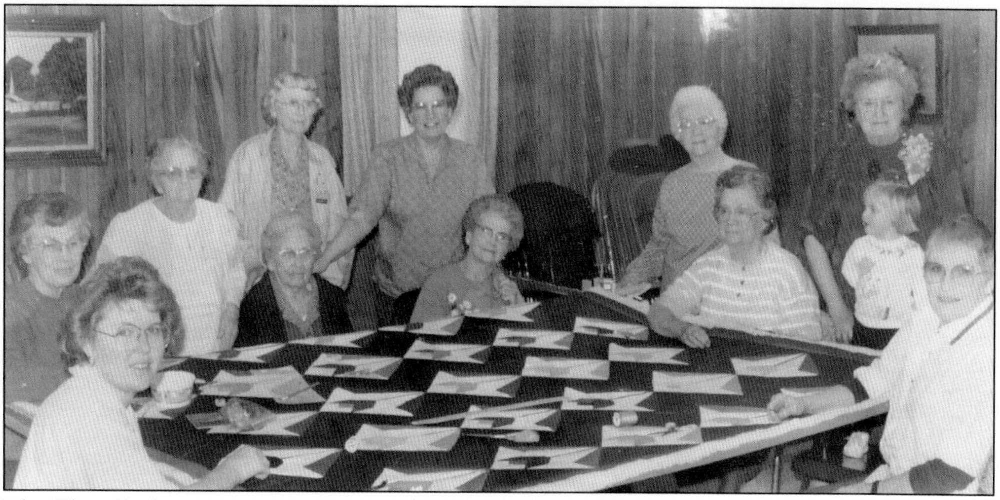

The Blair Quilters group was organized by the ladies of the Women's Missionary Auxiliary of the Blair (Good Hope) Baptist Church in the early 1960s and was active until about 2008. The quilters pictured here are, from left to right, (first row) Donna Bomar, Hildred Dempsey, Lona Dillon, Lois Powers, Ruth Powers, T9C McWilliams, unidentified child, and Carol Ann Corley; (second row) Cozette Stephano, Lou Nell Billingsley, Jewel Baker, and Doris Askins. (Courtesy of Lou Nell Billingsley.)

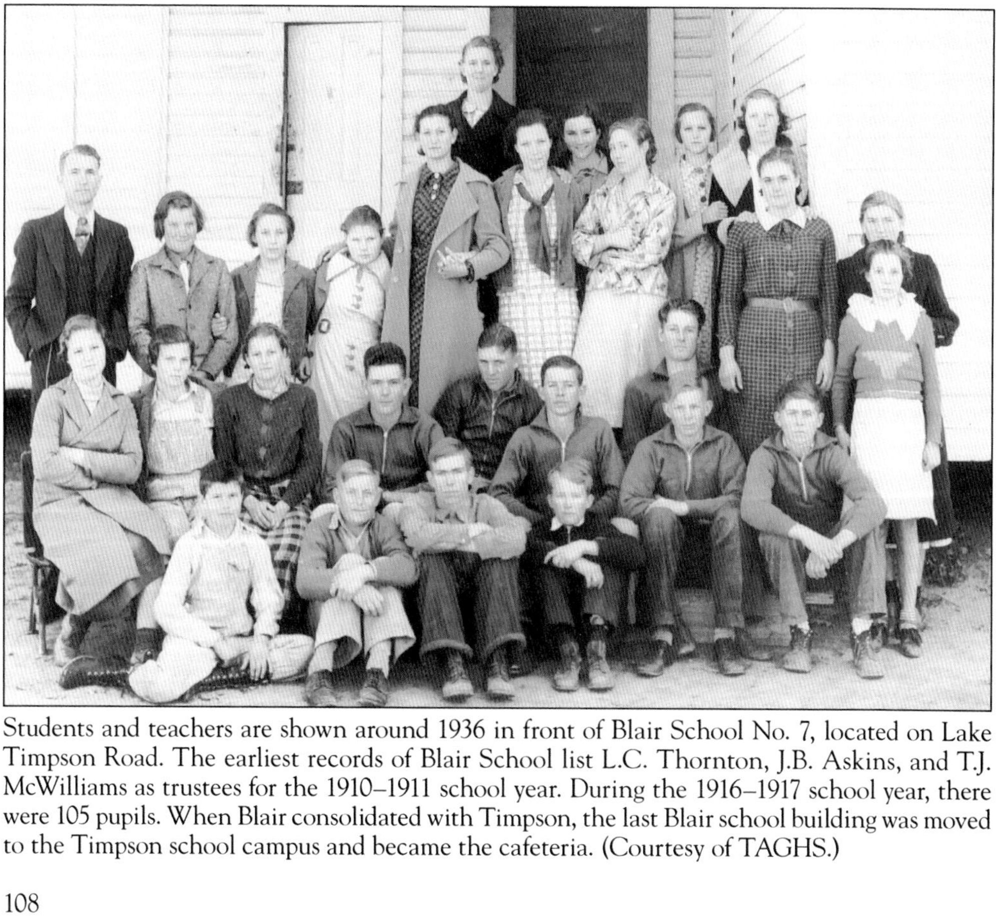

Students and teachers are shown around 1936 in front of Blair School No. 7, located on Lake Timpson Road. The earliest records of Blair School list L.C. Thornton, J.B. Askins, and T.J. McWilliams as trustees for the 1910–1911 school year. During the 1916–1917 school year, there were 105 pupils. When Blair consolidated with Timpson, the last Blair school building was moved to the Timpson school campus and became the cafeteria. (Courtesy of TAGHS.)

Seven

Small-Town Heyday

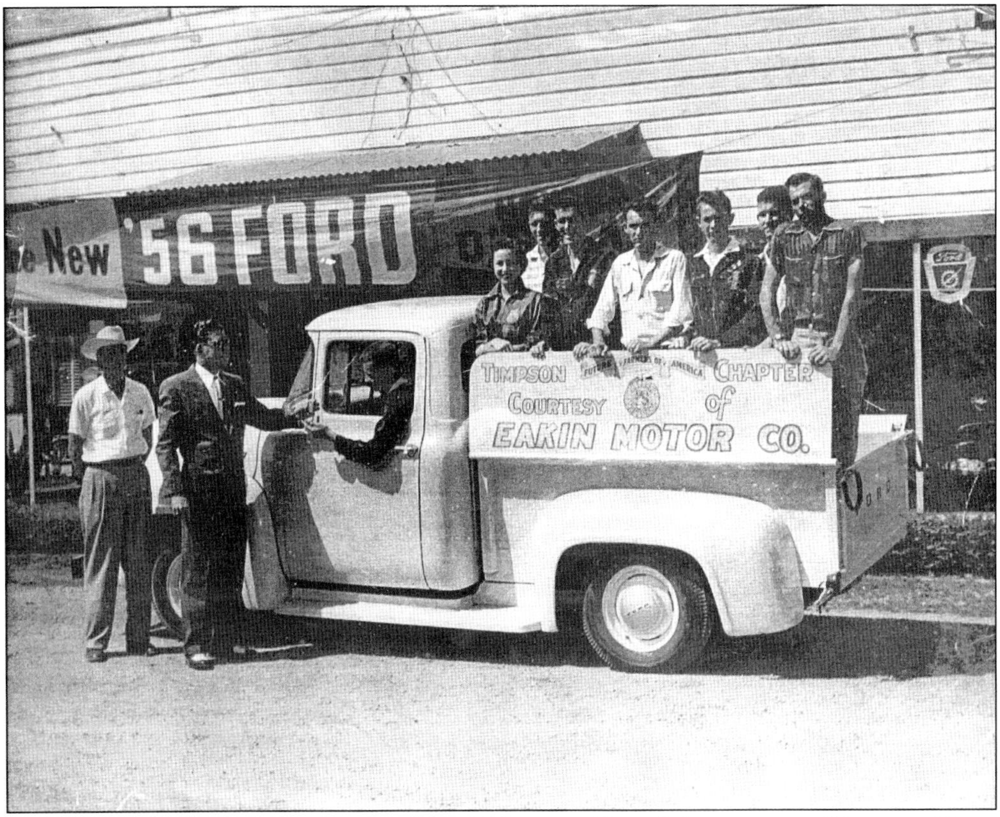

Eakin Motor Company opened in March 1955. Lovis and Lem Eakin, owners of Timpson Motor Company since 1946, relocated their business to Highway 59, becoming a new Ford Dealership. Shown here are, from left to right, Cecil Wharton (FFA teacher), and Lovis Eakin (sponsor), FFA students, and their sweetheart, Ina Dora Baker. Lovis Eakin died in 1977 and the business closed in 1982. (Courtesy of TAGHS.)

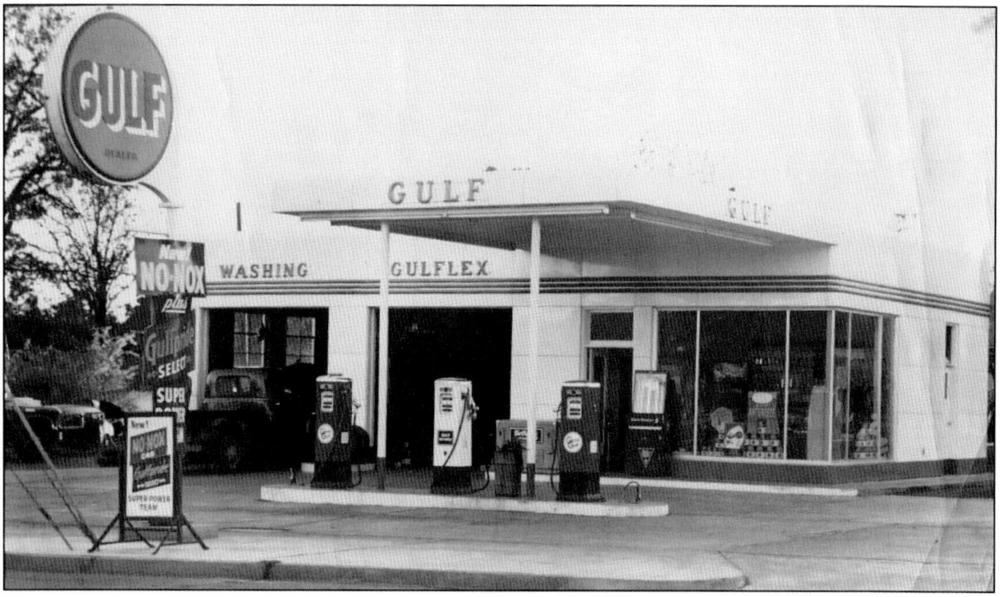

In the 1950s, cars were classic, and so was this modern Gulf Station on the corner of Jacob and South First Streets. Probably built when Robert Billingsley was owner (from 1953 to 1971), the station sat on the site of an earlier station operated by Sam Snelson in 1940, Horace Bryan in 1948, Henry Frazier in 1959, and John Winbery in 1950. Larry Bearden ran it in 1957 and 1958, as did Roy Hutto after 1971. (Courtesy of TAGHS.)

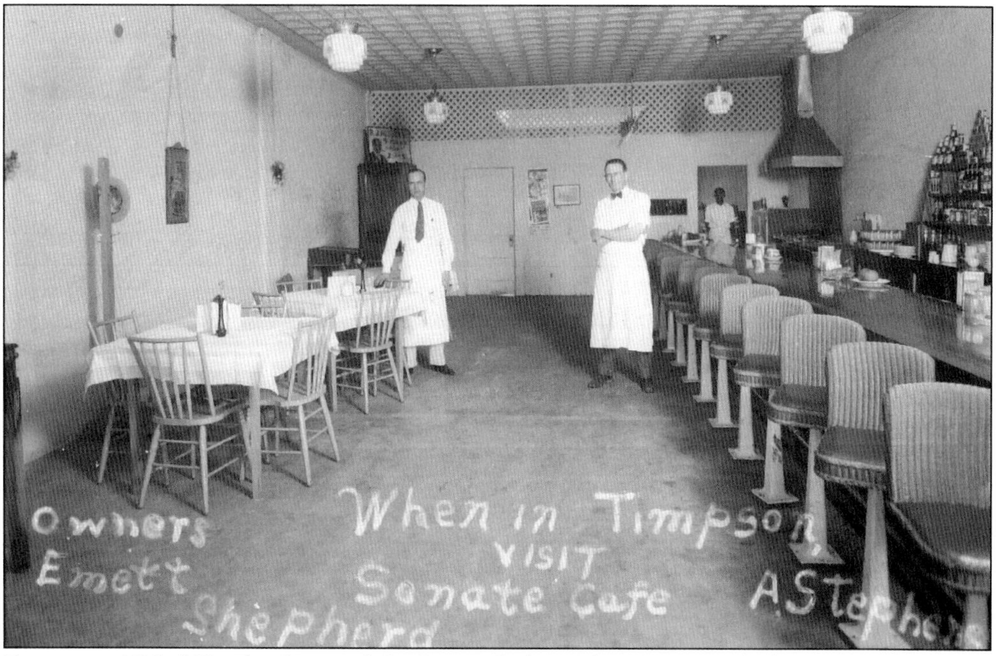

Emmett and Ethel Shepherd opened the Senate Cafe on Plaza Street in the late 1920s. This 1930s photograph shows partners Austin Stephens (left) and Emmett Shepherd. Of interest was their business card, advertising "Ladies Rest Room." Stephens had other business interests as well. In the 1930s, he owned the first and only miniature golf course in Timpson, located across from the school on McLaughlin Street. (Courtesy of David Shepherd.)

Donald Amos opened Timpson's first modern supermarket, Amos Foods, in 1967, where the Blankenship Building had previously stood. Amos is pictured here inside his well-stocked store. Later, he sold the store to Stanley Amos and Michael Johnson, who renamed the store Food Mart. The space now houses McDonald and Sons Auto Parts and Ace Hardware. (Courtesy of Lou Nell Billingsley.)

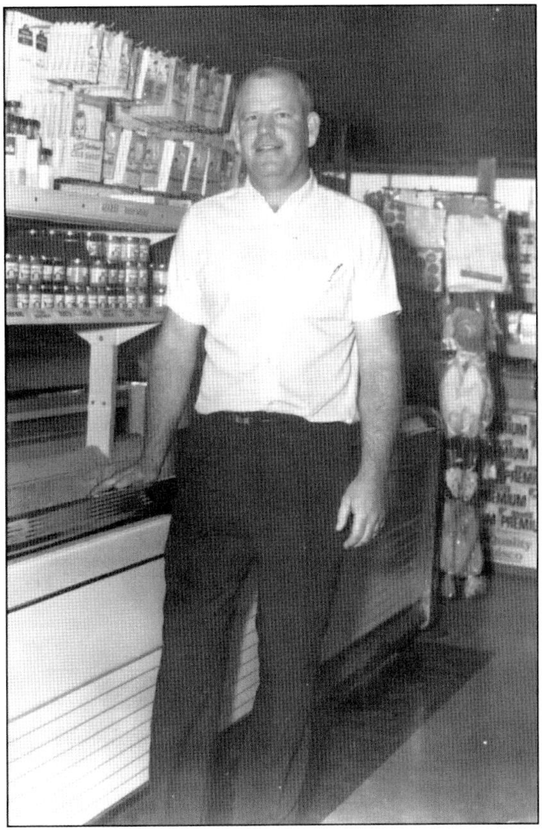

In 1946, Mack Taylor, who was associated with the Taylor Estate in Timpson, opened a store on Jacob Street in the one-story Burns building. Mack's "five and dime" carried the usual items found in a variety store, along with decorated flower arrangements, cards, gift sets, and candies. Shown here are Mack Taylor (left) and Gladys Clay. Another clerk, not shown, was Maurice McGraw. (Courtesy of Bobbie and Travis Clay.)

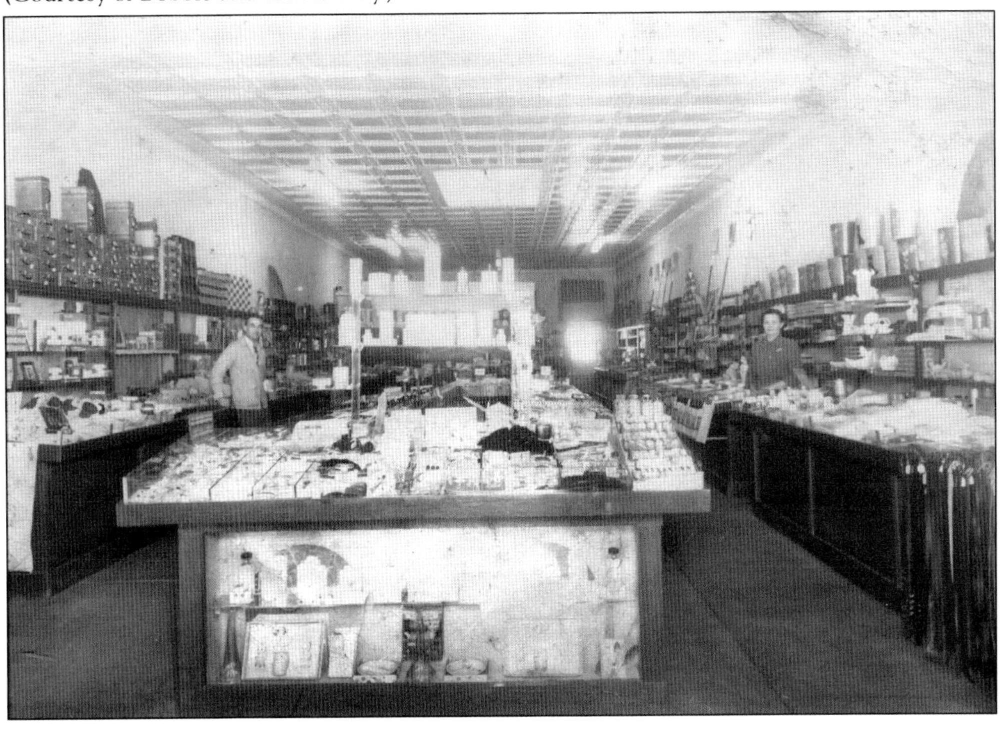

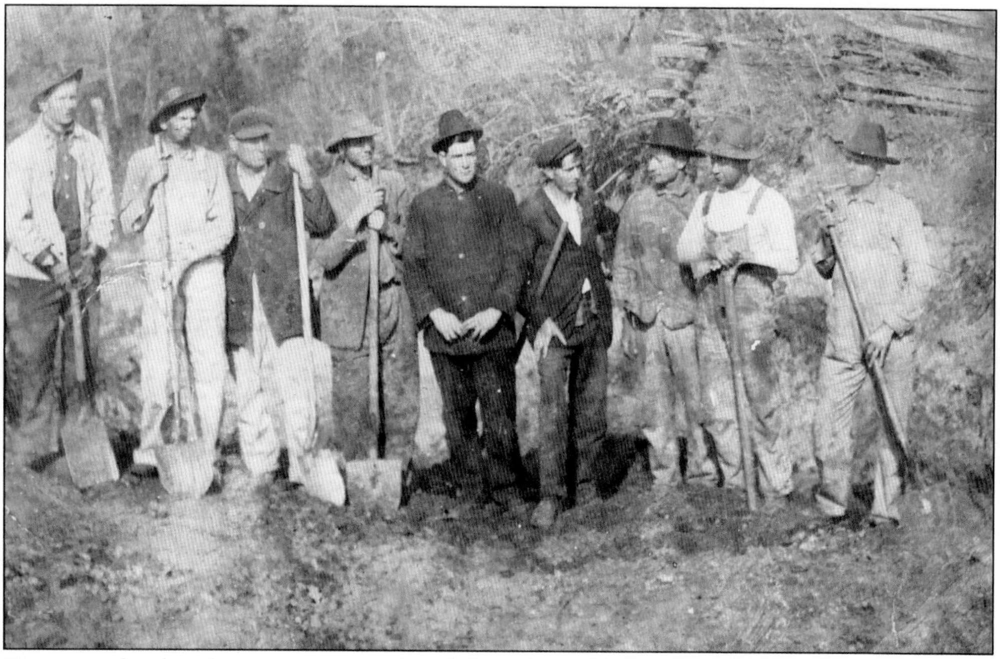

Times were hard, and many were unemployed, from the mid-1930s through the early 1940s. Any job was welcome, and many were fortunate to obtain work through the Works Progress Administration (WPA). This crew cleared roadways and planted trees. In this photograph, William Downing, second from left, and J.D. Bates, in the middle wearing dark clothing and hat, are identified. (Courtesy of Jan Magness Barrett and Bobby Hudson.)

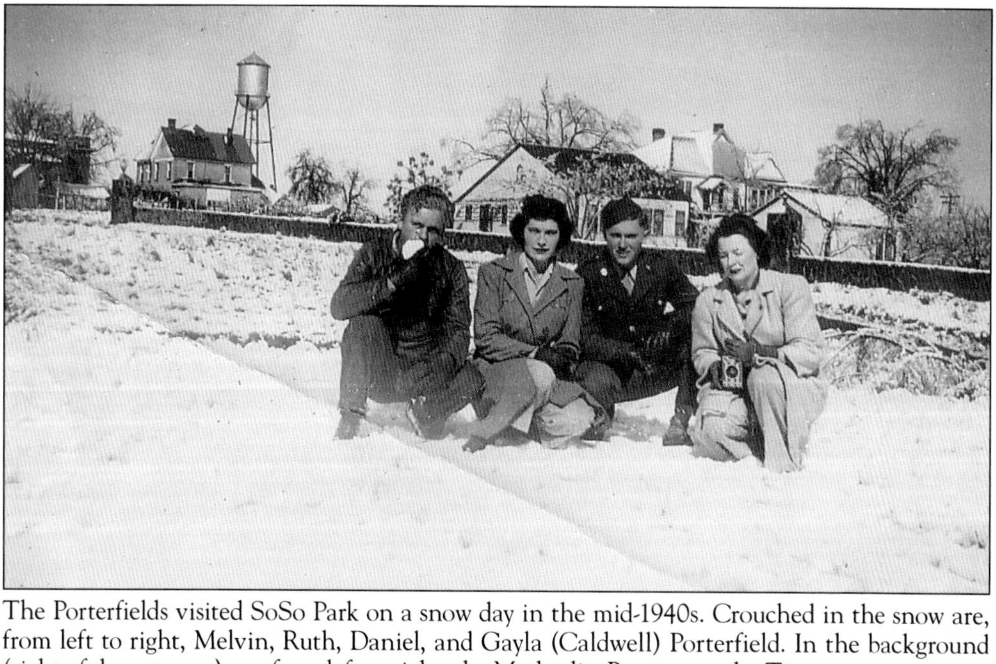

The Porterfields visited SoSo Park on a snow day in the mid-1940s. Crouched in the snow are, from left to right, Melvin, Ruth, Daniel, and Gayla (Caldwell) Porterfield. In the background (right of the gatepost) are, from left to right, the Methodist Parsonage, the Timpson teapot water tower, the Victor A. Hebert home (built in 1939–1940), and the Johnson-Whiteside Hospital. (Courtesy of Mary Ann Ramsey.)

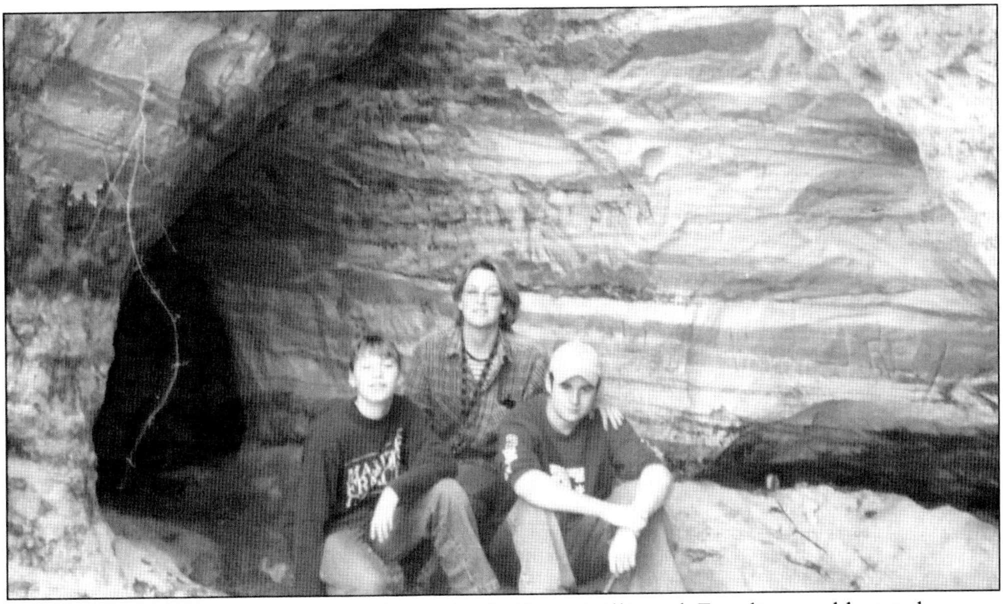

Cave Springs, unknown to many, is located off of Rose Hill Road. Families would visit the cave, bring a picnic lunch, and enjoy the cool spring that flowed from the cave. The striated rock around the entrance has shades of grey and coral coloring. Enjoying the experience in 2000 are, from left to right, Haley Sparks, Sharon Miller, and Chris Sparks. (Courtesy of Jeanette Beniot.)

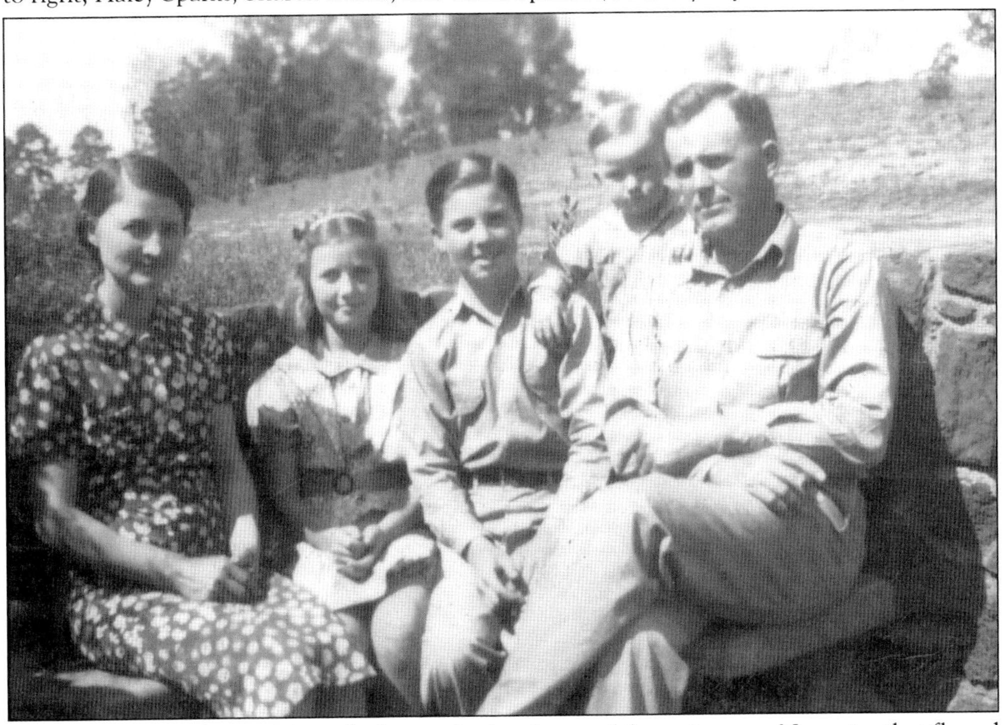

Most families traveling to Nacogdoches, or farther, knew of the spring near Naconice that flowed constantly beside Highway 35 (later US 59). A pipe brought the water through a native rock wall built by the Works Progress Administration in the 1930s. Shown here are, from left to right, Leta, Thelma, Charles, Joe Dan, and Otto Hairgrove. (Courtesy of Cecil Swann Hairgrove.)

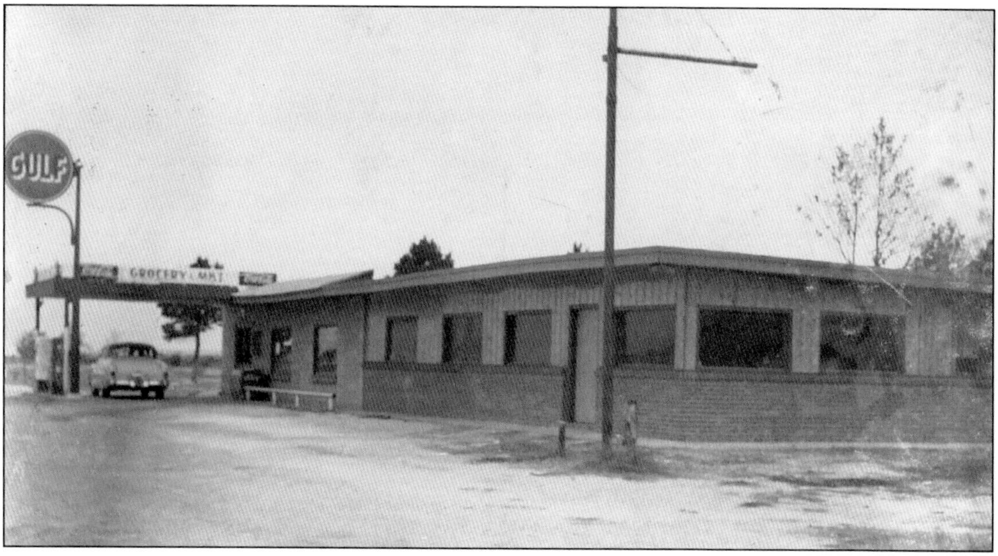

In 1945, Talmadge Young built a filling station and a small store on US 59, south of Timpson. This business burned and was replaced in 1955 with a station and café with a banquet room that seated 100. Many local banquets, meetings, and other events were held in the banquet room. In 1985, the highway department purchased the land in order to enlarge US 59. (Courtesy of Barbara Young Bogue.)

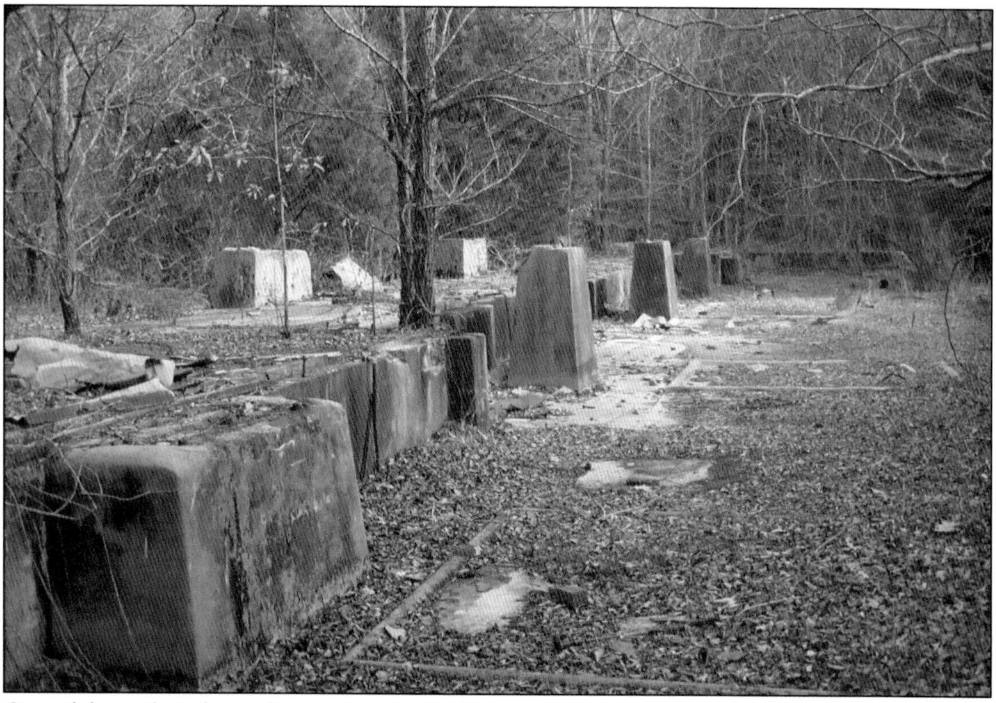

One of the early industrial operations in the Timpson area was the Gulf Oil Pump Station, built sometime between 1913 and 1915 and located in the Weaver Community. Several houses were built nearby for workers' families. The station ran day and night. In the 1960s, the station was leased to Spurlock Oil Company, then sold to Texas Eastern, and later torn down. Shown here are some remains in 2011. (Photograph by Jim Barrett.)

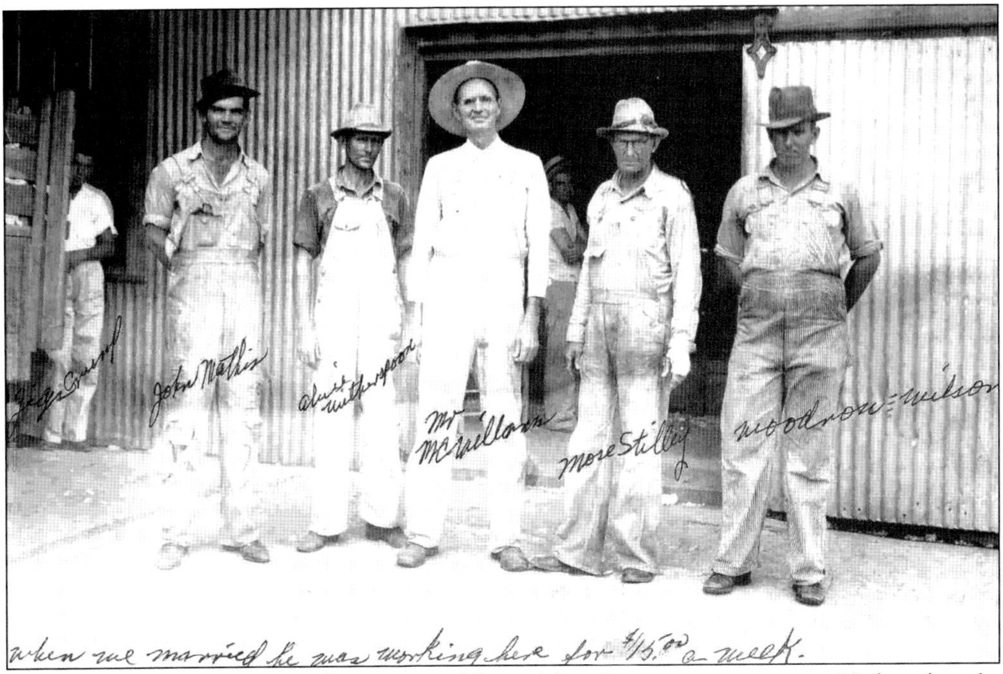

Lorenzo Dow McWilliams cut fencepost and farmed for a living as a young man. He later bought the first cotton gin in Stockman. He built a state-of the-art Fairbanks gin in Timpson and ran it as long as cotton was available. Shown at the gin in the early 1940s are, from left to right, Jigges Crump, John Mathis, Alvy Witherspoon, McWilliams, unidentified, Mose Stilley, and Woodrow Wilson. (Courtesy of Sandra Brownlow.)

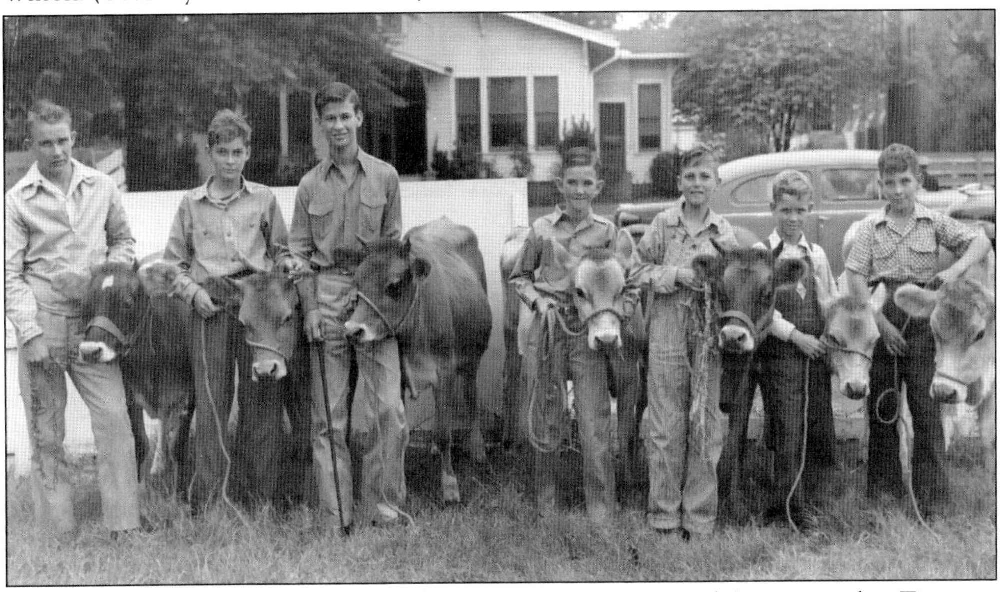

Agriculture and animal husbandry are favorite 4-H projects in rural America and in Timpson, Texas. Through a project, a 4-H member learns responsibility, working with others, learning by doing, and other valuable life skills. These 4-H members are shown with the animals they have fed and cared for. The only young man identified in this photograph is Maurice Fitts, at the far left. (Courtesy of L.G. and Billie Joy Allen.)

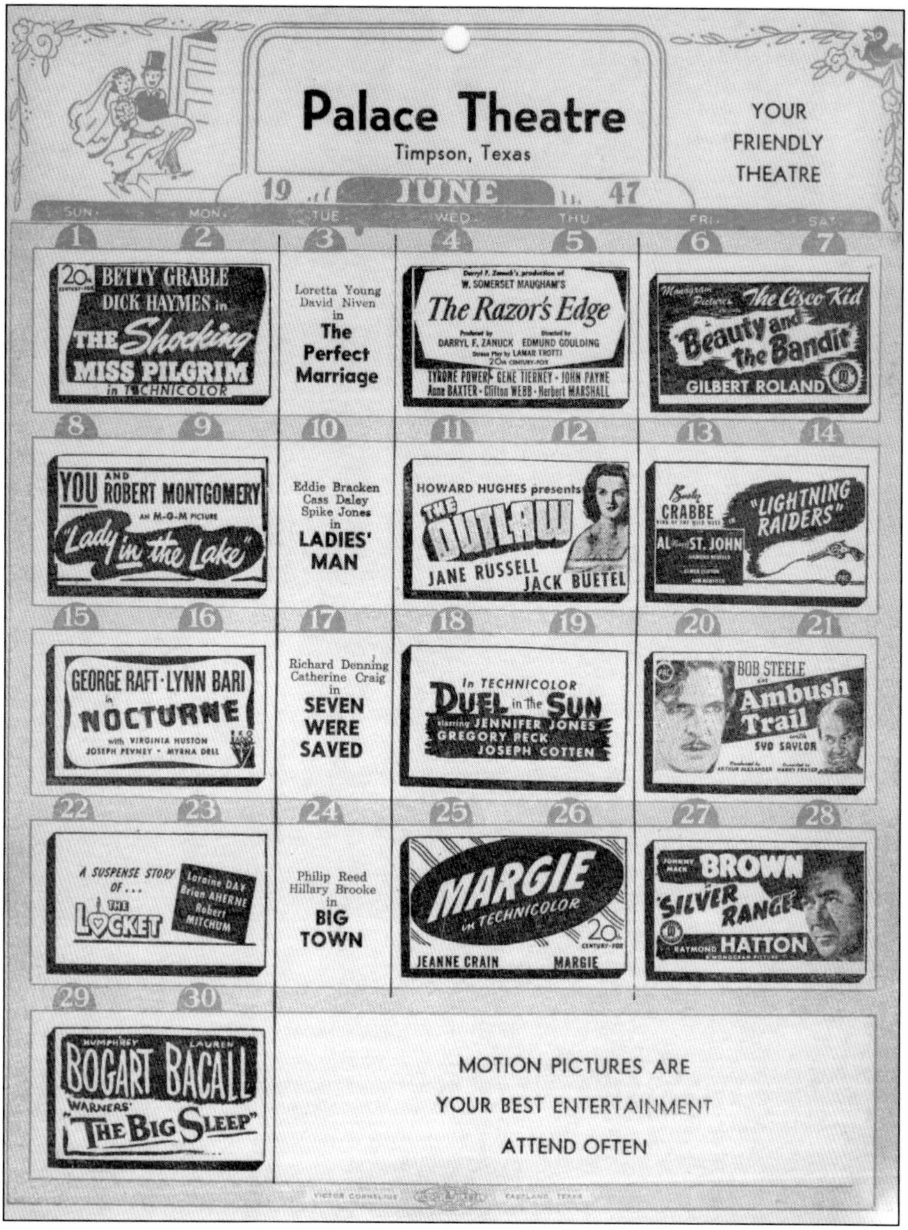

Records show that Timpson has had a theater since 1914, located near the center of the block on Jacob Street. It has changed hands and names several times, being known as the Cozy in 1914, the Crown in 1916, the Victory in 1929, and the Texas in 1932. In 1933, it became the Palace Theatre. The building burned in 1943 and in 1946, but was quickly rebuilt each time. In 1942, admission was 28¢ for adults, 17¢ for the balcony, and 9¢ for children. The theater was open each weekday in the evening for two features. On Saturday, the theater opened at midday for two features, then closed and reopened in the evening for two features and reopened again for a midnight show. On Sunday, there were two features in the afternoon and one feature after church in the evening. On the date of this movie calendar, June 1947, the Palace was the only theater in Timpson. In 1949, two more theaters joined it, the Fox Theatre and the Joy Theatre. (Courtesy of Bobby Dean Brunson.)

Jacob "Jake" Gasway, a Timpson High School graduate, joined the Wallace Brothers Circus in the early 1950s. He performed in the center ring with his tight wire act and was featured as one of the jugglers. He also performed with the Daily Brothers Circus. This handbill announces a 1951 performance by 21-year-old talent Jake Gasway. All three theaters in Timpson had a stage for live performances. (Courtesy of Paul Wendell Amos.)

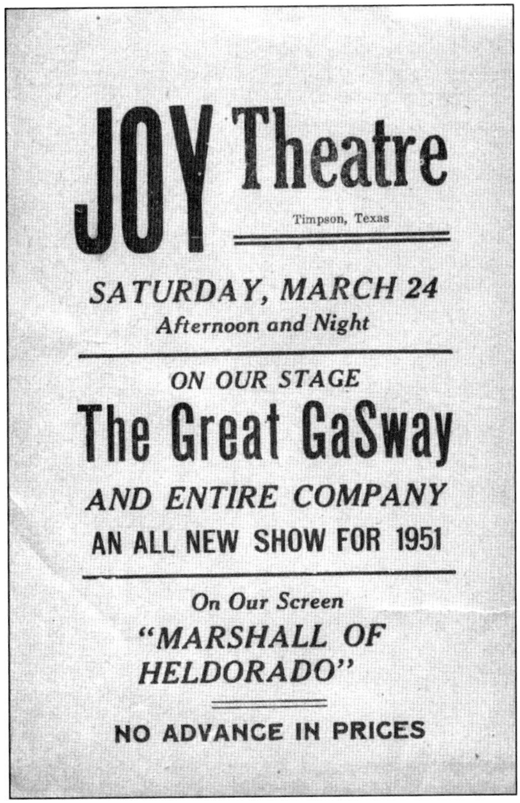

JOY Theatre

Timpson, Texas

SATURDAY, MARCH 24

Afternoon and Night

ON OUR STAGE

The Great GaSway

AND ENTIRE COMPANY

AN ALL NEW SHOW FOR 1951

On Our Screen

"MARSHALL OF HELDORADO"

NO ADVANCE IN PRICES

After World War II was over, local baseball resumed. In 1948, this team was part of the Piney Woods League that included Timpson, Garrison, Martinsville, Mt. Enterprise, Laneville, and Cushing. Zannie B. Crump, former manager and coach, named the team the Timpson Rockets. Local merchants donated new uniforms, and "Uncle Willie" Tyer furnished the location and materials for a new ballpark. (Courtesy of Juanita R. Green.)

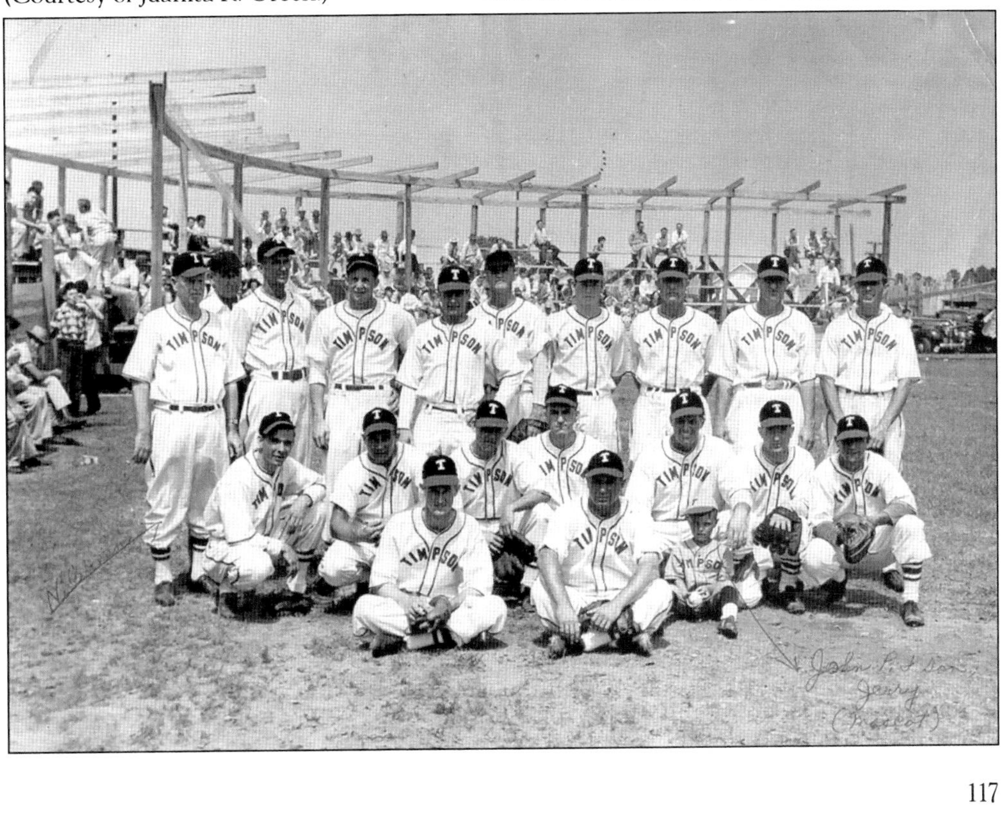

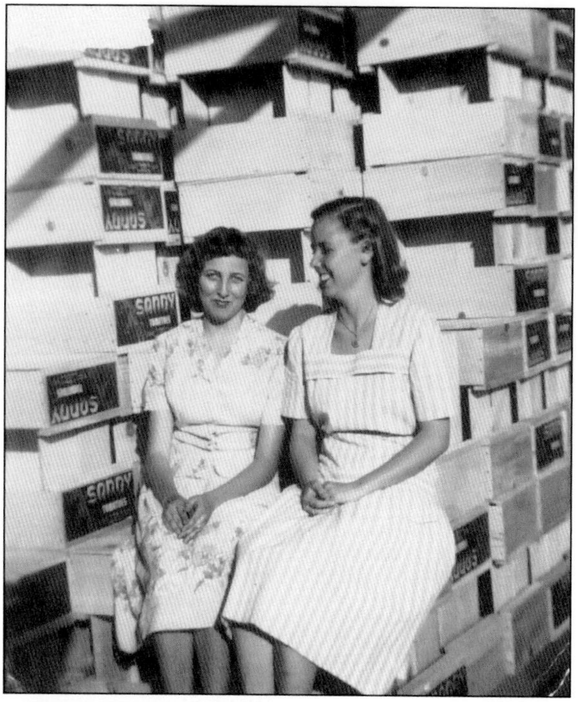

Maude Hooper (left) and sister Marian Hooper sit surrounded by tomato crates with a "Sunny Tomatoes" label. As teenagers, they worked for Hairston's Tomato Shed. Marian was a packer, Maude kept the manifest (a record of who packed each crate that went into the boxcar); brother Gene worked in the boxcar, stacking and reinforcing the crates to keep them in place. (Courtesy of Marian Hooper Bodiford.)

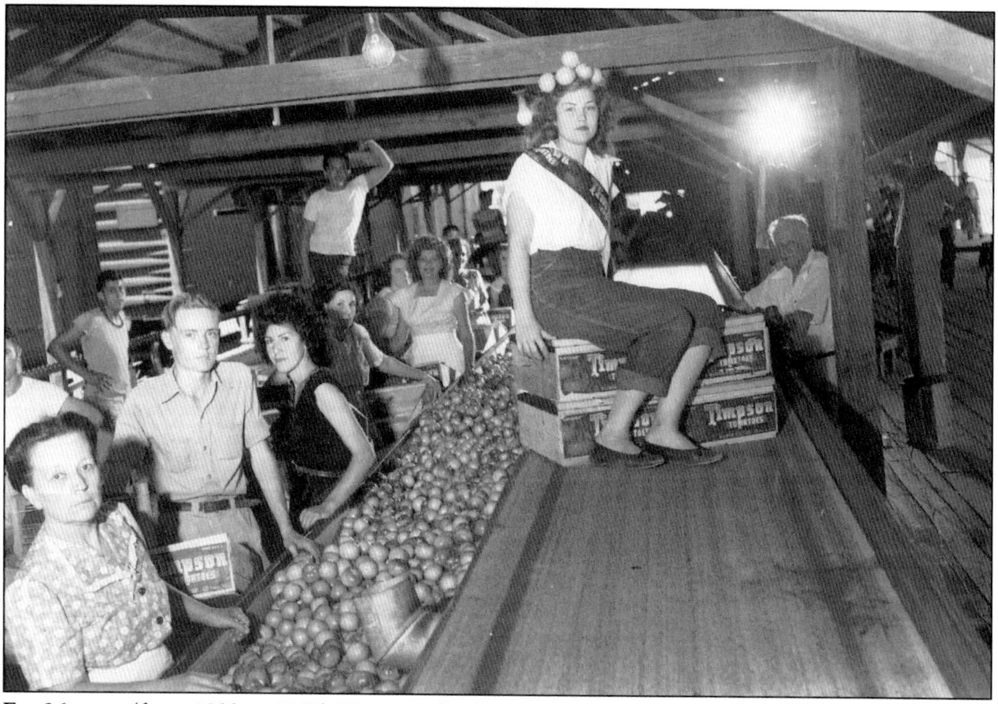

For 26 years (from 1933 to 1959), Timpson had a green-wrap tomato business, shipping tomatoes across the nation by refrigerated railcar. Between three and seven packing sheds operated at a time. Growers arrived early to get the best prices, and the last truckload was often unloaded in the wee hours of the next day. The 1949 tomato queen, Wilma Hairgrove, is shown here sitting on the tomato conveyor belt at McElwain shed. (Courtesy of TAGHS.)

Timpson Boy Scout Troop 113, formed in 1928, is shown raising the flag at Camp Tonkawa, their summer camp from the 1940s until it closed in the early 1960s. During World War II, the Scouts raised money by collecting scrap metal, paper, and by selling bonds for the war effort. They served at funerals for our fallen soldiers and raised the flag on Memorial Day. (Courtesy of Timpson First United Methodist Church.)

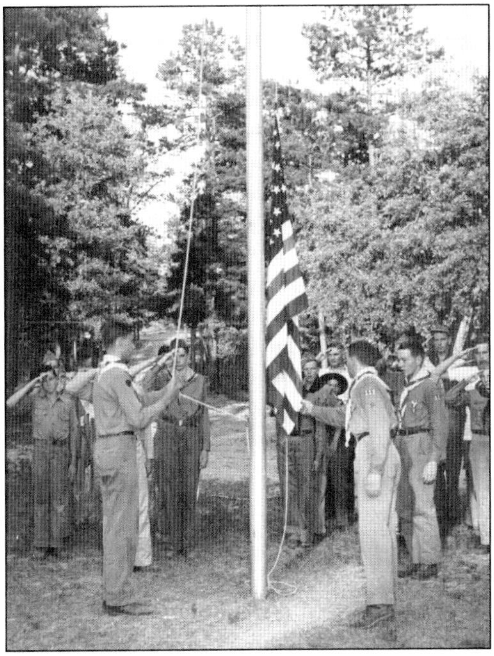

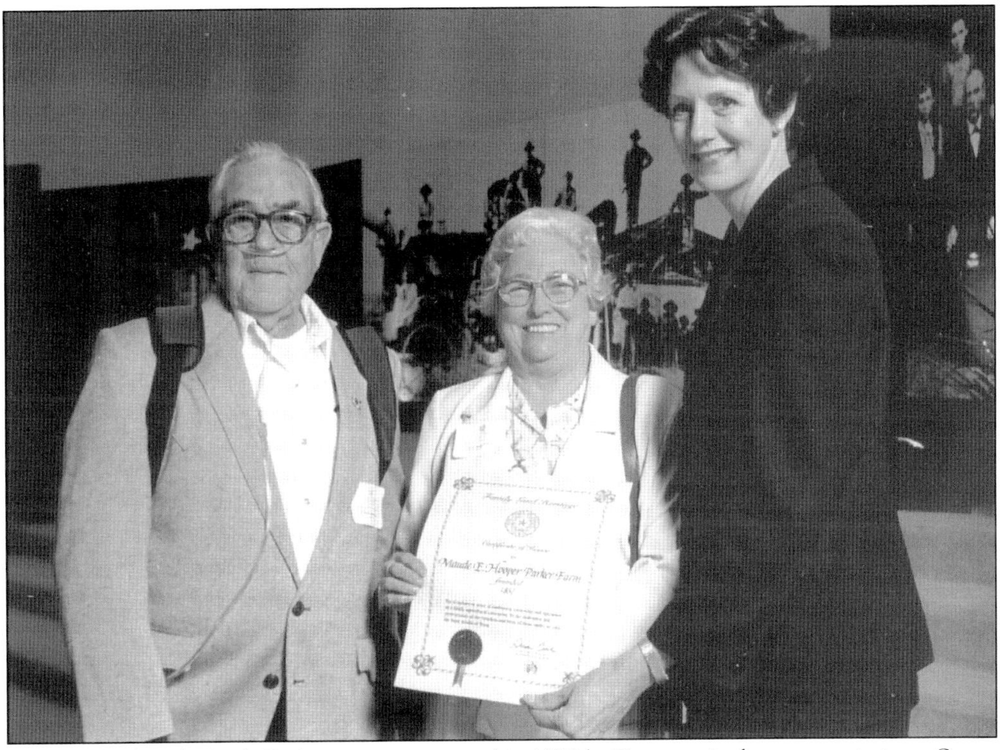

Howard (left) and Maude Parker were recognized in 1999 by Texas agriculture commissioner Susan Combs. The Maude E. Hooper Parker Farm (1858) had been in continuous farm operation for over 100 years. Other local Land Heritage properties are Morrison Farm (1855), Green Ranch (1838), Hairgrove Place (1859), Tyson Ranch (1876), Charles W. Askins Farm (1850), Harris Farm (1882), Joel M. Hairgrove Jr. Farm (1887), and the Hairgrove Farm. (Courtesy of Maude Parker.)

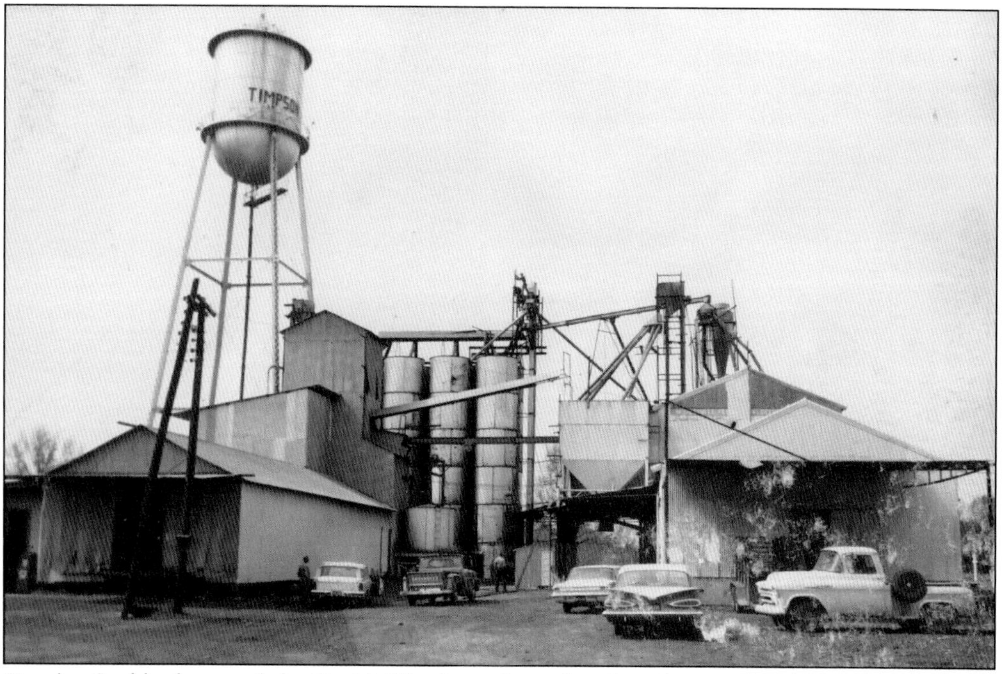

Pancho Goddard opened the Feed Mill, along the railroad tracks near Jacob Street, in 1953. It closed in the 1970s and reopened in 1980 or 1981. The mill made feed for broiler house chickens, cattle, horses, sheep, and goats. Michael Thrift purchased half an interest in the mill in 1994, and full interest in 1998, operating the mill until it closed in 2001. The old metal skeleton was demolished in 2009. (Courtesy of TAGHS.)

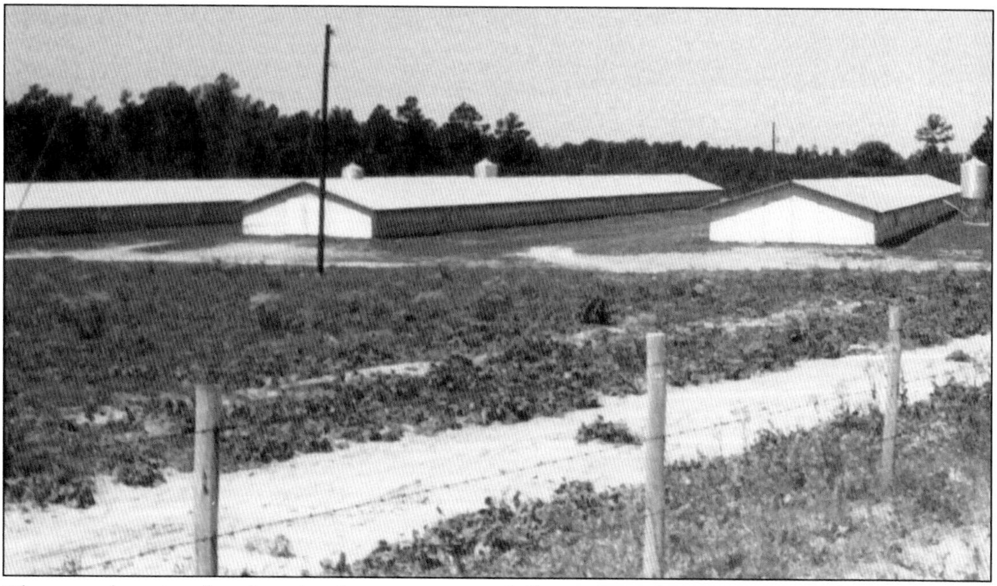

These modern, insulated poultry houses are very different from the tin open-air "chicken houses" many land owners built around Timpson in the early to mid-1950s. County agent John Moosberg introduced Shelby County residents to the potential profit in large-scale poultry production in 1948. The early results were so spectacular that chicken houses were soon a common sight around Timpson, and the East Texas broiler industry was born. (Courtesy of TAGHS.)

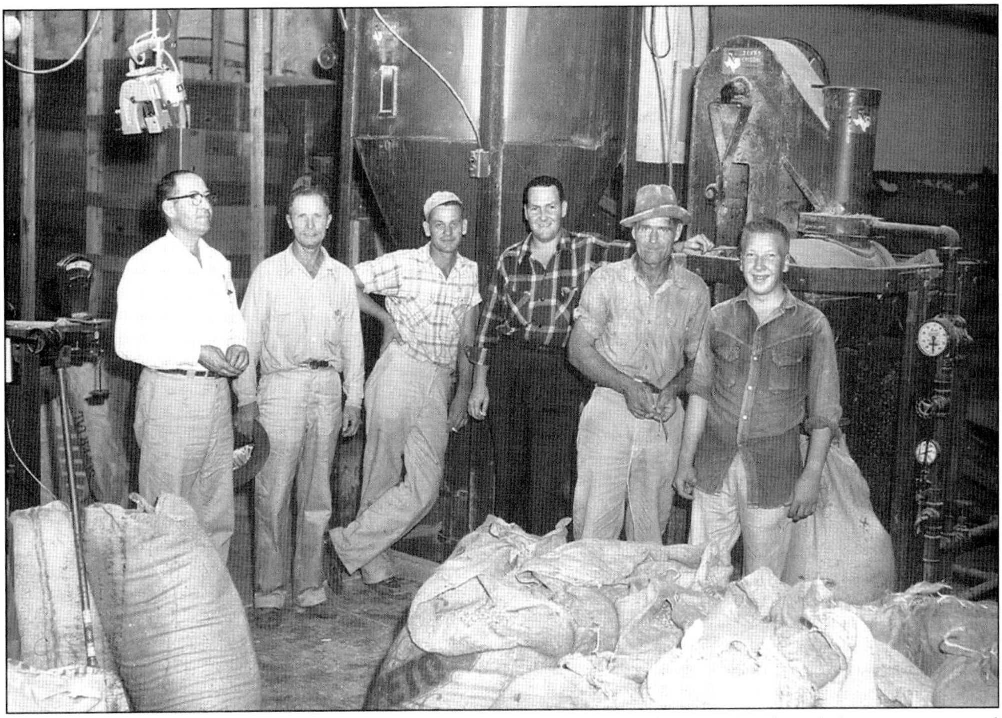

Yarbrough Milling Company, located in the old Armory building on Railroad Avenue, opened on October 30, 1954. The mill manufactured feed for livestock and poultry using the Swift Company formula. Owners were A.G. Yarbrough, Eugene Yarbrough and Louis Hancock. Shown here are, from left to right, Elmer Hancock, A.G. Yarbrough, Bud Crump, Louis Hancock, Dudley McDaniel, and Edward Pearley. This store was later owned by Poncho Goddard, then Bud Crump. (Courtesy of TAGHS.)

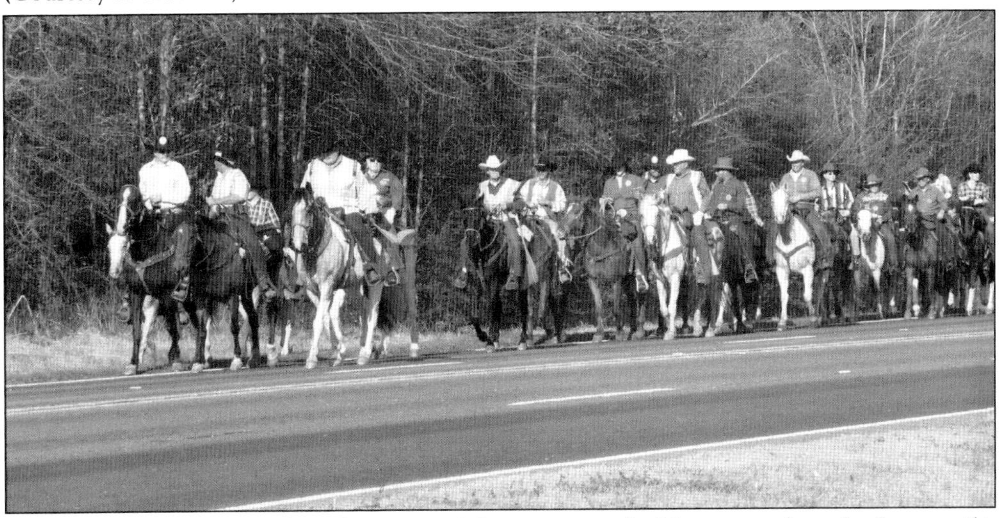

In 1955, a group of 19 men from Joaquin and Center set out for Houston on horseback to see if it could be done. The Old Spanish Trail Ride is an annual event that leaves Logansport, Louisiana, for the 250-mile ride to Houston for the Houston Stock Show and Rodeo Parade. This 2011 group is almost to the Bobo historical marker, a rest stop on the first day of the ride. (Photograph by Tempie Green Pike.)

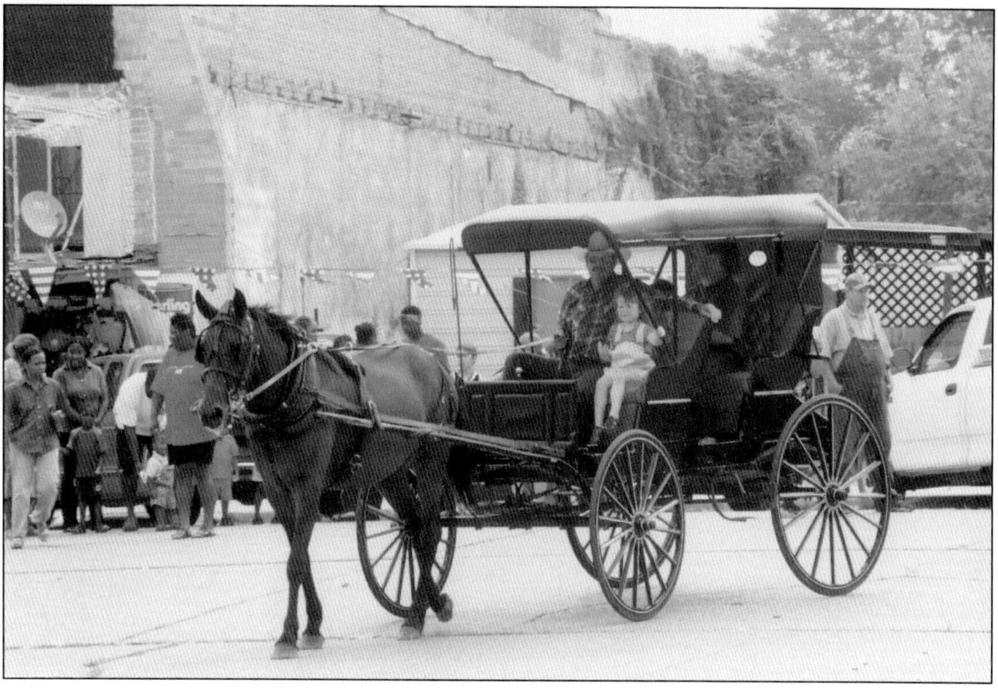

When Timpson was founded, in 1885, Billy the Kid had been dead only four years and cattle were still being driven up the Chisholm Trail. To celebrate Timpson's Western heritage, a first annual Frontier Days celebration was held in 1962. Among the festivities is a parade featuring period costumes, mounted cowboys, and vintage conveyances such as this horse-drawn surrey. (Courtesy of TAGHS.)

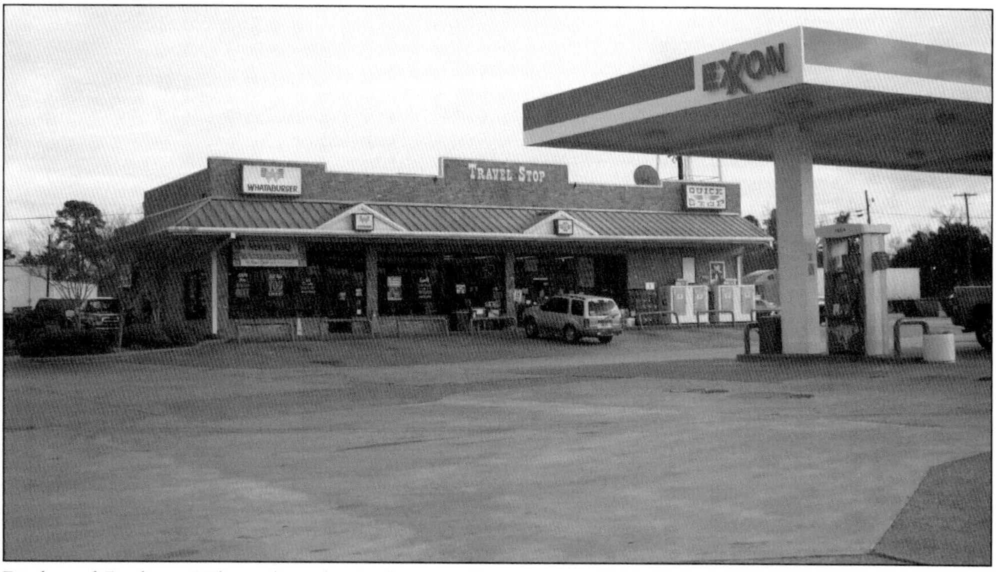

Bink and Barbara Gibson bought six lots on the corner of US 59 and TX 87 in 1979 and built a convenience store. Daughters Hope Lewis and Robin Crawford ran the store. Crawford acquired full ownership in 1996 and added a carwash. Following a fire in 1998, a new washateria and a new store building were constructed. It opened in 1999 and houses the Quick Stop business and a Whataburger. (Photograph by Shannon Ramsey.)

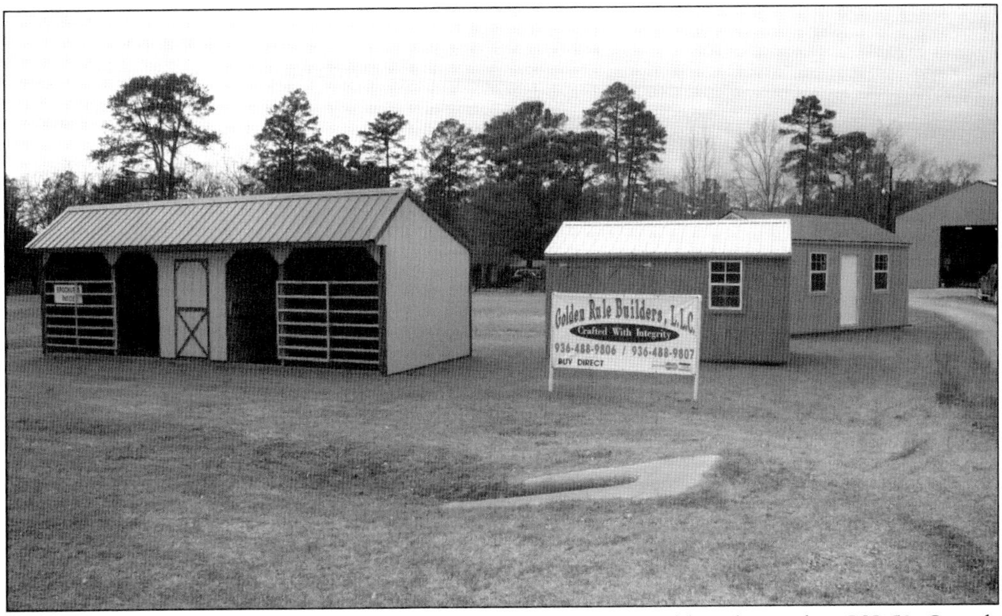

One of the newer businesses in Timpson is the Golden Rule Builders, located on US 59. Gareth and Brian Yoder moved their business from Grandview, Texas, to Timpson in July 2010. The company manufactures maintenance-free portable horse barns and portable storage buildings. Most of the construction is completed inside a spacious production shop and then trucked to the final destination. The company also builds on-site to custom specifications. (Photograph by Shannon Ramsey.)

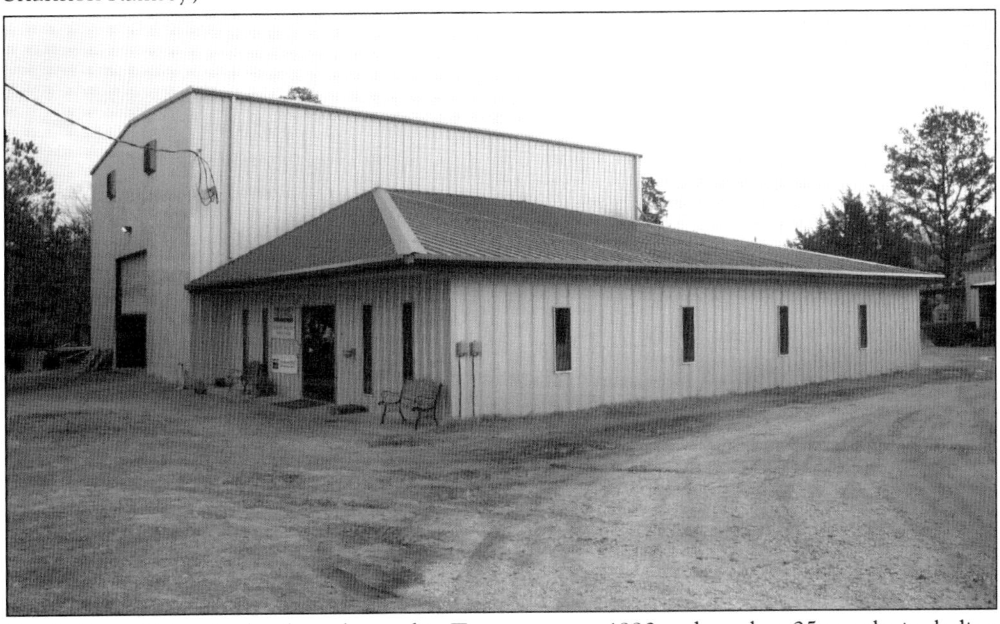

Smith Sawmill Service has been located in Timpson since 1990 and employs 25 people, including owners Paul and Debra Smith and their son, Michael. They service and supply mills all over the United States with saws, knives, equipment, and Paul's patented parts. Smith got his early training working at one of the local sawmills, where his dad, Bobby Smith, and grandfather, Robert Smith, both worked. (Photograph by Shannon Ramsey.)

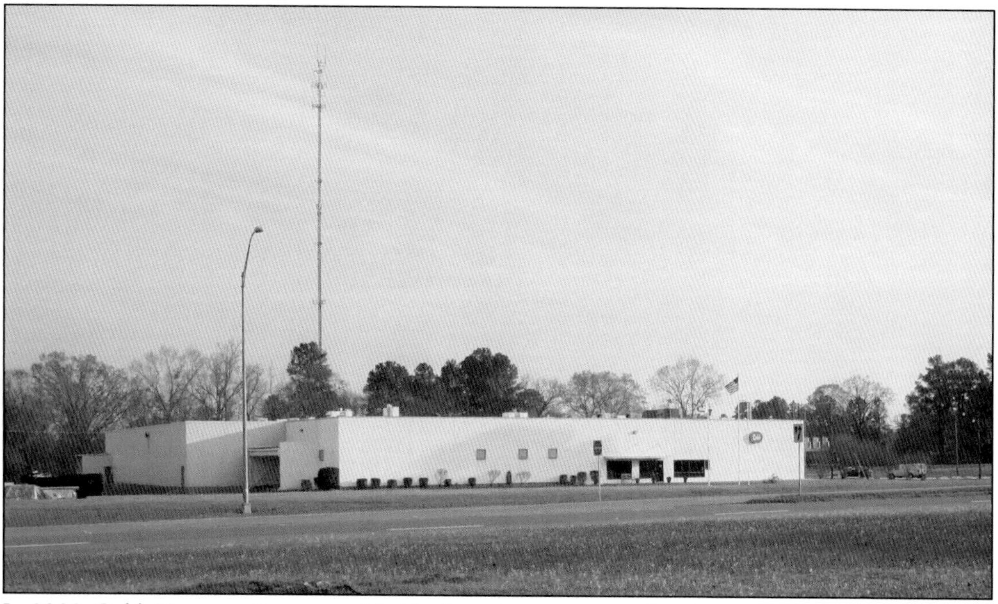

In 2000, Cobb-Vantress, Inc., a worldwide American company headquartered in Siloam Springs, Arkansas, purchased this business, located on US 59, south of town, and the farm on Highway 84 from Avian Farms. Cobb is a breeder-broiler and research company. They deliver one-day-old parent stock baby chicks to growers throughout the southwest region of the United States. Hatchery manager Tracy Hooper and approximately 90 other area employees work here. (Courtesy of TAGHS.)

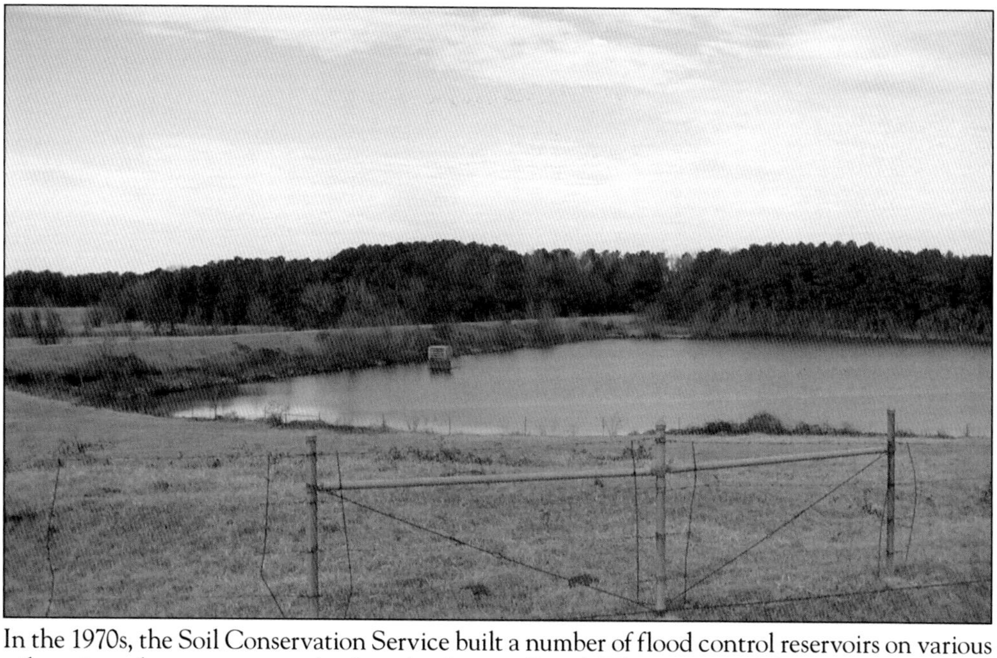

In the 1970s, the Soil Conservation Service built a number of flood control reservoirs on various tributaries to larger waterways (such as the Attoyac River). The purpose of these reservoirs was to control flooding along the larger waterways. A tower, with gates for adjusting the flow of water, was placed in the reservoir. Local reservoirs are located in the communities of Weaver, Silas, and Arcadia. (Photograph by Jim Barrett.)

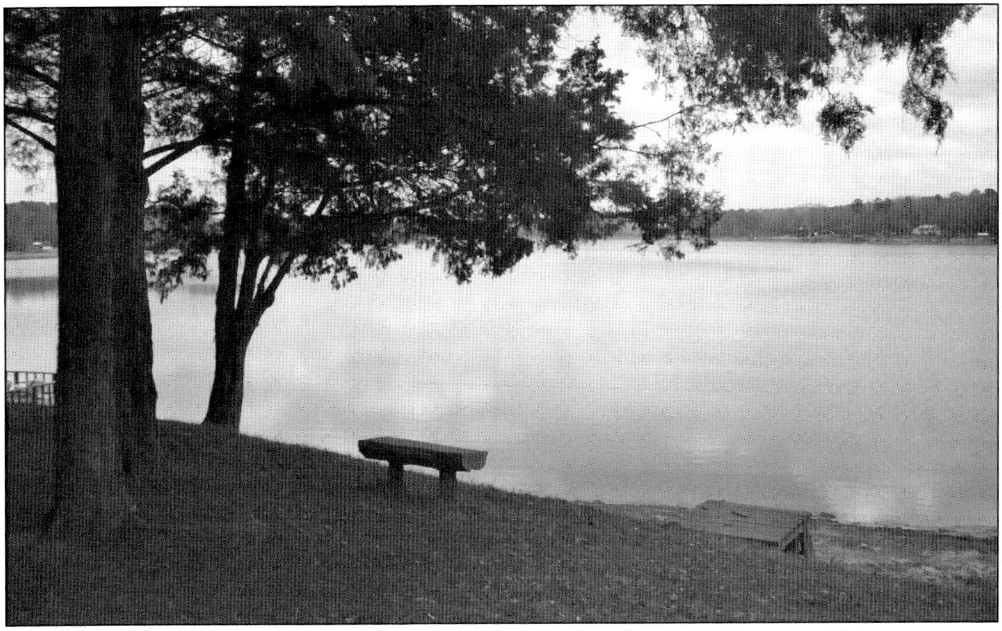

Voters approved a bond issue of $275,000 in 1954 to build Lake Timpson, a 234-acre project. Completed in September 1956, the area received over 19 inches of rain on April 27, 1957, filling the lake to overflowing. Lake Timpson is a recreational lake, where fishing is a favorite sport. The lake contains largemouth bass, crappie, catfish, bluegills, and redear sunfish. (Photograph by Jim Patterson.)

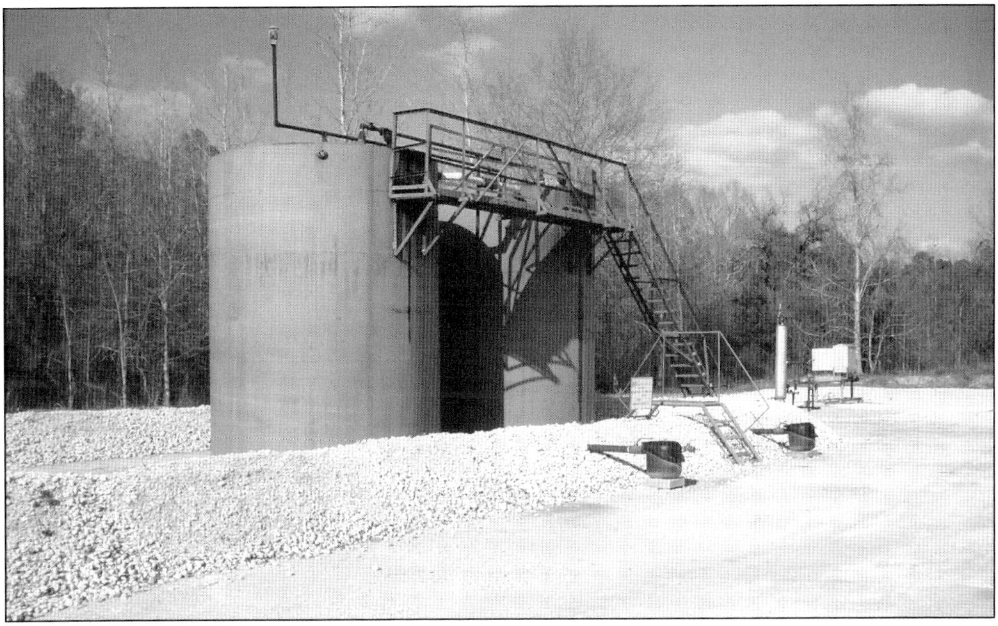

For 70 years, the huge oil and gas pools discovered in the counties to the north of Shelby in the 1930s seemed to stop at our county line. Timpson had to wait until the 21st century and the discovery of a major natural gas deposit in the Haynesville Shale, over 10,000 feet below the town, to participate. Gas wells such as this one are now a common sight surrounding Timpson. (Photograph by Jim Patterson.)

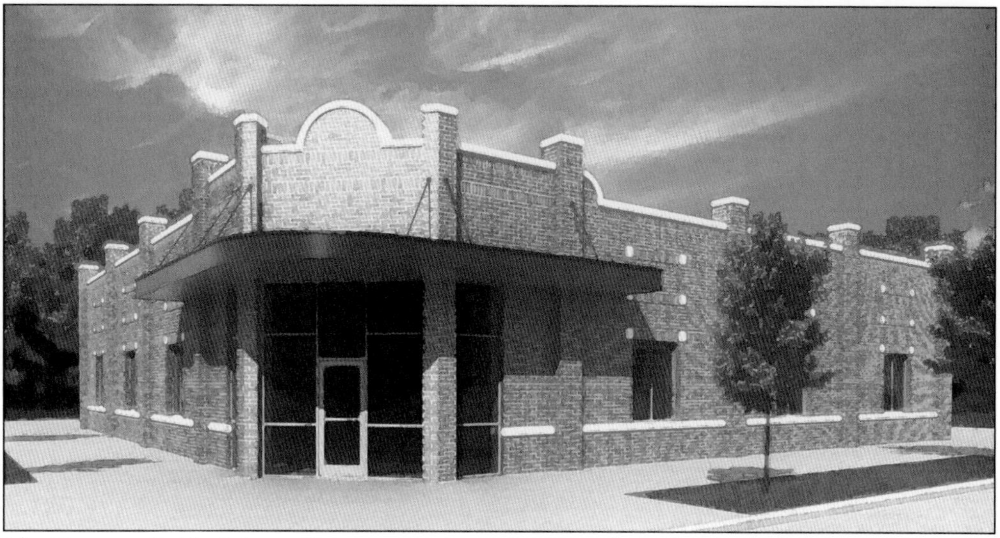

The Timpson Public Library District was created in 2002 through a local election allowing it to receive .005 percent sales tax in public funding. In 2003, a public library was opened downtown on Bremond Street. Fundraising events have included annual banquets and several home tours. The board and library volunteers serve without pay. Recent approval of a grant-loan combination from the USDA will make this proposed building a reality in 2012. (Courtesy of Timpson Public Library.)

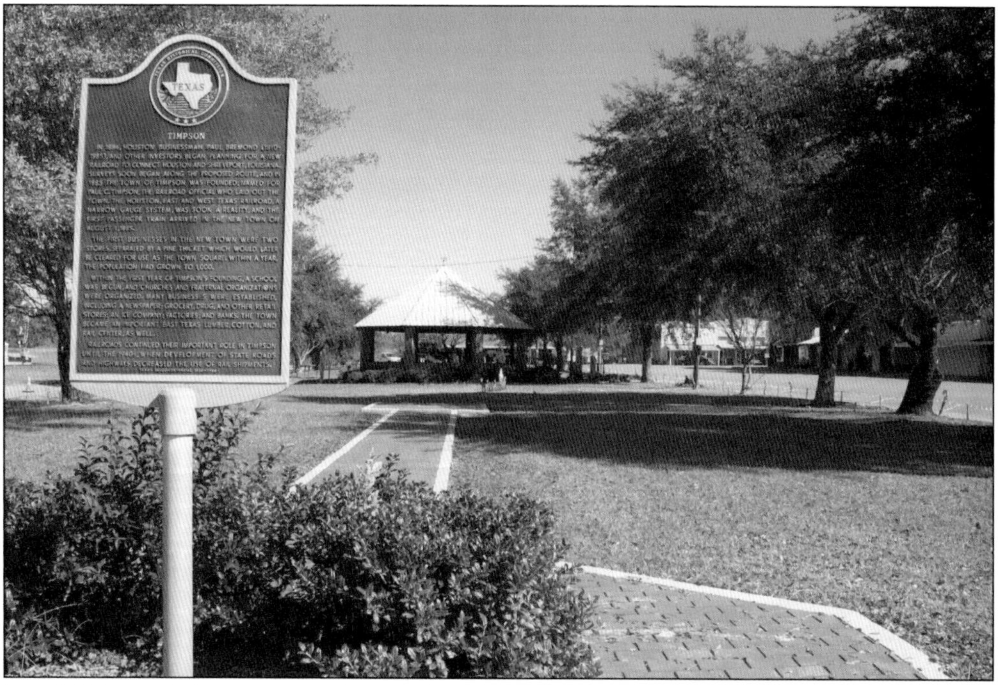

The "Walk of Reflection" was dedicated on July 4, 2009, during the Timpson Frontier Day celebration. The walk was placed in Park Plaza, beginning at the Timpson Historical Marker. The purpose of the chamber of commerce project was to provide a permanent place for hometown citizens and visitors alike to reflect on the history of our community and its people. Phase I included 144 engraved bricks and recognized 233 individuals. (Photograph by Kelsey Brae Rogers.)

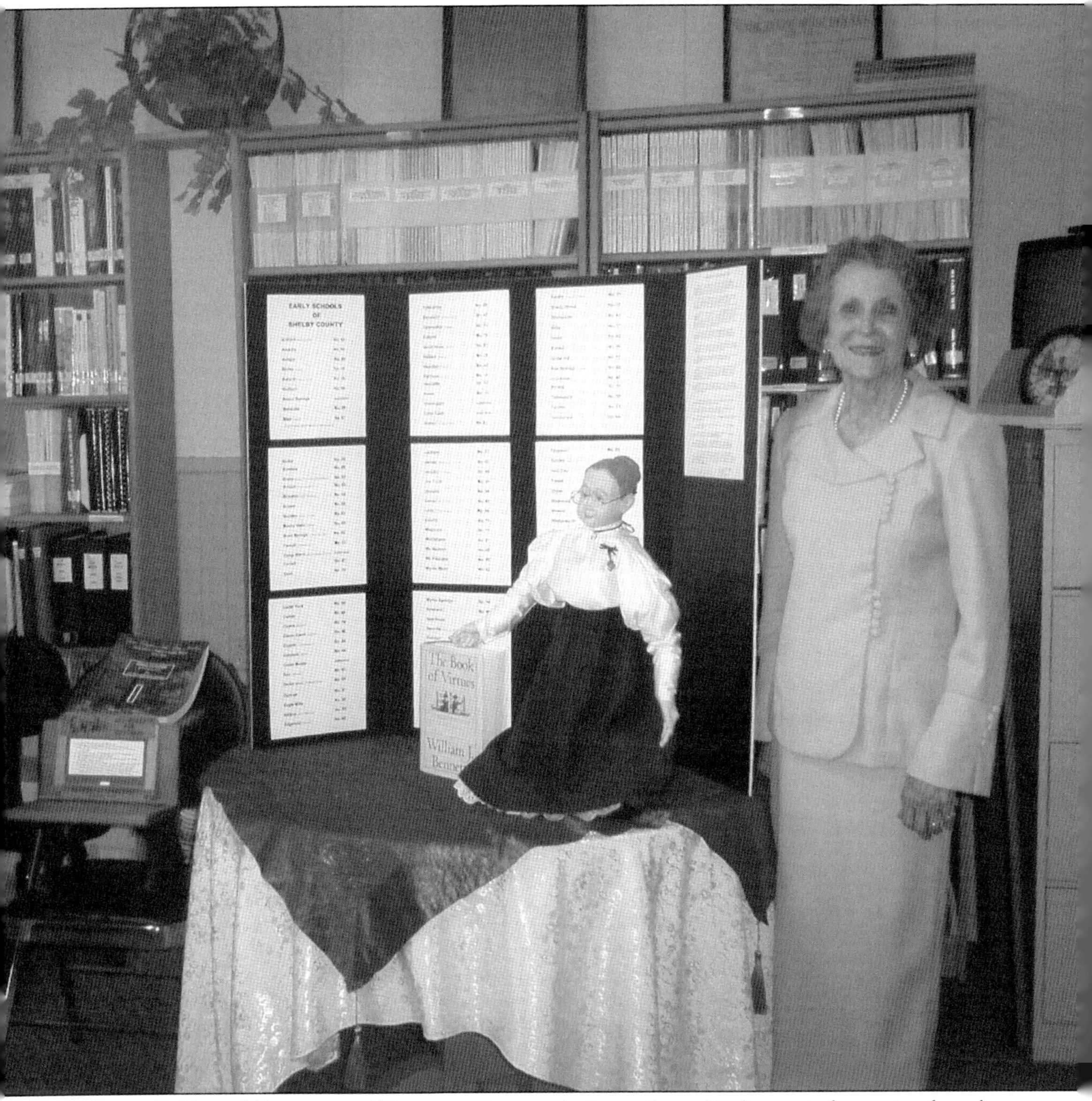

Fannie Baldwin Watson, a well-known educator, is shown here displaying information from her latest research on 19th century rural schools in Shelby County. Her presentation was done at the Timpson Area Genealogical and Heritage Society monthly meeting on May 20, 2009. TAGHS was established in 1991 to gather and preserve the history of the area and to provide instruction and training in genealogy research. Toward those ends, TAGHS has indexed over 25 cemeteries, written and published *Timpson, Texas Area History, 1880–2002*, and digitized over 50 years of local newspapers. The society has operated a genealogy library since its inception. Now housed in a downtown building, along with the Timpson Chamber of Commerce, it will become a part of the Timpson Public Library when the new building is completed in 2012. TAGHS provides a quarterly newsletter to its over 200 members throughout the nation. Meetings are held monthly on the third Wednesday at 2:00 p.m. in the genealogy library at 191 Bremond Street. The mailing address is P.O. Box 726, Timpson, Texas, 75975. The phone number is (936) 254-3500, and the e-mail address is timpsgen@sbcglobal.net. (Courtesy of TAGHS.)

MADE IN THE USA

Arcadia Publishing, the leading local history publisher in the United States, is committed to making history accessible and meaningful through publishing books that celebrate and preserve the heritage of America's people and places. Consistent with our mission to preserve history on a local level, this book was printed in South Carolina on American-made paper and manufactured entirely in the United States.

This book carries the accredited Forest Stewardship Council (FSC) label and is printed on 100 percent FSC-certified paper. Products carrying the FSC label are independently certified to assure consumers that they come from forests that are managed to meet the social, economic, and ecological needs of present and future generations.

FSC
Mixed Sources
Product group from well-managed forests and other controlled sources
Cert no. SW-COC-001530
www.fsc.org
© 1996 Forest Stewardship Council